Tragic Choices

THE FELS LECTURES ON PUBLIC POLICY ANALYSIS

Tragic Choices

GUIDO CALABRESI
and
PHILIP BOBBITT

W · W · NORTON & COMPANY · NEW YORK

Library of Congress Cataloging in Publication Data
Calabresi, Guido, 1932–
    Tragic choices.
    (The Fels lectures on public policy analysis)
    1. Policy sciences.   2. Decision-making.
I. Bobbitt, Philip, joint author.   II. Title.
III. Series.
H61.C23 1978   658.4′03   77-13603
ISBN 0-393-05649-X
ISBN 0-393-09085-X pbk.

FIRST EDITION

To our parents

Contents

Acknowledgments

An invitation to give the Fels Lectures in Public Policy Analysis at the University of Pennsylvania in 1973 first gave me the opportunity to address in a systematic way the issues dealt with in this book. I am particularly grateful to Julius Margolis, who was the director of the Fels Center of Government for his understanding support at the very beginning of this project. Subsequently, in 1974 and 1975 in talks at the Joseph and Rose Kennedy Institute of Human Reproduction and Bioethics, Georgetown University (André E. Hellegers, M.D., director); at the University of Ottawa, Canada; and at the annual meeting of the Population Association of America (under the sponsorship of the Population Council, Inc.), parts of this essay were developed further. Generous support for the project, and especially for the comparative aspects of it, was given by the National Science Foundation under Grant No. GS-35948.

I cannot begin to list all those of my friends and colleagues who have at various times read parts of this book and made valuable suggestions. They will recognize their contributions and know how much I appreciate their help. I wish especially to thank Dean Abraham Goldstein and Dean Harry H. Wellington of the Yale Law School. Their friendship, support, and generosity have been essential to me. So, also, has been the help and friendship given me by Professor Mauro Cappelletti of the European University Institute and the University of Florence, who made available the facilities of the Centro Studi di Diritto Processuale Comparato in Florence, of which he is director.

Librarian and Associate Dean Arthur A. Charpentier, of the Yale Law School, and his whole staff were of great assistance, as was Roberta Rawle Longinotti, my secretary when I was in Florence. The patience, dedication, and willingness to decipher and type draft after draft at inconvenient times of Susan Lucibelli, my secretary at the Yale Law School, deserve particular mention.

Many students at the Yale Law School, and elsewhere, were of great help in the writing of this book, some by participation in seminars and courses, others, as research assistants. I am particularly grateful to Jonathan Marks, George Miller, and Bruce Boisture, each of whose help at different times over three or four years, was invaluable to the work.

What can I say of my coauthor, Philip Bobbitt? He began as a student who was sufficiently bothered by the flaws which he perceived in an early version of this work that he determined to correct them, first as a critic in conversations and then as a research assistant. In time, when this book, both in style and content, had become as much his as mine, he became in name what he already was in fact, a coauthor. There are (such is always the case in works which are jointly written) parts of the essay attributable to Philip which I would have treated differently, but I am certain that it is a far better book than it could have been without his insights and collaboration.

Finally, I thank my wife, Anne, whose help in this, as in all things, has been and is indispensable.

Guido Calabresi

Woodbridge, Connecticut
July 1977

This book offers a general theoretical account of how societies cope with decisions which they regard as tragic. Whatever contributions I may have made to this account derive principally from discussions with Guido Calabresi beginning in

1974 and continuing up to the latest impassioned telephone call. Beyond my acknowledgment of this rare and rewarding collaboration I am indebted to so many people for aid in the preparation of the manuscript that I risk embarrassing omission by naming a few. Perhaps by mentioning at least some, I gesture toward all.

I thank Deans Abraham Goldstein and Harry Wellington of the Yale Law School for their role in my support during my time in New Haven. Also Professor Steven Duke and his family who lent me quarters during my last three-month sojourn working on the manuscript. At the University of Texas Law School, Dean Ernest Smith has been especially helpful. Without his encouragement and the support provided by a grant from the Fund of the Texas Law School Foundation, work would have been much more difficult. My research assistants, Jean Noonan and Laura Richardson, were of considerable assistance in reading the manuscript at various stages. My students at the Law School contributed both through their papers and comments in my seminar to my understanding of the subjects treated in this book. Katherine Burghard assisted in proofs.

Associate Librarian Robert Berring, and Associate Dean and Librarian Roy Mersky, of the Texas Law School, provided efficient and indefatigable assistance.

My secretary, Pat Ponkoney, deserves thanks and admiration for having weathered so equably the sore testing of typing repeated drafts.

Also, I must thank the Honorable Henry J. Friendly, Senior Judge of the Second Circuit Court of Appeals, for permitting me to leave my clerking duties to resume work on the manuscript.

My debt to my great teachers is unanalyzable. Yet I could not acknowledge aid from any source without mention of Professors Charles L. Black, Jr., Grant Gilmore, and Jan Deutsch.

To Anne Calabresi is owed gratitude for her suggestions, which have much improved this book.

But beyond telling I owe most to the strength and patient care of Bonnie MacDougall of Columbia University and the Chapin School, with whom I daily discussed the subjects herein and on whom I so deeply relied.

If this work has not one exclusive meaning and does not necessarily tend to a definite conclusion, I do not regret an hour of having labored in its subject.

Philip Chase Bobbitt

Austin, Texas
July 1977

Tragic Choices

[Man] finds no resting place, no haven from calamity,
But something often dearer still than life
The darkness hides and mist encompasses . . . no man
Can tell us of the stuff of it, expounding
What is, and what is not: we know nothing of it.
Idly we drift, on idle stories carried.

—Euripides, *Hippolytus*, 11. 189–97

1

INTRODUCTION

W<small>E CANNOT KNOW</small> why the world suffers. But we can know how the world decides that suffering shall come to some persons and not to others. While the world permits sufferers to be chosen, something beyond their agony is earned, something even beyond the satisfaction of the world's needs and desires. For it is in the choosing that enduring societies preserve or destroy those values that suffering and necessity expose. In this way societies are defined, for it is by the values that are foregone no less than by those that are preserved at tremendous cost that we know a society's character.

In the essay that follows, we study scarcities which make particularly painful choices necessary. These choices are sometimes tragic and sometimes not. We will attempt no simple definition to separate the difficult choice from the tragic, or the trivial from the difficult. We will instead, use examples of choices we believe to be tragic in particular societies and speak of their characteristics. Soon enough the reader will come to recognize those choices which in his society are tragic.

There are difficulties in this approach. Examples too often are taken to imply prescription or solution, and we have few prescriptions and no solutions. More important, the use of examples may lead the reader to conclude that what we mean by tragic is subjective to each individual, that tragic choices are those that each of us finds appalling. Instead, we intend to discuss the tragedies of cultures; it is the values accepted by a society as fundamental that mark some choices as tragic. The critic of social values may object strongly to decisions his society finds quite acceptable, and readily approve of other choices that his society must make and yet cannot stomach; moreover, he may be right. But it is not with him or with our own imperatives that we are concerned; it is rather with those choices which the society finds intolerable.

Tragic choices come about in this way. Though scarcity can often be avoided for some goods by making them available without cost to everyone, it cannot be evaded for all goods. In the distribution of scarce goods society has to decide which methods of allotment to use, and of course each of these methods—markets, political allocations, lotteries, and so forth—may be modified, or combined with another. The distribution of some goods entails great suffering or death. When attention is riveted on such distributions they arouse emotions of compassion, outrage, and terror.[1] It is then that conflicts are laid bare between on the one hand, those values by which society determined the beneficiaries of the distributions, and (with nature) the perimeters of scarcity, and on the other hand, those humanistic moral values which prize life and well-being.

In such conflicts, at such junctures, societies confront the tragic choice. They must attempt to make allocations in ways that preserve the moral foundations of social collaboration. If this is successfully done, the tragic choice is transformed into an allocation which does not appear to implicate moral contradictions. Morally debasing outcomes are averted. But unless the values held in tension have changed, the illusion that denies their conflict gives way and the transformation will have only been a postponement. When emotions are again focused on the tragic choice, action will again be required. "We have a prospect of insuperable moral difficulty, a nightmare of justice in which the assertion of any right involves a further wrong, in which fate is set against fate in an intolerable necessary sequence of violence."[2]

Thus the detail of the pattern of tragic choices is movement. In them society confronts the grave and constant in human suffering. Action in the context of necessary scarcity brings ultimate values, the values by which a society defines itself, into conflict. We ask, "What course without evils?"[3] but we know that no true answer will give us comfort. As one critic has put it, "Basic to the tragic form is its recognition of the inevitability of paradox, of unresolved tensions and ambiguities, of opposites in precarious balance. Like the arch, tragedy never rests."[4]

Tragic choices show two kinds of moving progressions. First, there is society's oscillation between the two sorts of decisions it must make about the scarce good. It must decide how much of it will be produced, within the limits set by natural scarcity, and also who shall get what is made. In this book the former decision is called a first-order determination and the latter a second-order determination or decision. Secondly, there is the motion that is composed of the succession of decision, rationalization, and violence as quiet replaces anxiety and is replaced by it when society evades, confronts, and remakes the tragic choice.

These two movements, and the concepts they entail, are the patterns within which the various methods of allocation operate. In any particular example, such methods and movements form the plot and story line of the tragic choice. Since they are therefore fundamental to the analysis of this book, which focuses principally on the methods of allocation, we may properly devote some preliminary attention to their further description.

The first movement, as we have said, traces the interplay between two different levels of allocation. First-order determinations define the global setting, whether existentially imposed, as in a condition of absolute natural scarcity, or, as is the more common case, one chosen on the basis of relative priorities within the larger context of ultimate natural scarcities, for instance, a population-restrictive policy which sets acceptable rates of procreation in a society. Second-order determinations allocate the available resources as defined by the first order, for instance, who may have children, how many, when, and so forth. Unless imposed by absolute natural scarcity, all first-order determinations contradict the postulate that a particular good is priceless. And all second-order determinations, unless they are supported by a totally dominant conception of appropriate distribution—of hierarchy and equality—mar some distributional ideals of the society.

These two kinds of determination are found in any allocation. Typically, in the nontragic choice, they are united, made by the same institution and in the same way. The economist's classical market serves to determine how many ships and how much sealing wax will be produced, as well as who shall have how much of each. The decision, arrived at through a political process, to award medical licenses to persons who meet certain set standards—which can be modified so that a particular number is achieved—serves both to decide how many doctors there will be and who they will be.

It is characteristic of tragic decisions, however, that first- and second-order determinations are made separately. This allows for the more complex mixtures of allocation approaches which are brought to bear on the tragic choice, and it permits a society to cleave to a different mixture of values at each order. Indeed, when the first-order determination of a tragic choice appears to be no more than a dependent function of the second order, it will usually be the case that the connection is illusory, serving to obscure the fact of tragic scarcity and—while the illusion lasts—evading the tragic choice. Thus we comfort ourselves in the belief that our society does not establish an acceptable number of auto deaths, but that this figure results from thousands of independent, atomistic actions.

Of course there is considerable fluidity between the two kinds of determinations. It is all very well to decide that families must average no more than 2.1 children, and to devise methods for allocating the right to have them, but unless the first-order result, the figure of 2.1, has been arrived at by reference to some external absolute—a religious command, for example—the costs entailed in achieving the second-order decisions are bound to influence the first-order determination, and 2.1 may give way to 2.3 or 1.8.

This fluid relationship accounts for the paradoxical fact that societies often refuse to permit the production of the full amount of the scarce resource that could be made available without creating other unacceptable scarcities. Assume, for example, that a society could without difficulty withstand a procreation rate which yielded an average of 2.5 children per family, but that such a determination made for some very difficult second-order choices; however, setting the first-order figure so that a 2.0 per family number is derived, avoids these choices. It is quite plausible that such a society would revise downward the first-order determination in order to smooth second-order decisions and thereby lessen their costs.

The division between first and second order, and the interplay between them, helps explain behavior in many tragic situations. We often move in what appear to be erratic jumps, valuing life at a rather low level in some circumstances at the first order and at a high level in other situations. But if one realizes that at very high and very low first-order levels, relatively easy second-order choices are possible, while this is not so at intermediate levels, then the discontinuity becomes explicable. Of course this does not fully explain the differences in the value we place on life in different situations; why, for instance, the United States will spend a million dollars to rescue a single, downed balloonist but will not appropriate a similar sum to provide shore patrols. These differences depend in part also on the second movement which characterizes tragic choices, the progression from attempt to desperate attempt to avoid tragedy that forms the sequence of decision in the tragic context.

Such a progression seeks to change our perception of the particular tragic dilemma. By making the result seem necessary, unavoidable, rather than chosen, it attempts to convert what is tragically chosen into what is merely a fatal misfortune. But usually this will be no more than a subterfuge, for, although scarcity is a fact, a particular first-order decision is seldom necessary in any strict sense. True, there are instances of such absolute necessity like the triage decisions required by a plague or a famine. If artificial kidneys required the use of some unsynthesizable element of which there was only a small amount, then societies could only make so many artificial kidneys regardless of the resources they were willing to divert to that end. A determination to produce that number which exhausted the rare element might still not achieve a sufficiency that would permit us to treat all patients suffering from renal failure. But such natural scarcity is not often the limiting fact. More frequently scarcity—and the necessity of picking sufferers it imposes—even if absolute at a particular moment in time (as with the number of physicians capable of performing a kidney transplant), is not absolute over time. More commonly still, scarcity is not the result of any absolute lack of a resource but rather of the decision by society that it is not prepared to forgo other goods and benefits in a number sufficient to remove the scarcity.

This last situation poses the most difficult choices since responsibility is not, in such a case, as easily evaded. Scarcity in general remains a fact of life, but in the particular tragic situation, scarcity and suffering are not merely imposed: The society incurs them by its own decision or, at the least, society finally wills to accept them as "properly pertaining to the nature of things, including [society's] own deepest nature."[5] It is then that we observe most dramatically the second movement we described, the progression from decision to rationalization to violence which in succeeding cycles characterizes the development of the tragic choice, the flight which evidences the attempt to transform a tragic dilemma into a situation in which the conflict of values is not exposed and which the society will not find tragic.

The attempt depends upon, and presupposes, for its plausibility, the fact that at the fringes of virtually all tragic situations are decisions which are not viewed as tragic. It does not appear to be tragic in the United States to fail to provide dialysis for a person in whom such treatment is unlikely to work. Nor is it tragic to draft young men in wartime while exempting very old men when it is believed that the young make much better soldiers. Both these decisions determine who is given a greater chance to live. Yet neither seems to implicate a conflict in American values; it would be otherwise if the kidney were given to a wealthy recipient rather than to a poorer patient on the ground that the kidney was more likely to work in a wealthier man because he could afford to rest, have private nurses, and so forth.

Whether the decision is perceived as tragic—whether it evokes ruth and arouses terror and outrage even when basic values are, in fact, placed in conflict—is a function of what methods are used to cope with the fatal scarcity. If the tragic decision is justified by an explanation which does not implicate moral conflict, then the violence which follows will not give rise to tragedy—for a time. But "whatever subtleties this clever age invents,"[6] unless the society changes its values, the sequence must be repeated whenever the explanation is intensely questioned or when fresh life-taking decisions are made.

The extent to which such methods succeed in an ameliorative role, even for a time, depends on how they accommodate cultural values. In the examples given, the American respect for efficiency seemed for a moment to be the effective factor which enabled a movement away from a tragic outcome. And this was so even though the principal humanistic value at stake was, as it is in every tragic situation, life, or its correlative, well-being. (In fact, societies are often able to avert tragic outcomes because many different values are placed on life, and the absolute value which a humanistic society accords to life does not determine its value in a particular situation.) But we saw quickly enough that the movement could not permanently be accomplished by the use of relative terms (such as efficiency) alone. Instead it is other kinds of values—notions of honesty and equality—which prove to be the crucial ones in the tragic context.

In the examples given above—the kidney and military service allocations—it seemed as if the value accorded efficiency would give us a neutral criterion whose application would not direct attention to any inadequate first-order or improper second-order determinations, but would arouse no more than pity and sorrow for those who would suffer. Yet the criterion failed and the ameliorative quality ceased with it, when efficiency-guided distributions correlated with wealth difference.

We may conclude that it was not merely the esteem Americans accord efficiency which enabled us to choose an allocation method which averted tragic results. Rather it was the way in which reliance on efficiency tacitly placed two other values in support of the allocation, namely those of honesty and equal treatment. These values play a unique role in the making of tragic choices, for they are structural premises designed to moot, or at least set the terms of, any particular ordering of preferences. As such they animate both resolutions of tragic conflict and the attack on such resolutions.

As we shall see, a conception of equality (or its converse, of hierarchy) often may achieve such a consensus in a society that its invocation in justification of a particular allocation can be used to avert a tragic outcome. Yet because even this conception is held in tension with other, antagonistic conceptions of equality, the resolution gained is temporary and the city is under siege almost as soon as it has been subdued.

Honesty is also ambivalent. It has the remarkable quality that it is capable of being abandoned with regard to some questions without being destroyed everywhere. Thus it can often be of service to the tragic choice by being neglected— indeed the usefulness of some allocation methods depends almost entirely on the charade that they serve the purposes they say they do. But the trick of dishonesty depends on assumptions of honesty; when these are questioned, honesty serves as a powerful engine of attack on the allocation.

In the kidney example a tragic outcome was avoided because it was believed that treating differently patients in whom the kidney would work from those in whom it would not amounted to treating people equally who were relevantly equal, and discriminating between those groups which were, relevantly, unequal. Furthermore, it was believed that the aim of the application of this distinction was to achieve maximum success from a limited number of artificial kidneys and not to serve other, covert purposes. When it became apparent that the rich were being separated out, whether or not this implied that decision makers had been dishonest about their motives, and even if such discrimination achieved maximum efficiency,[7] the discriminating criterion and therefore the allocation method became intolerable.

This particular conception of egalitarianism, which one might call a corrected egalitarianism, plays an unusually influential role in the American concept of equality.[8] It accepts the general premise of formal egalitarianism that discrimination is proper so long as likes are treated alike, but corrects the operation of this premise by rejecting it whenever methods applying it happen to produce results which correlate the permissible category of discrimination—health, for example— with an impermissible one, such as wealth or race. Every culture's concept of equality is an amalgam of such paradigms: Simple or naïve egalitarianism treats everyone alike and admits of no discrimination; laissez-faire egalitarianism requires equal opportunity to move within categories which may be properly the basis for discrimination, but begins in a context of variegated starting points, for instance, existing wealth distributions. Although no society could hold fully to one of these caricatures, concepts of equality do differ from society to society, in great measure as to which of these conceptions is most influential. Because allocations are taking place, the outcome of the tragic choice depends mainly on its relationship to a particular culture's notion of when it is right to accord some men a good and let others suffer, and sometimes die, without it; because most societies give precedence to some conceptions of equality, or hierarchy, over others, some such allocations can avoid tragedy at least for a time; but because no society adheres wholly to one conception of equality, many allocations remain tragic or revert quickly to tragedy.

Thus notions of equality are not the structural values which ultimately prove decisive in fashioning methods to cope with tragic choices. They are relatively fixed standards which guide the popular perception of allocation methods and to which such methods stand in a certain relationship. Rather it is honesty whose many uses are of most aid in society's struggle with tragic choice.

Honesty is not merely the backdrop against which tragic decisions are made, though it is surely this, as one quickly sees when it is doubted. Honesty is also the light which colors society's perception of the allocations achieved by such decisions. Evasion, disguise, temporizing, deception are all ways by which artfully chosen allocation methods can avoid the appearance of failing to reconcile values in conflict. Indeed, how could this not be so if society must confront suffering without being willing to discard its values every time it cannot uphold them? Averting the eyes enables us to save some lives even when we will not save all.

Honesty is the most influential brace in the tragic equilibrium. Though subterfuge may bring us peace, for a while, it is honesty which causes the tragic choice to reappear. It is honesty which must be protected from those allocation methods which taint it, while using its legitimating prestige to deal with immediate problems, because if altered, honesty loses its analytical power to deal with future problems quite unlike the ones we presently face and flatter ourselves that we understand. It is more than the instrument, it is measurement itself, for it is honesty which allows us to see clearly, and occasionally appreciate, the ways, some subtle and some not honest, by which societies must cope. We want to live, but we cannot. We want men to be equal, but they are not. We want suffering to end, but it will not. Honesty permits us to know what is to be accepted and, accepting, to reclaim our humanity and struggle against indignity.[9]

We stand in two relations to tragic choices. We are spectators, in anguish or disinterest. We are also participants in indirect and not so indirect ways. Usually we are more aware of our occasional role as direct participants, even perpetrators, than we are conscious of the many indirect ways in which the spectator becomes a part of the decision-making process. One purpose of this book is to acquaint spectators with those analytical perspectives which will enable us to appreciate the tragic struggle, the civilized and sometimes ennobling efforts by which a society preserves its traditions and values while replacing them to accommodate change and necessity.

Another purpose is to allow us, as citizens, to accept responsibility for tragic choices decided in our names. Then, as spectators, we can observe a culture, composed of ourselves, acting to save ultimate values from necessary desolation. "There is a magnificence [in these situations] in the power to rise, in the anguished acceptance that must always . . . precede the winning of dignity. For it is here before necessity that old morality is unmade and then remade into a new thing."[10]

The rest of this book concentrates on the processes of allocation. This is not an effort to offer solutions to particular problems, but rather, by looking at tragic situations, to illuminate the approaches we use to allocate both tragically scarce and trivially scarce resources.

We shall see what a market looks like, not when it is used to allocate cameras or fast cars, but when it is used to allocate a scarce life-saving resource. We will see what comes of using accountable political decisions not to distribute voting rights, but the right to have children. We shall ask how legal institutions, like juries, look when they are called upon to determine, not if a person is a petty thief and fit to be jailed for a year, but whether his life can be sacrificed because a certain number of victims must be found.[11] We shall consider what all these devices look like when each assigns tragic goods without benefit of that compensating diversity which ameliorates trivial allocations, namely, that other goods will be allocated through other approaches, and thereby rough fairness will out.

By studying these approaches and institutions in tragic contexts, where they cannot work well, we may more easily see those intrinsic strengths and limitations which are concealed when we merely observe what such approaches do acceptably.[12]

We will quickly be immersed in the analyses of methods. Terms will be invented and common terms used in strange contexts. It is of course notorious that one can arrive at "an over-simplified metaphysics from the obsession with 'things' and their 'qualities' ";[13] analogous illusions tempt the lawyer and the economist who treat hearts and watches as goods. Also, there is the temptation to assume that an account of a phenomenon—here, a decision or allocation process—tells us why it exists, or, in a fundamental sense, explains it.[14] We do not offer such explanations. Instead, the analyses in this book are overlays, maps organizing a turbulent landscape. The shapes we impose are familiar, yet new profiles emerge. From their study we may learn to recognize the motive, elemental forces which restless tragedy serves.

2

PURE ALLOCATION
APPROACHES

THE QUESTION of how allocation decisions are made in nontragic contexts by most societies, opens to view the special problems of decision-making devices in the tragic context. We shall begin by describing four general approaches to allocation. Each is, to some extent, a caricature of the actual processes used; but while the deviations from pure approaches in nontragic situations may often properly be ascribed to technical defects or to failings in the application of the particular approach, the failings of each of these approaches in the tragic context reflect basic features of the approaches themselves.

The Pure Market

At first glance, market mechanisms have strong appeal: The lack of overt coercion and the decentralized nature of market decisions act to absolve societies from responsibility for outcomes. Individuals appear to be the principal actors, and while society may be said to have set the stage, attention is riveted on individual choosers who, it is assumed, are acting to further their own goals. And yet we need only consider proposals such as: Everyone can be drafted to serve in wartime but anyone can buy his way out, or cancer chemotherapy will be auctioned to the highest bidder, to see how limited is the appeal of the market in a tragic situation. It is well to restate some of the reasons for these limitations in order to see what ameliorative modifications may be available.

For the market to achieve a first-order determination some cost figure for the resources required to produce the scarce good must be established by the market. Unless a market can, at a reasonable cost, be set up to determine these costs, the first-order determination will be made in a collective, nonmarket way, thereby affecting critically the desirability of a market approach at the level of the second-order determinations. Much of the advantage of market procedures is unavailable to us if we cannot, for example, determine the social cost of one more newborn child simply by letting a market aggregate the individual costs to those of us already here.[1]

Another, more significant problem with market determinations we shall call the *costs of costing*. The difficulty described in the preceding paragraph arose because it is sometimes impossible for the market accurately to assign costs to certain goods and bads so that we can determine how many of each we wish. The present problem reflects, instead, the external costs—moralisms and the affront to values, for example—of market determinations that say or imply that the value of a life or of some precious activity integral to life is reducible to a money figure. Even if the first-order determination has been satisfactorily made through a collective, nonmarket decision, this difficulty remains, and limits the desirability of second-order market allocations. In effect, a market at the second order, because it requires that a price be used, brutally emphasizes the first-order decision's implicit rejection of the pricelessness of the good being allocated.

At least as important as a limitation of the market is its dependence on the existing distribution of wealth. This dependence is accentuated when the market is used to make only the second-order determinations; once the first-order determinations are made collectively, it is implausible to say that by using the market we have merely given a resource to those who are willing to give up what it takes to produce it. Instead we are openly testing relative desire and this test is necessarily warped if the measure of desire—a single dollar, for example—has a different importance for different choosers.

It is no use to reply that the market simply measures whether each individual believes that he will be better off with the goods he must forgo to outbid others, or without them and with the resource itself. And this is true even though there are reasons supporting the reply, for the reasons are sufficiently intricate as to be generally inaccessible or so attenuated as to sound fishy.

To put it another way, when tragic choices are made through the pure market within an existing distribution of wealth, costs arise which are external to the immediate decision makers and are borne instead by the rest of us. These external costs may limit our willingness to permit a market: The social costs of indentured labor, for example, surely include one's outrage at inducing the poor to sell themselves, and this cost must be considered before the society allows peonage. The willingness of a poor man, confronting a tragic situation, to choose money rather than the tragically scarce resource always represents an unquiet indictment of society's distribution of wealth. That willingness, when it follows a first-order determination which has been made collectively, is a yet more insistent accusation; it presents the wrenching spectacle of a rich man and a poor man bidding against each other for life. Yet the degree of redistribution of wealth necessary to avoid such external costs would itself be too costly. It might require a virtual equivalence of wealth such that incentives to produce would not survive.

It would not be enough to allocate the scarce resource to the relatively poor bidder without requiring him to match the bid of his wealthy competitor; he must continue to be favored until he no longer needs and hence no longer prefers other goods more than the scarce resource. Otherwise the wealthier bidder will simply buy the resource from him instead of from the auctioneer. Such subsequent exchanges might be prohibited, but the need for prohibition only serves to emphasize that society—for its own reasons—is preventing all the bidding participants, including the poorest, from doing precisely as they wish—from accomplishing that rare feat, making what, but for the frustration and demoralization involved, would be a Pareto superior move.[2]

We are, in other words, dealing with situations in which we

are unwilling to bear either the external costs of a market allocation of the tragically scarce resource or the external costs of a wealth distribution sufficiently egalitarian to avoid such costs. We will have occasion later to discuss this problem of *merit wants*.[3] For the present it is enough to note that if the market is used to make the first-order *and* the second-order determinations, the conflict is to some degree hidden; if the latter only, the costs of the conflict are dramatically highlighted.

Finally, the market presumes that, in allocation decisions there are no valid reasons other than each individual's relative desire to obtain the scarce good or avoid the bad. Madame DeFarge and Madame Curie are on the same footing. Yet we may believe that there are external benefits to keeping Madame Curie in good health that the pure market cannot translate into incentives affecting her atomistic decision. Such external benefits (or costs) are in addition to those which arise because market choices are made on the basis of an existing distribution of wealth, and may therefore require modifications even in markets which are totally neutral with respect to wealth distribution.[4] Modifications designed not to equalize wealth but instead to influence individual choices, though technically feasible, raise the specter of a collectively imposed in-egalitarianism. They proclaim the greater worth of Madame Curie to society.

We shall return to a discussion of these problems in Chapter 3 when we examine the modifications of the pure market by which it may be adapted to cope with the tragic situation.

The Accountable Political Approach

In many nontragic decisions we do not use markets, but allocate instead according to standards set up through a responsible political process. In wartime, the United States has decided in a centralized, political way not only how much gasoline should go to civilian use but also to what categories of people how much should go. The political decision was accountable, or *responsible,* in the sense that an explanation for the standards was expected and was, in fact, given. Whenever we decide the number of people who may hold certain governmental positions and then allocate those positions according to examinations which reflect discernible standards, we are making both first- and second-order determinations in an accountable political way. It is just as much this sort of decision if the standards explicitly depend on preferences for particular groups, like veterans or the disabled. The political process has set guidelines for allocation and given reasons to justify both how many of certain goods or bads will be needed and who will get them.

Intertwined with tragic choices are many closely related allocations which can be made through accountable political processes, without involving tragedy.[5] The decision to give priority for the use of kidney machines to those who will most benefit medically was this kind of allocation. To many that decision involved no conflict and hence no sacrifice of basic values.[6] Similarly, the deferment and exemption system formerly employed by the selective service laws represents the same sort of political choice: When deferments or exemptions operate to exclude the aged, the seriously handicapped, or the very young, or perhaps even conscientious objectors, from military service, the criteria for discrimination are not the result of tragic choices. But when conscription operates, as it occasionally has, to exclude farmers, geniuses, or engineers from the risk of wartime death because they are felt to have a greater social utility at home, many would feel that that determination is the outcome of a tragic allocation. Just as the pure market was used to assign wartime service during the Civil War, such pure, responsible political devices have been used at different times in our history to make tragic choices.[7]

As we shall see, this approach has substantial defects when used in the tragic situation. We should like first to mention, however, two general defects of accountable political decision making which are not specific to tragic allocations.

The general shortcoming of responsible political decision making is that the process itself is easily overburdened. Even if one believes that any single allocation decision is best made through an accountable political determination, it is very unlikely that such a decision will also be well made if a hundred or a thousand other decisions are to be made by the same process. The choice of an allocation mechanism must be prefaced by the recognition that there are many other decisions to be made. Therefore one must determine the comparative advantage of using political devices. This problem though is not specific to tragic allocations.[8]

A second general difficulty with this approach results from its unaccomplishable need for information gathering. In part, this is a problem of centralization. If the object of political decision making is to allocate according to individual desires for a good, then the process requires learning a lot about many individuals. The same is true if the object is to allocate according to some measure of the social usefulness of each individual's having the good. The problem is the same whether we are allocating the right to have more shoes or more children, but it is especially relevant to tragic choices because the decentralization devices which we use in nontragic decisions to resolve this problem will prove unacceptable in the tragic context, for reasons which we shall discuss. (We may be content to have a local bureaucrat determine the relative usefulness of our having shoes, by reference to responsible, centrally made standards, but not tolerate that same person's deciding the relative usefulness of our survival.) Yet absent decentralization, it is virtually impossible to determine each individual's relative desire to survive. While the market finds it difficult to take into account the social utility of an allocation apart from individual expressions of desire, the political process, in a tragic context, is substantially handicapped in considering individual desires to determine social utility.

This problem of decentralization is principally a matter of the second-order determination. The first-order decision is not dependent on the same degree of specific knowledge of individual differences. So long as the accountable political decision makers have some measure of average desires for various goods and the average social utility of having more or less of each, they can make the first-order determination at a centralized level.

The political approach has special difficulties when it is employed to make tragic decisions. These are the problems of an exposed inegalitarianism and of exposed decisions against life, and they are the direct analogues of merit wants and costing of lives which were mentioned in the preceding section.

The very fact that the goods and bads involved in tragic allocations were often considered merit wants in the context of market choices suggests that their allocation in any way other than through simple egalitarianism poses difficulties.[9] In some instances the goods would not be merit goods were they allocated according to some other unequal distribution, different from the dominant wealth distribution. Then either an alternative market or a political allocation might avoid the conflict; a nontragic solution would exist. This is the case where such conventionally accepted standards as age and health are employed as means of allocating wartime service. But it is not the case where external costs attach whenever a nonequal distribution of certain goods or bads is made, and this is true whether the external costs are of the traditional sort or of the variety we have called moralisms.

If a society values simple equality as a fundamental standard, some goods or bads must be allocated on that basis. Yet unless simple egalitarianism is totally dominant, allocation according to its dictates will violate other deeply held conceptions of equality. A society which attempts to adhere to plural conceptions of equality—all held, as it were, in tension—must find any exposed allocation damaging. The goods and bads involved in tragic choices are, moreover, those very goods whose allocation, however done, is most destructive of some of the conflicting egalitarian values. Thus a society like ours may not give precedence to simple egalitarianism among conflicting concep-

tions of equality. Yet that same society may find it impossible to
say that mathematicians may have more children than porters
and justify this rule by reference to the relative value to society
of the children of both groups. The assertion clearly contradicts
the desire of that society to view mathematicians and porters
simply as equals. As such, the allocation undermines all the
institutions which depend on simple equality.

This does not mean that the problem must necessarily arise
whenever life or death is being allocated. In some societies the
greater importance of one category is fully acceptable and
allocations consistent with that status evoke no fundamental
conflicts. In other societies there is a trade-off, so that one
category is preferred in some choices and discriminated against
in others. But most of these situations occur in hierarchic
societies where caste prescribes role,[10] and it is hard to see how
a society that views its members as created equal can accept
such trade-offs in tragic goods without dissonance.[11] It might be
that allocations based on relative individual desires to have the
good or to avoid the bad would not violate any of our conceptions of egalitarianism and would be acceptable in the United
States. But even if that were the case, such judgments of
individual desire are extremely hard for responsible political
processes to make, while most markets which would make
them begin from the inegalitarian premise of unequal distribution of wealth. Still, our intuitive notions that allocations based
on individual desires, as against social utility, are more consistent with those conceptions of egalitarianism which are captured in the phrases "all men are created equal" and "to each
according to his need" suggest ways in which markets and
political processes may be modified to reduce the tragic character of some choices at the second-order level.

A final point should be emphasized. The problem of preferring one group to another may be compounded by the very fact
that it is the political process that is being used. The inegalitarian choice is not just occurring either as the aggregate or the
simple expression of individual choices, rather it is being made

by the whole society in its most responsible way. The state is declaring in unmistakable terms the greater importance of one category over another.

Allocation through responsible political processes does not avoid the market defect of directly valuing things; lives, for example, we prefer to think of as beyond price. When an accountable political process reaches the conclusion that convicts will be used in ultrahazardous industries, a destruction of our values has taken place distinct from any lack of egalitarianism in the determination. Such a second-order decision makes clear and unmistakable the first-order determination that certain lives are worth risking. If the political process refuses to provide a group such as the aged with hemodialysis, the clear assertion has been made that some lives are not worth saving. To the extent that our lives and institutions depend on the notion that life is beyond price, such a refusal to save lives is horribly costly. The offense can be limited by dramatic reaffirmations of the value of life in other contexts. A fortune may be spent to save the convict caught in a jailhouse fire. But for the society as a whole, to reconcile the two decisions rationally as well as emotionally is extraordinarily difficult, and the frequent result will be that the lower value becomes dominant, across the board.[12]

The analogous defect of the market—that once a price for a life in a given context is determined, it is hard not to have that price seem to represent the value of life in general—may be greater or less depending on how obviously lives are being costed. So for the political process, the offense may be greater or less depending on how obvious and exposed the political decision. This aspect was clearly intuited by Justice Potter Stewart in the Pentagon Papers Case when he noted from the bench the difficulties that "a judicial sentencing to death of a hundred people" for the sake of freedom of speech would imply, if secret news of troop convoys were publicly printed.[13]

Before we leave this first look at accountable political decision making, we should note that the crucial defects of such decisions in tragic contexts are not as much in play at the first-order level of decision as they are at the second order. We have already mentioned why the problem of individual desires is not as severe. And the egalitarian ideal is not questioned by a decision which limits the total number of vaccine doses or infantry divisions. The second-order decision necessarily implied by the first-order determination may pit the egalitarian ideal against other values (life, honesty) or may bring different conceptions of egalitarianism into conflict with one another, but the first-order decision need not logically or, strangely enough, emotionally, require that egalitarianism be undermined. The relationship between the first-order determination and the costs of too clearly valuing the priceless is more complex. The first-order decision, by limiting population for example, necessarily prevents some people from procreating, and yet because another level of decision making must occur (one that can be made in a totally different way by different institutions) before someone is actually barred from having children, the conflict of values seems to be stayed until the second-order decision.

Consider the different attitude we all share toward the failure of Congress to pass truly effective safety legislation, as against the attitude we would have were it unwilling to appropriate funds for the rescue of a trapped hostage. Lives may be discarded in both examples, but the choice is less exposed in the first case and therefore less destructive of some of the basic values involved. To return to Justice Stewart, an absolute rule forbidding prior censorship which can be statistically shown to cost many hundreds of lives strikes us differently from a decision in a specific case to allow publication when we know that a hundred lives will be lost as a result.[14]

Certain general characteristics limit uses of the responsible political approach. To these are added the substantial shortcomings of that approach when applied to second-order tragic determinations. There may be societies that are capable of the detached rationality that would permit a legislature to authorize uncontrolled medical experimentation with the ter-

minally ill, sterilization of the dull-witted, or the abandonment
of vacationers lost at sea on the basis of a narrow cost-benefit
analysis. [15] We are not such a society and therefore our political
processes alone will not serve us in such dilemmas, tragic
dramas unresolvable in a culture for whom scarcity is, for the
present, neither a memory nor an expectation.

The Lottery

A third approach to decision making is the lottery, a choice
not to choose. This approach mirrors a simple, sweeping conception of egalitarianism, since allocation by lot treats everyone
within the eligible group in the same way. Either all have an
equal chance at the pay-off or pay-offs are distributed in an
equal amount to all group members. Exclusion from the eligible group represents a decision that the member is sufficiently,
relevantly dissimilar to compel special treatment. The fewer
relevant differences that are recognized, the greater is the
likelihood of absurd or costly results from a second-order determination.

American egalitarianism is neither absolute nor simple,
however, and it is not the only value at stake. Indeed, the agony
of the tragic choice reflects precisely the conflict of discrete
values to which we are committed. The lottery does not help us
resolve the conflicts which inhere at the first-order decision
level. At best, lot systems are only useful for second-order
determinations, but there the lottery poses the problem that,
despite the egalitarian basis of our society, we view people as
different from one another. To the extent that such dissimilarities are perceived as compatible with other views about
the general equality of man (and recognition of these differences is fundamental to some conceptions of egalitarianism), [16] a
political decision may set limits on the lottery pool (for
example, the exemption of the blind from wartime service). But
such a two-stage combination of approaches does not succeed
when the relevant dissimilarities are either inaccessible to
political decision makers (ascertaining, for example, the rela-

tive desire to serve in the military) or where their recognition is perceived as violative of egalitarian ideals (the exemption from service of a gifted research biologist). In such cases, inclusion of relevantly dissimilar individuals in the pool can bring about absurd results. (The "dove" who is a highly educated musician may be sent to war, while the "hawk" who is a crack shot may remain at home.)

Absurd results confer political benefits, however, in that they confirm the incorruptibility of the decision process. In addition they reinforce those values which caused the society to wish to treat as similar individuals who, for other purposes, are obviously dissimilar. Moreover, to the extent lottery mechanisms treat as the same people who are relevantly in the same situation, and are generally so perceived, those choices are nontragic.

Nevertheless, lot systems, at the level of the second order, display defects that resemble those associated with markets and accountable political processes. In the market it was difficult to recognize those differences among individuals which were not expressed in atomistic choices. Conversely, the political process could not easily handle differences based on individual desires. Lotteries are blind to both sorts of differences. Randomness epitomizes a conception of egalitarianism that treats everyone alike. As such, it clashes with other conceptions, like "to each according to his need," which require differentiation.

In addition to the potentially high costs of randomness, lot systems usually dramatize the first-order determination. A lottery for the available artificial kidney machines brings into high relief the preliminary choice to provide an insufficient number of machines to serve everyone. This can be as destructive as giving an exact price to lives or judicially sentencing a hundred people to death for the sake of freedom of the press. Whether the cost of this spotlight effect can be overborne by the advantages which accrue to second-order lottery determinations will depend, of course, on what kind of first-order choice is involved. The decision that three survivors of a shipwreck must be sacrificed to lighten the lifeboat is differently perceived, and differently taken, than would be the decision to send only thirty boats to Dunkirk.

A modification of lot systems that reduces this highlighting effect is a *first-come-first-served* method. Once the quantity of the tragically scarce resource is determined through a first-order decision, the second-order allocation consists simply in giving it out to all who ask for it as long as the supply lasts. This approach cannot be used where, as in childbearing, individuals can vary the time when they desire the resource. Additionally, it may be deeply inegalitarian if usable knowledge of the availability of the resource is unevenly distributed within the eligible group, particularly if the uneven distribution is linked to social or economic attributes.[17] But if such information is either broadly available or randomly distributed and the need for the resource is not triggered by the user, a first-come-first-served method approaches a pure lottery with the drawing made *ex machina*.

Like the pure lottery, however, first-come-first-served retains the defect that recipients treated as equals may in fact not be considered equals. Indeed, that defect may be more damaging because it will be hard to give effect to those differences which could be openly considered under a pure lottery. A pure lottery may exclude from the drawings for kidneys those who are substantially less likely to benefit from dialysis than the mass of would-be kidney recipients. But unless the likelihood of dialysis failure is so great as to warrant denial of the dialysis even when no better recipient is presently available, a first-come-first-served approach will make analogous exclusions extremely difficult. Should a second-rate recipient be excluded simply because we think it likely that a first-rater will come along later? Should a second-rate recipient be given the artificial kidney temporarily and then have it removed when a first-rater comes along? Either way, most of the benefits of first-come-first-served in de-emphasizing the first-order determination, to say nothing of avoiding hard second-order decisions, would be lost.[18] The exclusions that are relatively easy to accommodate in the lottery are harder to build in as modifications to a first-come-first-served approach. It is little wonder, then, that when a first-come-first-served approach has been used, even those second-order allocations which were susceptible to an accountable political approach annexed to a lottery have been too costly to make, and scarce artificial kidneys have been given to recipients who benefitted very little from them.[19]

Pure lotteries, by contrast, can readily incorporate market or political modifications. More importantly, they can frequently be appended *faute de mieux* to market and political decision procedures when the limits of mindful choice are reached in a tragic situation (choosing a hostage, for example, from among children). The blind working of the lottery is the feature critical to such combinations. Preliminary exclusions can be made through other methods in order to eliminate the possibility of absurd or too expensive winners. Beyond that, blindness is employed to express our refusal to make distinctions to which tragic consequences must attach: It allows us to choose when we can no longer tolerate choice.[20]

Although the lottery method may be combined with other approaches to help cope with the tragic situation, lottery methods themselves, unlike political and market approaches, cannot be significantly modified to adjust to the varying features of the tragic choice. The blind element is necessary and, ultimately, irreducible. This is both the virtue and the shortcoming of the lottery.

The Customary or Evolutionary Approach

This is less an approach in the manner of the preceding three than an attitude which may be given effect by any of the other methods, or their combinations. The attitude consists of the avoidance of self-conscious choice: The method of choosing is not explicitly chosen and may not even be known by the mass of the people. The actual allocations evolve in the society without any explicit selection.

The great advantage of this attitude is that so long as the belief in its society-intrinsic character holds, it seems to avoid the costs of fundamental values in conflict. We do not know for example that market incentives determine the production of children in America and these incentives are rarely perceived as having been set up or chosen for such a purpose; therefore the value conflicts typical of allocating the rights to have children at either the first- or second-order level are not precipitated. But the fact of the matter is that the costs of bringing up children, which have been unself-consciously assigned to some categories of parents but not to others, act as a real market control on procreation. The very rich bear somewhat greater per capita costs of rearing children than middle-income groups, but not to any degree proportionate to their greater wealth. The very poor, at least on some views of the matter, may actually have market incentives to create children.[21] That the resulting allocation may or may not be desired or desirable is less important than the fact that no explicit choice of it was made.

Some may argue that our determination of the number of children is essentially the result of a pure market, that we have internalized the cost of additional children to the parents and that individual families are deciding for themselves and for society the correct first-order determination, the total number of children the society will have. We may test this assertion in a simple, intuitive way. The question is, "Do we tolerate a range of procreation, say 1.8 to 2.3 per family, because we believe it to be the result of individual expressions, or have we intuitively determined that that range is what is appropriate, and accepted the systems of incentives which have evolved, because they bring it about?" Were it the first, we would be inclined to accept a change in the rate of procreation to 0.8 or to 6.3 per family; it would be the result of the aggregate of individual reactions to costs placed on them and we would have no predetermined correct level of procreation. The pure market would be taken to have indicated that *that* was the correct first-order decision. If instead, as we suggest would be the case, such a result would be taken to indicate that something had gone horribly wrong, we would have a strong indication that the second explanation was correct.

If the distribution of bearing and rearing children is, in part, a result of unchosen market pressures, our definition of *death* has resulted from unchosen nonmarket choices. For most of man's history death has been a simple notion, more an empirical observation than a concept. One could have, we suppose, tried to define what rule determined death, but the fact of the matter was that the definition used was essentially vague. The errors such a definition might engender were less important than that those errors could not be explicitly attributed to the conscious choice of a particular definition of death which would kill some who were still living.

The nonmarket customary approach often takes the form of moral suasion. This means of allocation is probably as significant in our current system of population control as the unchosen market incentives we have mentioned; at other times, it has served to allocate service in the military. In each case, the people who respond to moral suasion, the good citizens, are not necessarily those to whom we would consciously allocate fewer children or greater wartime risks; but the advantage, as with unchosen market incentives, lies less in how the allocation is made or in its results, than that it may appear not to have been made at all. Thus the possibly absurd outcomes may be less harmful than the deliberate, blind results of a lottery.

The precariousness of customary approaches should be obvious. Any loss of innocence not only destroys the value of the approach, but also suggests that we were kept innocent. As soon as people begin to realize that children are in fact allocated according to a complex system of moral suasion and market incentives and that this allocation operates to the benefit of some and to the detriment of others, criticism of the allocation is inevitable, and the critics will rightly charge that the allocation could have been changed by state action. At this point a choice not to choose, a choice to remain as we are, becomes itself a clear decision and as such is subject to the same costs as chosen allocations. It was only our ignorance of the costly choices imbedded in the unchosen *status quo* that had materially reduced the price in ideals.

This problem may again be exemplified in the context of defining death. A new definition is proposed and is immediately attacked on the ground that, in a miniscule number of cases, the definition would doom people who could return to what all would accept as life. The change may even be taken to represent a decision to kill a few people in order to facilitate transplants. Then someone asks, "What is the present definition and how often does *it* doom people who are alive?" Ignorance or innocence is lost and we are now faced with the fact that, no matter how we choose, some living people will be killed as a result of our choice.[22]

This is not to say that we should not have emerged from naïvete to sophistication. Whether the Tree of Knowledge is the Tree of Life depends on whether, now that we are aware of what we are doing, we can do sufficiently better to make up for the costs of clearly choosing. But whether we can or not, we cannot turn back: We now know that either way, we are choosing to take some people's lives. We have moved beyond the customary situation.

We should distinguish one aspect of tragic choices that is often confused with the customary approach but is in fact quite different. We are very often, in tragic situations, faced with the choice between a device which allocates well, but whose flaws are also certain, and a device which does less well, but which is theoretically perfectible. In the context of jeopardizing lives, we may choose the perfectible approach even though it costs lives because it represents a less clear choice to sacrifice life. Whether we will do this or not depends on many factors, including the actual likelihood of the perfectibility, the comparative number of lives required by each device, and so forth. The common preference for such perfectible devices over more efficient but predictably flawed mechanisms will be discussed later in the context of the uses of *fault* language in tragic choices. We mention it here because, not infrequently, customary allocation devices are of the theoretically perfectible kind.

For instance, the success or failure of the traditional definition of death depended on the sensitive abilities of doctor and nurse. This possibility of perfectibility may be a valid reason for retaining what just came to be the allocation method, even when we are faced with an explicit choice. It is a reason, however, logically different from the observation that when we were ignorant that a choice was being made at all, we were avoiding some societal harms, quite apart from whether the nonchoice brought about theoretically perfectible or necessarily imperfect results.

The customary approach leaves us one other question. Should we sacrifice this approach, and its substantial benefits in preventing the tragic situation, by the mass distribution of disillusioning information? Should researchers point out that the failure to eliminate grade crossings is as certain a killing as the unwillingness to produce kidney machines?

Choice, however costly, is liberating and leads to progress; nonchoice allows those already in power to hide the allocations they favor. The failure to make society aware of its implicit choices will diminish, with each averting of the eyes, the values of openness and honesty. To this one might reply, "Man chooses badly, and what is left to evolve will better reflect the complexity of competing outcomes than the poor planning of policy makers who must schematize a dimly grasped reality."[23]

This conflict is by no means confined to tragic situations. It occurs when some argue for a gold standard and others for a rational monetary system. It occurs between those who urge relatively formalistic legal systems, which answer primarily to their own logical rules and aesthetics, and those who support more functional approaches to law. When the dilemma occurs in the context of tragic choices, it is, however, especially difficult, for there, to one's doubts about man's ability to choose intelligently, one can add the very real costs entailed by the knowledge that a choice is being made.

Yet we are born to reason and any attempt to keep someone from pointing out the unchosen choices that are being made is bound to fail. At the same time, our vision is limited, and so at any time many unchosen choices will exist which have not yet been found out. As a result, there will always be customary resolutions waiting to be exposed and in whose existence some will take comfort.

Conclusion

In this chapter we have discussed four methods of allocation. The pure market attempts to resolve conflicts in tragic situations by according pre-eminence to individual expressions of wants. It fails because the summing up of such expressions fails to accommodate social goals and fails even to represent what individuals want. Its operation runs counter to some important conceptions of egalitarianism and it too clearly prices that to which we should like to ascribe infinite value.

An accountable political process does not succeed because it cannot readily give effect to individual desires. It is also flawed, as it straightforwardly involves the whole society, the state, in preferring some individuals to others and in choosing to discard what ideally we would assert to be inalienable.

Lotteries deify absolute equality, but in so doing offend other conceptions of egalitarianism and emphasize society's unwillingness to spend enough to treat everyone decently as well as alike.

The customary approach represents a totally different attitude. It is unconcerned with individual desires or collective optima in its allocations; it is concerned only with not choosing. This means that it may bring about results which are as mindless as those of lotteries or which are manipulable by those in power. It avoids the costs of costing, but at the cost of honesty and openness. And honesty and openness are structural values which define a society at least as much as "the sanctity of life" and "all men are created equal." They are no more absolute than the other values. But a society consistently forgoes them only at great peril, for without them who is to say when or how any values are affirmed. Since honesty and openness are not absolute, the customary approach is not without merit, but it, too, ultimately, destroys some values to which we must cleave.

In coping with tragic situations we are not limited, however, to pure approaches. Both market and political decision processes may be significantly modified to counter their principal defects. Neither the lottery nor customary approaches are subject to much variation (except as one views their use in combination with other procedures as a variation). The next two chapters discuss those approaches which are amenable to major modifications, the market and the political processes.

3

MODIFIED POLITICAL DEVICES[1]

Decentralization

Decentralization is an obvious modification of the accountable political approach and takes one of two forms, depending on whether it is motivated by a desire to base decisions on the standards of the local community or by the belief that centralized standards are better effectuated if some necessary *facts* are determined locally. In either form, decentralization promises to allow a more discriminating choice, and to offer wider possibilities for experimentation. The first form encourages experimentation with different grounds for allocations, the second, with different fact-finding devices. But the very statement of such possibilities should suggest some of the problems decentralization does not solve, as well as those which it adds to the existing list.

In the first place, decentralization does not resolve the fundamental conflict between our commitment to inconsistent egalitarianisms and the necessary inegalitarianism implicit in the recognition of the distinctions decentralization is meant to facilitate. The decision to allow the sighted to have children and deny this right to the hereditarily blind is a costly one even if it emerges from a local board applying responsibly determined standards. Granted, the difficulty may be somewhat different if the standards are determined locally. While a local determination may enforce parochial prejudices, it does have the advantage of avoiding the national statement that, for example, the sighted are worth more than the blind. Instead, the less toxic assertion is made that in Connecticut or in Texas the sighted are more highly valued. But this more restricted declaration has its own costs. We are one nation, and it is offensive to have fundamental allocations depend on the chance of where in the land one lives. The judicial history of the Fourteenth Amend-

ment may be characterized as the development of the sense
that whatever its advantages, this kind of decentralization will
not be permitted when certain allocations are involved. That is,
our society has come to believe, and hold as a fundamental
value itself, that with regard to such allocations people should
be treated the same regardless of where they are, or where they
came from, within the country.[2] It follows, therefore, that the
modification of an accountable political approach by a decentralization in the fashioning of standards rarely ameliorates the
egalitarian dilemma present in tragic choices.

Decentralization is more promising when it is employed to
improve fact-finding rather than set standards. For example,
substantial leeway may be given to accountable local bodies in
fashioning ways of determining whether an individual con-
scientiously objects to military service. But this presumes that
conscientious objection is itself an acceptable ground for differentiation, and frequently in tragic choices such acceptable
standards are not available.

Moreover, localized fact-finding is especially susceptible to
some of the general shortcomings of the decentralizing modification. If the virtue of the decentralizing modification is its
ability to ascertain facts otherwise unavailable or unclear to
more distant decision makers, this virtue is flawed by the
doubts which accompany any fact-finding that is unverifiable.
The more decentralized the process becomes, the less sure we
are that the acceptable national rules are in fact being applied;
the suspicion of bias, advantage, or corruption is heightened—
and more so still when what is at stake is so significant. Nonmarket allocations are always subject to perversion by market
influences such as bribes, favors, gifts, and political contributions. Distance implies detachment and propinquity implies
opportunity. The more decentralized and unverifiable the fact-
finding and the application of a standard, the more some people
will claim, at no small social harm, that the whole process is
crooked. We shall have more to say about this when we discuss
aresponsible decision making.[3]

Responsible decentralization adds costs of another kind, the process costs of appearing before the decision maker. There are emotional costs to subjecting oneself to the sort of local fact-finding required in the decentralized tragic decision. And there are costs of access to the decider and, more specifically, costs of equal access.

We may understand such emotional costs if we contemplate what it means to have to appear before a tribunal to justify our right to have children. Privacy is essential to human dignity in many tragic situations, and any requirement that we bare ourselves before some board violates that dignity. Dignity is more likely despoiled in the situation posited because a responsible decentralized agency must justify its conclusions and hence, inevitably, do some public baring of the facts in individual cases. We are little assuaged in this concern by the realization that not all tragic choices share this problem to the same extent, any more than they equally share any problem.[4]

The costs of access may seem more pedestrian but they are no less troublesome. In nontragic contexts we encounter them in the current controversies over court costs and legal aid. The more decentralized and individualized a decision, the more expensive it is likely to be in terms of purely administrative costs. That we all know. What is often forgotten is the equally true fact that the more decisions are individualized, the more equality of representation before the decision maker becomes crucial. This has frequently been ignored because legal thinking has structured the discussion of the individuality of decision making along the familiar lines of the categorical judge-made decision versus the relatively individualized jury decision.[5] And here legal scholars have been inclined to focus on the nature of the decider rather than the disconcerting and just-perceptible possibility that greater jury flexibility might require a greater equality of representation. Such a possibility has been obscured as the jury has been presumed, because of its composition, to be more responsive to those less likely to have effective access.[6] Today, however, one can discern in arguments for no-fault divorce, or even no-fault auto insurance (though the position is rarely explicitly made), that the lack of individuation such reforms may effect can be justified precisely because those who could afford representation had too great an advantage in the old systems.[7] When we decide to decentralize decision making in the tragic context in order to make judgments of social utility or individual desire more sensitive to individual distinctions, we have also decided either to pay very high administrative costs or to add another inequality to those implicit in the recognition of such distinctions, namely, the unequal ability to present one's case.

Both the emotional costs and the costs of access are examples of what we shall term process costs. Apart from the question of who gets the scarce resource in a tragic situation, there is the essential decision as to who shall bear the cost of the procedure by which the resource is allocated.[8] Sometimes these process costs can be shifted; sometimes they are an unseverable part of the chosen procedure. A procedure which invades the privacy of those who seek the right to have children injures even those who win that right; insult is added to injury for those who don't. A procedure which entails high cost of access will, unless these costs are borne by the state, create financial hardships for those who can barely pay for a lawyer and add one more insult to those who cannot. The problem of process costs, however, does not apply only to decentralized, responsible political processes. Hence, we will deal with it in greater detail later.[9]

To say that there are costs is not to say they are not worth paying.[10] When the modification of accountable political processes by decentralized decision making brings sufficient benefits, the expense of equal access may be worth bearing. An instance of this would be the application of fairly clear indices of individual desire or social utility when their use would not entail too great privacy costs or too great, and too offensive, inegalitarian premises. One thinks, for example, of the decentralized determination of whether a kidney transplant will "take," and prove compatible with the tissues of the recipient.

Decentralization the American Way: The Aresponsible Agency or Jury

What we shall call the aresponsible agency is a typically American mode of decentralizing political decisions. The jury, in one of its aspects, is the prototype of this variant and the myth of the jury is the source of the use and adaptation of aresponsible agencies in a variety of tragic contexts.

The aresponsible agency generally has three features: It is representative, decentralized, and it gives no reasons for its decisions. Its representative quality is supposed to give effect to what society views as relevant differences among individuals. Because the agency is decentralized, it is able to make individuated decisions. And giving no reasons, it avoids, or at least mitigates, the conflict between the wish to recognize differences and the desire to affirm egalitarianism in all its forms. For though recognition of differences does occur in the decisions, that recognition needn't compel the rejection of egalitarian ideals. Too many distinctions are consistent with various conceptions of egalitarianism, while others, though inconsistent, come to be seen as such only if a number of decisions suggest a pattern. It is thus hard for anyone to be sure, in the first instance, that a jury has done anything inegalitarian.[11]

The jury's representativeness and lack of responsibility have at times been identified as the reason why certain decisions are committed to it.[12] It is the combining of these elements which is the source of the characteristic and powerful way in which the jury operates: Juries apply societal standards without ever telling us what these standards are, or even that they exist.[13] This is especially important in those situations in which the statement of standards would be terribly destructive. This has been the role of juries in euthanasia cases. Something of the same purpose was served by the untrammeled discretion which allowed juries to impose the death penalty within certain broadly defined classes of cases. Indeed, the Supreme Court's curtailment of this discretion may be illuminated by our subsequent discussion of the defects of aresponsible agencies.[14]

The myth of the jury has seemed so compelling that, in the United States, there has been strong pressure to deal with tragic choices by turning them over to jurylike bodies. Such pressures produced parajuries, such as the Seattle God Committee, which allocated artificial kidneys, and at times in our history draft boards with unfettered discretion.[15] The choice of the jury device, however, is seldom made with a sufficient understanding of those problems which an aresponsible agency does not solve, of those problems which are created by aresponsible decision making, and finally, of the differences between the potentially tragic situations with which juries have dealt relatively successfully and those decisions which have recently been given to parajuries to resolve.

The use of a jury or parajury does not avoid the process costs we have discussed in considering decentralized decision making in general; the problems of privacy and of access to representation remain essentially as severe as before.

One can imagine the parajury being given only the most general guidelines (analogous to the charge a judge gives a jury in a lawsuit). These guidelines would be based on distinctions which could be incorporated in the responsible decision-making process; once given them, the parajury would be left to its own devices as to how to decide the allocation. In such a situation the applicant is bound to feel pressure to bare his soul in order to be sure that everything relevant is before the deciders. The often humiliating costs of such testimony are immense. These costs may be somewhat less than if the parajury were required to give reasons for its decision because the secret-sharing is at least confined to a small group. But this easing may be more than counterbalanced by the pressures which secrecy creates. The applicant, precisely because he

does not know why previous applicants lost or won probably
exposes himself more than he would have done before an
accountable decision maker. If he, nevertheless, loses, and
without explanation, the demoralization will be particularly
intense.

Of course, not all tragic decisions entail the same privacy
costs. Medical experiments with humans, for example, often
require decisions based on less intimate information than, say,
decisions allotting the right to procreate. Even personal data
relevant to the experimentation decision are commonly
semipublic because the individuals involved have, in practice,
divulged them to doctors and nurses for purposes extraneous to
the allocation, for treatment rather than decision.[16] We do not
mean to make too much of this difference, but only to suggest
what we will discuss in greater detail later on, that the suitabil-
ity and costs of each technique for tragic decisions vary with the
tragic choice.

The problem of representation before the decision-making
body is as acute for an aresponsible agency as it was for a
decentralized responsible agency. Since people are not equal in
their ability to state their cases, we are again faced with the
necessity either of accepting *sub silentio* the notion that the
ability to state a case is an acceptable criterion for allocating the
good[17] or making sure that everyone is approximately equally
represented. The literature on legal aid is sufficiently vast and
the attempts to avoid the dilemma are sufficiently current to
indicate what a mare's nest this question presents.[18] Slogans
like "divorce at will" or "abortion at one's own discretion"
which buy equality at the cost of hiding real differences are a
sort of despairing response to the problem of unequal representation.

To the problems with which we have become familiar in the
political process, the aresponsible agency adds some which are
especially its own. They derive, quite simply, from the lack of
accountability, and as such are necessary features of the approach. After an aresponsible, representative agency has for

some years been used to make tragic choices, either of two things will happen: A pattern of decisions will emerge or it will not. Both possibilities weaken the parajury by undermining its credibility as an unbiased, rational agency, capable of making socially admissible choices.

If a pattern emerges it becomes clear that the use of the aresponsible agency was simply a roundabout way of saying that the winners (as revealed by the pattern) were to be preferred to the losers. Once again, the egalitarian dilemma comes to the fore. Although it may be somewhat mitigated because a series of representative agencies, rather than the government as such, have decreed the result and because a preference can change as subtly as it was created, as values among jurymen change, the egalitarian dilemma is also accentuated by these features. A critic may properly say, "If a pattern of preference does exist, then at least we should be sure that the preferences correspond to rankings determined in a truly representative, and even national, fashion." If we, in fact, favor husband-killers to wife-killers, we should know whether this would be supported by a national policy determined through a responsible political process;[19] by leaving it up to the jury, we permit local prejudices of the very sort forbidden by the Fourteenth Amendment to triumph.[20] Even when the results fall short of that constitutional barrier, we are still allowing standards to be set in a way which is less representative than we might prefer. The recent and not-so-recent accusations of prejudicial draft boards and juries reflect this problem.[21]

Where no pattern of decision can be discerned, a mirror difficulty arises. One grows to suspect that the parajury is either mindless, arbitrary, or corrupt. The extraordinary degree of faith Americans have in the jury seems to ameliorate this problem in the United States. In countries like Italy, for instance, arbitrariness or favoritism would be assumed if aresponsible decision making processes were consciously employed. As one would expect, such processes are not used there to make tragic choices. But the problem exists, to some extent, for us too.

Every lawyer tells a story akin to the tale of a jury deciding a paternity suit against a man and then turning around and granting a divorce to the man's wife on the ground of his impotence.

More seriously, the 1972 opinions of the Supreme Court in the capital punishment cases ambidextrously prompt both this criticism and that based on the presence of a pattern.[22] While the attack on the jury's discretionary use of the capital penalty was in part based on the observation of intolerable discrimination,[23] Justice Potter Stewart's opinion was instead based on the notion that having the decision to die made in a patternless way constituted a cruel and unusual punishment. His oft-quoted phrase that being sentenced to death was like "being hit by lightning" and, therefore, unconstitutional, suggests a striking counterpoint to the claims of the black appellant that a pattern of discrimination had arisen and therefore the death sentences were unconstitutional.[24] As we shall see, the jury is significantly different from the parajury which, in turn, is more vulnerable to both these kinds of criticisms. And in the tragic context generally, no less than in the capital context, high stakes heighten scrutiny.

Patternless tragic decisions, moreover, exacerbate one of the process costs to human emotions we have already mentioned. Deep anxiety and frustration are a necessary part of a process which makes a crucial decision against someone, but which fails to explain why. One needn't read Kafka to get a sense of the costs of such a process; we have all experienced analogous frustrations with results which, because unexplained, seem arbitrary. The more crucial the result, the more pressure one feels to bare one's soul to try to gain a favorable judgment; and the more one can perceive real or imagined differences in the relative ability to state one's case, the higher these frustration costs are likely to be. And these are borne by the very people who already bear the costs of losing out on the allocation of the tragically scarce resource.

Yet aresponsible agencies are useful. And surely we cannot be barred from employing flawed methods since they are all we shall have in the tragic decision. We know that juries have long been used successfully in the operation of the criminal law, often in situations which share some of the features of tragic choices. But there is at least one significant difference between such situations and true tragic choices. This difference accounts for the most important limitation in the use of aresponsible agencies in tragic decisions.

In situations of tragic choice the aresponsible agency must allocate. It must pick a certain number to live and another number to die, it must give children to some and deny them to others, in such a way that the total number approaches an acceptable first-order decision. We do not think of the process of our criminal law in such terms. Cases are not given to juries because, as in the *Mikado*, "a victim must be found." We shall see that this need to select, to allocate, significantly structures both the aresponsible agency and its dialogue with its critics, who demand patterns and are horrified by those they find.

The necessity to allocate requires some degree of continuity within the aresponsible agency, for a discontinuous aresponsible agency, even though it be circumscribed by guidelines in choosing between possible applicants, would tend simply to grant the scarce goods to the applicant immediately before it.[25] If there is total discontinuity, if each jury decides only whether a particular applicant should have the essential resource, this tendency is of course heightened. The allocation will then either resolve itself into a first-come-first-served allotment or will require more goods than were made available by the first-order decision.

Assuming that neither of these is acceptable—if we had wanted first-come-first-served, we would have set it up in the first place; and, though some modifications of first-order determinations under pressure from aresponsible second-order decisions are likely and acceptable,[26] the modifications required by the use of unfettered, discontinuous aresponsible agencies imply the total elimination of scarcity; that is, the elimination of the tragic dilemma altogether at the first-order level—two remedies are available. We can restructure the question put to the discontinuous aresponsible agency. Instead of being asked to allocate scarce goods among applicants on the basis of their worthiness relative to each other, the agency is asked to determine if a particular applicant is, in absolute terms, sufficiently worthy to be given the goods. This is the sort of determination made by a jury in a criminal trial that must come to a decision whether to convict a criminal because he is guilty and not because he is guiltier than those who may be tried later. If the standards for absolute worthiness are set high enough, each aresponsible agency can be permitted to decide even just a single case.[27] Such a modification accounts for our frequent use of moral terms like *fault* and *worthiness* in tragic choices.

The second remedy aims directly at the feature of discontinuity since, to the extent that we are unwilling to convert the tragic choice from an allocation decision to a worthiness-dependent decision, no acceptable equilibrium is likely to be found absent some continuing responsibility of the deciders. The aresponsible agency must be brought face to face with the consequence that granting a scarce life-saving transplant to Marshall today will mean that they have committed themselves to deprive Taney tomorrow, whom they deem more deserving.[28]

Continuity, in turn, accentuates those problems which arise both from the presence and the absence of outcome patterns. Continuity pricks our concern over the nonrepresentative character of the aresponsible agency; if a series of juries is viewed as representative, then the pattern of decisions which emerges from that series can also be taken to reflect the values of the community. Similarly, the lack of a pattern may be viewed as reflecting values so sensitive to the nuances of slightly varying facts, or in such flux, as to disrupt any discernible pattern. These are values which true juries of one's peers discern at any given moment in the life of the community. Unfortunately, neither of these defenses to pattern-based criti-

cisms of aresponsible agencies is at all plausible if the agency
has any substantial continuity, since the defenses depend on a
thoroughgoing representativeness which no long-sitting parajury can possess.

Furthermore, continuity of aresponsible decision making
affords greater opportunities for caprice and corruption.
Whether or not these sins are actually committed, the suspicion
that they have been committed is virtually inevitable. Thus,
though a discernible pattern in the decisions of a continuous
aresponsible agency may prompt criticism, the absence of such
a pattern is worse. The pattern can be taken as a sign of bias
(because the composition of the agency is not representative of
the community as a whole) or even as a sign that the agency is on
retainer to the advantaged group. But the lack of a pattern is
taken as clear evidence that each case is decided merely on the
basis of favoritism.

We face, then, three possibilities. Either we abandon altogether the use of aresponsible agencies, or we try to modify
them further, or we restructure the tragic allocation into the
sort of decision made in the criminal law, that is, we transform
the situation from an allocation requiring an assessment of
relative worthiness, to a decision requiring a determination of
absolute worthiness or absolute fault, which can be satisfactorily assigned to a true jury.

First Modification: The Para-aresponsible Agency

As one might expect, each of the three possibilities has been
tried: Aresponsible agencies have been abandoned; the issue
has been converted from one of allocation to one of absolute
worthiness; agencies have been modified to enable true allocations. The hospital committee overseeing medical experiments, and the committee which decides who will get the
transplant or the artificial organ, and even the local draft board
(during those periods when it was accorded virtually unfettered
discretion) are examples of modified aresponsible agencies.

The modifications which permit such agencies to function successfully in true allocation situations are governed, of course, by the contours of the particular tragic situation. At a minimum, a degree of continuity over a number of allocations must be provided. This requires a substantial overlap of membership in the decisions of many cases. The total number of such cases must be large enough so that the allocations respect the first-order determination limiting the resources available. If the tragic situation is such that this number of cases comes up over a relatively short period of time, true allocations of scarce resources can take place, while the membership of the aresponsible agency need not be too long-lived. The members of a committee distributing scarce foods in a famine need serve only relatively brief terms to appreciate the consequences of a too-quick disbursement to the first applicants. The committee is therefore put in a position to decide relative worthiness and yet it need not remain the decider for too long. If, after a series of decisions, the membership changes, some of the advantages of the true jury can be retained even in the context of actual allocation decisions.

Nevertheless, adapted aresponsible agencies are likely to be representative in a quite different sense from juries. Because the tragic allocation requires some continuity, these agencies tend to have a sizable number of technical experts among their memberships.[29] We do not believe that this is because the questions they are called upon to answer are, in fact, more technical or require more expert knowledge than those faced by true juries. Rather, we suspect that while it is the need for continuity which limits the degree of true representativeness possible, this lack of representativeness can be justified or explained away by invoking the need for experts. The presence of experts, furthermore, permits the inference to be drawn that the resulting aresponsible decision is based on minute and therefore nonpatterned concatenations of technical data. This inference serves much the same purpose as its true jury analogue which justifies unpatterned decisions as reflect-

ing fragmented, or at least extremely complex, combinations of
values. Like a true jury, use of experts may allow us to prefer
Story to Stone without implying that Storys and Stones are not
in every sense equals.

Since the presence of experts further limits the availability
of peer-representative members, the remaining representation
on these agencies will typically be the result of a conscious
attempt to include representatives of relevant groups or views,
and not of the random selection typified by the jury. The
minister, the social worker, the various relevant minorities, are
all put on the committee intentionally. Thus, with fewer members and without the full benefit of the crucial representativeness achieved through use of a series of juries,[30] it is nonetheless hoped to create an aresponsible agency which will seem to
be representative. The interested citizen, it is hoped, will
think, "They can't all be bought, or all share the same biases,
and if there were something really rotten going on, at least the
person on the committee with whom I identify would object."

Limited continuity, the presence of experts and of intentionally chosen representatives all combine, however, to evoke
clamor for agency responsibility. Such pressures are not un-
known in true jury situations; note the occasional demand for
interrogatories or for the right to question individual jury
members after a verdict. They are on the whole limited because
with true juries, aresponsibility works fairly well and its advantages are fairly clear. The modified aresponsible agency has no
such status. And so, to the traditional reasons for asking for
responsibility—control of arbitrariness, venality, and corruption—new grounds are added.

If decisions are made by experts on the basis of technical
differences which do not implicate questions of egalitarianism,
is it really likely that, if the experts told us why they chose as
they did, over time a pattern would remain so ineffable? If a
pattern were described, then a responsible choice could be
made on whether such reasons were consistent with prevailing
or dominant conceptions of egalitarianism—such as, for exam-

ple, age and conscription for combat service. Furthermore, if self-conscious appointment rather than representation arrived at by a series of random selections determines agency member-ship, shouldn't we assure ourselves that the groups chosen to be represented are in fact those that need representation? And how can we know this unless we can examine the reasons which moved the representatives to decide particular cases as they did? Finally, where there is no continuity at all, as with true juries, the harm done by an individual aberrant jury is quite limited, but this is not true of agencies with some continuity. Some classes of applicants will inevitably be treated differently from classes who appeared before the previous committee or will face a succeeding committee. Such disparities appear more outrageous if the decider has life over a group of cases than if it is clearly an *ad hoc* decider like the true jury.[31] If we knew what prompted each committee's decisions, and made that crucial data available to subsequent committees, such disparities pre-sumably would be reduced.

And so it is that a good part of the literature on para-aresponsible agencies is devoted to ways of making them more responsible. But if we had wanted responsible decision making in the first place, we would not have chosen these agencies. It was because we were unwilling to endure clear statements like "persons with perfect pitch are going to be preferred to dia-betics" that we failed to choose hierarchic, responsible, politi-cal decisions and chose instead the device of the committee.[32]

This conflict provokes us to search for ways of achieving some of the advantages of responsibility without forfeiting the aresponsible feature of parajuries which is their principal ap-peal. The techniques which have developed limit responsibility by assigning it: (a) in a different time frame; (b) to an elite with criticism available in a limited forum; and (c) to a body required to state justifications which, since they are nonreviewable and therefore likely to be merely self-serving explanations may still contain asides by which reactions to the true grounds of deci-sion are tested. Each of these approaches may be used in

conjunction with the others. They are all rather old hat to
lawyers, who know them as functions of the quite different
process by which judges are kept both independent and responsible; and though control of the judiciary does not present
the same problems as do parajuries, these devices may increase
the ability of parajuries to draw those—and only those—
distinctions society wants. It remains to be seen whether these
adaptations can operate without the demoralization which
those distinctions entail when drawn too openly, and without
violating grossly the values of honesty and openness.

The principal advantage of assigning responsibility within a
different time frame accrues from the passage of time; it permits
the description of the actors involved in abstract terms and
thereby encourages the perception of the tragic choice in
theoretical terms; and it allows criticism of past decisions without indicting present decision making. The scholarly commen-
tary on tragic choices amply documents the vast difference it
makes to society whether lives are confronted as statistical or
real.[33]

Various explanations for this difference have been given,
but, whichever explanation one is inclined to accept, the conflicts between values symbolizing rights to equal treatment and
to survival as incommensurables are more obliquely revealed
when statistical decisions affecting lives are involved. To the
extent that the reasons the adapted aresponsible agency is
required to give for choosing particular winners and losers are
viewed as abstract discussions, and evoke the same response as
decisions affecting statistical lives, the extinction or denial of
values implicit in responsible decision making is diminished.
The very abstractness of the decision may, however, lead to its
being perceived as a generalization of preference, from individuals to classes. The cost of such generalizations is not slight,
but it is at least possible that the adapted aresponsible agency
can find a channel—between unacceptable generalized hierarchic decisions (e.g., the refusal to ransom foot soldiers) and the
equally unacceptable deliberate execution of an individual—

through the reification of its individual decisions in abstract terms at a much later time when the human beings involved are no longer news. Perhaps in this way some control and openness are salvaged.[34]

A roughly similar tack is taken by directing responsibility to an elite and confining criticism within a limited forum. Learned discourse on even the most dramatic problems is frequently abstract, boring, and lengthy. And the very fact that the criticism is by a limited group acts to contain the damage to values. The same elite which engages in criticism may be sophisticatedly aware that choosing survivors, and hence nonsurvivors, in a tragic situation implies no lack of parity between groups across a spectrum of other contexts and may also be aware that clear choices for death, say, do not universally diminish the value of life; less harm is then done by shifting responsibility to this elite, away from a larger group which may not be able to make such nice distinctions. We assume for the moment that situation 1, in which one class is favored over another, and situation 2, in which they must be treated equally, are different, but that what we have elsewhere called the costs of apparent inconsistency are considerable.[35] Responsibility to an elite may avoid such costs of naïveté.

The shortcomings of assigning responsibility to a priesthood are substantial. The very definition of such a priesthood offends many conceptions of egalitarianism; and if, to mitigate this offense, the right to criticize must be formally open to everyone, it is nevertheless true that the opinions of the agency are likely to be expressed in language accessible only to critics who are specially trained. This makes pleas for openness and honesty sound ironical or even pointless.

Of greater significance, however, elite criticism is unresponsive to the very needs which led to the call for more responsibility in the first place. It may achieve some control of corruption; it may also give that degree of continuity of decision making, among short-lived adapted aresponsible agencies, required to avoid abrupt turnabouts. But what does it do for representativeness? Unless the elite itself represents the mass of views, elite criticism simply reinforces those decisions of the agency which serve primarily elite purposes or ideals.[36]

Finally, we have doubts that the elite is, in fact, more able to handle the tragedy implicit in some choices. Can one be so sure that the elite will not confuse a preference for one group over another, which arises in the tragic context, with a general hierarchic preference, or that an elite will not mistake necessity for a sign that the sanctity of life and its interdependent values are unimportant in nontragic situations as well? We are far from sanguine about this. Logic relentlessly and inappropriately pursued to its end can as readily lead to destructive results as can muddled emotions. But rebuttals by dissenters in the elite by means of an emotive appeal to the broader constituency simply put us right back where we started.[37]

Responsibility discharged by self-serving explanations which contain asides which are to be tested as grounds for decisions is the third way which might be used to adapt semicontinuous aresponsible agencies to partial responsibility. Such asides permit reaction to possible reasons for a particular preference without suggesting that such reasons will, in fact, decide any real case. This procedure abstracts the tragic choice and makes it possible to canvass reaction indicating what are relevant, acceptable grounds for distinctions, without committing the formal basis of decisions to those grounds and thereby accepting obviously hierarchic standards. Since such asides are a matter for general discussion, this device permits feedback from a broad array of sources and, indeed, may seem more promising in achieving representativeness than does elite criticism. But since the grounds for decision in such a process are intentionally disingenuous, this feedback over the mass of cases may well be bought at the price of forfeiting control over individual decisions, and undermining honesty. Fears of agency corruption, or even simple willfulness and arbitrariness return to the fore. The alarums sounded against manipulative judicial opinions and rules, though dealing with a different set of institutions and issues, should alert us to analogous dangers here.[38]

In practice, all three of these devices may be used in various combination. There is nothing inconsistent between criticism in a different time frame and criticism by an elite; there is not even a necessary inconsistency between elite criticism of the given grounds for a decision, perhaps in a different time frame, and public discussion of the asides which the deciders assert did not control the instant case, but which might be relevant in the future. It is not clear, however, whether such amalgams amplify the power of each modification or the flaws of each. Isadora Duncan is said to have written George Bernard Shaw proposing an assignation, saying, "A child with my body and your brains would surely be perfection." Shaw replied, "But what if it should have my body and your brains?"

In this discussion of adapted aresponsible agencies, we have had several occasions to suggest the relevance of criticisms directed to difficulties associated with judicial decision making. Is, then, the model for those decentralized, adapted aresponsible agencies that of a modified court rather than of a modified jury? We do not think so. While important decisions have been left to courts in our society, these decisions are very different from those which we encounter in tragic situations. The desirability of case-by-case decisions, of interstitial deciding, of updating outworn rules, of moving in areas of legislative lack of interest or of political stalemate: these, and the many other grounds for judicial lawmaking, ultimately, require clear, logical, and fairly generalized statements of why a decision was reached.[39] The reasons for using adapted aresponsible agencies to make tragic choices may be traced instead to the desire to make the grounds for decisions less direct and perhaps even less obvious, while at the same time trying to make sure that the decisions are based on broadly held social values. It is in fact rather hard to conceive of a body constituted as a court being deemed appropriate to decide a tragic choice of the kind allocating an artificial organ or the right to have children unless—and

by hypothesis we have ruled this out in this part of the book—
the initial standards for choice were responsibly set by the
legislature.

Administrative agencies seem similar to adapted aresponsible agencies, but they do such a variety of tasks that it is rather
hard to pin down just what one means by the term. Some
decisions by these agencies are certainly allocation decisions;
for instance, which airline gets which routes, which company
gets which television channel, who is to get a bus franchise, and
so forth. These are also the decisions in which administrative
agency actions are most suspect. They are suspect not because
the implicit preferences offend our multifaceted sense of
egalitarianism, but because it is very hard to tell whether, for
example, Braniff International will in fact serve Dallas better
than Texas International, since the responsibly set standards
for what is better are often so vague. Representativeness and
control are fundamental requisites of any administrative agency
allocation process to insure that generally held views of what is
better will be determinative and to check pressures toward
favoritism. But it would be a mistake to confuse the administrative agency's need for these elements with similar requirements of para-aresponsible agencies when making tragic
choices, for traditional administrative agencies encounter no
inherent contradiction in stating the "better" on the basis of
which the allocation is to be made. There may be conflicting
views, or it may be hard to express clearly what is desired, and
these difficulties may lead to the suspicion that the agency is not
doing its job, but these are, of course, defects of an entirely
different sort.[40]

Second Modification: Translation of the Allocation Decision into a Worthiness Decision

A second possibility open to us modifies the choice itself,
instead of the jury, in an effort to make the choice more amenable to traditional, jurylike decisions. This modification con-

verts the allocation decision based on relative worthiness into a decision based on absolute worthiness, such that worthiness or fault are so defined that, in practice, enough applicants will be found wanting so that the constraints imposed by the first-order determination will be satisfied. Without actually allocating, a series of aresponsible agencies can then act as a series of true juries.

This technique depends on the persuasiveness of the proposition that individuals who are denied the scarce goods could, through their own behavior, put themselves in the favored category. The greater the plausibility of this notion, the less this technique seems a subterfuge, the less the responsible political decision to base the result on absolute worthiness violates egalitarian principles. We all know enough about our use of moral terms in common language, however, to realize that often absolute terms are applied to human acts even though the odds vary dramatically that different categories of people, classified by non-moral indicia, will be found worthy; and we acknowledge that such differences are based on factors as to which individuals have little control.[41] A fault approach often simply reflects a hidden political choice to prefer one group to another, which avoids affronting egalitarian conceptions because the responsible decision was cast in terms which seemed to make the preferred position open to anyone. There are limits even to the short-run utility of such subterfuges; if the right to bear and care for children were made dependent on "a showing of good moral character and the completion of a satisfactory essay discussing the role of the superego in child development," both being arguably relevant to parenthood, we would object, on egalitarian grounds, as soon as it became apparent that moral character and essay writing reflected traits that tended to be paired with particular socioeconomic groups.

Conversely, such approaches are especially favored when achieving the fault or absolute worthiness standards acts to increase the amount of the scarce resource available or to reduce the cost of its availability, thereby not only diminishing the inegalitarian features of a tragic choice, but also suggesting that no first-order determination need ever be made. Of course, at least in theory, the jury could always find every applicant worthy and so doing negate any implicit first-order determination. In fact, this open-ended view of the process is plausible only if there would be enough of the resource to go around, since the decision as to individual worthiness is subtly but ineluctably connected to the fact of scarcity, and this is apparent in remarks such as "Were everyone faultless there would be no accidents"; "Were everyone perfect parents with full knowledge of the responsibilities of parenthood, we could have unlimited childbearing and not overpopulate the world."

As we have noted, such perfectibility need not be truly realizable to be useful; indeed, we have seen that even when it is known that as a probabilistic, statistical fact one method of allocation would result in more of the scarce resource being available, nevertheless, an inferior but theoretically perfectible allocation may be preferred if achieved perfection would abolish scarcity. The reason for this phenomenon is clear: By attributing to individual failures the fact that every applicant will not receive the tragically scarce resource, the tragic outcome is made to seem consistent with the view that the competing values at stake represent incommensurables. The costs to a few individuals must often seem small indeed compared to the historic protection of the societal myth. It is, in one sense, cheaper to blame the criminal for his shortcomings and hence for his crime—even if this perpetuates high levels of offenses—than it is to admit that we are unwilling to spend what would be needed to eradicate crime (if this could be done), *and* spend what we are willing to spend, recognizing that a certain number of people will be raped or murdered.

The scandal of an absolute worthiness approach is its sacrifice of values of honesty and openness. If some categories of people are, in fact, substantially less likely to be able to meet standards of absolute worthiness than others, then only the appearance of egalitarianism has been preserved. Similarly, if perfectibility is a fantasy, if society would not tolerate the first-order demands required by jury findings that every candidate is worthy, then the first-order determination is avoided only through subterfuge.

But so long as the possibility of perfectibility is sufficiently great, and the ability to show oneself worthy or free from fault sufficiently widespread among different groups, the result will remain stable and nontragic. An absolute worthiness or fault approach has proved remarkably stable in some areas of criminal law (like drug addiction) when there is good reason to believe other approaches would be less costly were it not for the stark clarity of the tragic choices they would necessitate.[42] On the other hand, it strikes us as unlikely that an approach of this sort would succeed as a method of distributing rights to procreate. This may be, in part, because our approach to drugs has arisen from customary practices and therefore has the benefits of having come into being through a nonchoice; but even aside from this, the premise of perfectibility, like the premise that all have an equal chance to prove themselves worthy parents, is implausible enough to justify the hunch.

We have discussed this technique—the move from an allocation decision to an absolute worthiness determination—in the context of aresponsible agencies, because in America we have frequently used the jury to make just such decisions turning on absolute worthiness. The advantages of using a true, representative, aresponsible agency should be clear: There is no jury opinion which is open to the criticisms that perfectibility was a fraud and that a particular applicant lost out because he belonged to a group which finds it relatively more difficult to meet the standards of worthiness; and it is easier for representative, aresponsible agencies to compensate for initial disadvantage, without acknowledging that the standards themselves are biased, than it is for a responsible, opinion-writing decider to make similar allowances.

In fact, of course, a decision measuring absolute worthiness could be made in any nonmarket way and could use responsible or aresponsible nonrepresentative, decentralized deciders to apply the standard. Many societies, indeed, do not use the representative, aresponsible agency, the jury, to make such absolute worthiness decisions; courts are an example of one form partly responsible, generally nonrepresentative, decision making of this sort has taken. But it seems clear that the more a society holds a multifaceted egalitarianism dear, the more it is likely to employ a series of representative aresponsible agencies to apply standards of absolute worthiness.

The general flaws of such agencies discussed above remain: loss of privacy; the costs of equal access; and—somewhat muted because decisions are made by a series of aresponsible, representative agencies—the problems of corruption, arbitrariness, and lack of representativeness. When true juries have been used successfully, these faults have frequently been overlooked because critical discussions focused on the comparison of the aresponsible, representative agency with either a nonrepresentative, responsible decider (a court), or with a nonrepresentative, aresponsible decider (a bureaucracy).[43] In these contexts questions of equal access to, or privacy costs of, jury determinations seemed relatively unimportant. The alternative approaches under discussion presented still other, greater disadvantages to the groups who might suffer from lack of privacy or equal access before a jury and promised little better with respect even to these problems. When we consider, instead, new roles for the true representative aresponsible agency, we must ask ourselves whether (in view of these general flaws plus the danger that we may be acting as if we are not allocating when in fact we are), a different approach, which recognizes the allocation decision for what it is, might not be preferable.[44]

The appeal of a fault or worthiness approach, however, goes beyond the fact that it permits a greater use of an aresponsible agency; by transforming the decision, society attempts to deny the tragic element implicit in the choice. Society announces that *it* will not choose to sacrifice lives or fundamental rights, that *it* will not violate conceptions of equality, that the sacrifices which do occur are due not to a societal unwillingness to forgo other goods but to individual failings. One recalls Duerenmatt's *Visit*,[45] in which the ultimate victim's early wrong, which had been ignored for years during which he had been viewed as a worthy citizen, comes to be seen by the citizenry as a desperate moral failing which justifies his death. Obviously, such an approach debases honesty. Just as obviously, it adds to the tragic outcome borne by the chosen victim and his family much of the cost of the process as well. We do not think tragic choices are to be understood without realizing society's compounding of sacrifice with blame, of insult with injury if you will, in order to absolve itself. The literal origins in this practice of the word *scapegoat* should warn us of the awful dangers of its appeal.

If the scapegoat epitomizes one mode of handling tragic choices, the pure lamb or perfect sacrifice suggests another, rarer mode. This approach does not deny the nature of the tragedy: A life must be taken, someone must forgo a basic right. But demands for equal chance are quieted, paradoxically, by choosing for sacrifice the worthiest, the perfect. The value of life is exalted, equally paradoxically, by the dramatic example of society's willingness to give up its most precious lives, whenever any lives are to be taken. Societies like ours which determine the worthiness of their citizens by criteria that are in some measures utilitarian—that is, by usefulness to society in roles other than as sacrifices—will find this method of selecting a victim so costly that it must be reserved for extraordinary moments. In addition to the loss of valuable members of society, one can imagine the terrifying psychic costs consequent to dragging an unwilling victim to the sacrificial altar. The use of moral suasion to induce volunteers to offer themselves is a response to these latter costs. Some commentators, like Margaret Mead,[46] have recommended variants of this approach as procedures by which subjects should be chosen for medical

experiments. Instances in which the best have been induced to
volunteer for war—one thinks of the enthusiasm with which an
entire generation of young Englishmen went to France to fight
in 1914[47]—provide an arresting example of this method at
work.

Conclusion: Modified Political Devices

We can summarize the use of modified political devices,
and this third part of the book, in fairly short order. The
shortcomings of classic political decision making—the inability
to reflect distinctions with respect to the individual desire to
receive a good or avoid a bad, and the social utility of having a
good or a bad go to one individual rather than another—can be
ameliorated by methods of decentralization and individuation.
But these methods entail many difficulties. Representativeness
and control become elusive; it is costly to assure equality of
access to the deciders, privacy is jeopardized. Important as
these difficulties are, they do not reflect the principal limitations on using the political process as a technique for making
tragic decisions. These derive instead from the conflict of values
forced by a tragic choice. A responsible political process under-
lines the fact that life, for example, is not treated as an absolute,
and that some are deemed more deserving of it than others. To
veil these conflicts, various subterfuges are used. When a subterfuge is used, most often some real advantage exists beyond
the preservation of the myth. Maybe use of a fault standard in
tort law does make people behave better; perhaps a jury does
some things better than other institutions, quite apart from its
aresponsibility, and so on. Such advantages are essential, lest
the subterfuge so rot our commitment to honesty that all is
doubted. If the side advantages are, in fact, sufficiently great, it
is possible that a stable, nontragic solution can be found. Or the
subterfuge may be believed for a while and permit tolerable
decisions for as long. Or society may become more sensitive to
the importance of candor and honesty owing to events outside

the immediate subterfuge, so that even an effective subterfuge becomes intolerable and must be laid bare. Then the conflict the subterfuge was designed to mask becomes manifest, so that the usefulness of the approach is ended. We know that the choice was a tragic one and that we must look elsewhere for help.

4

MODIFIED MARKETS

The Limits of Pure Markets

THE OPENING CHAPTERS of elementary economics textbooks are devoted to sketching the wonderful workings of the invisible hand and how, given an initial distribution of wealth—that is, of both money and what we have elsewhere called entitlements—the pure market achieves Pareto optimality, allocating resources so that no one's lot can be improved without worsening someone else's. These same texts then usually point out the existence of deficiencies which require major or minor technical modifications of the market, for instance, externalities, public goods, monopolies, and the like.[1] Typically, however, the story is not interrupted to comment that the very existence of such defects indicates that it is too costly for the market, unaided, to correct them, for as Professor Ronald Coase has pointed out markets could cure all such defects if the cost of setting up the curative market were low enough.[2]

The implications of this sketch—of the arthritic invisible hand, one might say—are worth reviewing, since they have significance both for the usefulness of the Pareto standards, and for interventionist policies generally. Far from being an instrument by which the public policy decision of whether to intervene in the market is determined, or by which the workings of markets may be compared with proposed nonmarket methods, Pareto standards are virtually useless since a nonmarket can never be shown to be Pareto superior to the market and, more importantly, nor can the market ever be shown to be Pareto superior to a nonmarket.

A simple example of the former will serve. Suppose by overfishing a lake, the fishermen from the villages around it find their catches annually declining; no one village is willing, how-

ever, to cut back its fishing since the other villages may simply
take advantage of this; but it is clear that only a cutback will
allow the lake to replenish its population of fish so that, this
having been accomplished, the total yields for all villages will
be greater and the hours spent fishing actually less. Voluntary
mediation fails because some villages refuse to go along, hoping
perhaps that the rest will restrict their catch leaving those who
hold out free to fish as much as they wish. A perfect opportunity, one thinks, for the Game and Fish Commission. And so a
nonmarket method is employed: A rule is enforced limiting the
number of hours any fisherman may spend fishing. Soon yields
go up, and ultimately more fish are being caught by all with
fewer resources spent on their catching, surely a more efficient
result.

This intervention, however, cannot be shown to be Pareto
superior to the market result since one cannot know that the
fishermen who gave up their extra hours on the lake have been
fully compensated by the increased catch; the very fact that a
nonmarket intervention took place meant that the actual value
for each fisherman's loss, to him, was not arrived at through his
market action. And one need only consider the bargaining
position of the hold-out villages when the rest had voluntarily
agreed to limit their hours on the lake, to say nothing of considering the joys of the lake spray or the sunset on the water, to see
that the simple improvement in ultimate yield is not, necessarily, a full compensation for the right forgone. Nor can one reply
that these values, or their loss, can be ascertained by, for
example, simply questioning the losers. Pareto standards, having arisen out of the ideology of classical welfare economics, do
not grant to nonmarket expressions of preference—however
accurate they may in fact be, and one may justifiably doubt
that questionnaires, interviews, tests, and the like, perfectly
reflect true preferences—the axiomatic validity accorded those
revealed in market action.

If the Pareto standards are of no use to us in deciding
whether a nonmarket's results are Pareto superior to a mar-

ket's, neither are they a useful guide to what policies to pursue within the market or whether to use a market at all. (We emphasize that we are concerned with policies, that is, general structural changes, and not with tactical adjustments; there will always be new, Pareto superior deals to be made, but this is the art of the businessman, not of the economist.) While some commentators have concluded that Coase's theorem—which advises us that (assuming no transaction costs) the market will achieve Pareto optimality regardless of initial entitlements or liability rules—counsels abstention, one might equally draw the opposite conclusion.[3] Although a market may be Pareto optimal, this fact does not demonstrate that the cost incurred by the market's having arisen might not be greater than that of some alternative, nonmarket allocation system—and this crucial feature, the cost of setting up the market, is precisely what is assumed away by the theorem.[4] Moreover, those who lose because a nonmarket approach is eschewed cannot be compensated in any way that can be judged by Pareto standards.

That the Pareto standards are of no use to us in deciding whether or not to make structural changes within the market, or replace it altogether with respect to some allocations, should cause us no despair; it forces us to focus on the distributional consequences of policy choices hitherto obscured, or comfortably ignored, by a mistaken reliance on the Pareto criteria. We are now brought face to face with the logical corollary to Coase's theorem: Interventions, even when they are taken because exchanges judged beneficial on non-Pareto efficiency grounds will not otherwise occur, necessarily represent distributional decisions and must be evaluated accordingly. That is, one may not say that a policy benefits winners more than it harms uncompensated losers and simply leave it at that.

Without pursuing further the theoretical implications of Coase's theorem we will just reiterate that it reveals the bankruptcy of the neoclassical welfare economics' Pareto standards as guides for policy making. In their place, we should use something like the following: In any proposed reallocation of resources the winners must appear to be able to compensate the losers and the actual distributional change brought about must either be, in some sense, favorable or not so unfavorable as to outweigh, given interpersonal comparisons, the fact that some have gained more than others have lost. This efficiency standard may be awkwardly entitled potential Pareto superiority with tolerable distributional effects. We suggest that this is, in fact, the standard used whenever an intervention within a market or to set up a market is to be justified, at least so long as the money needed for the intervention is not unanimously given, that is, whenever some form of coercion is required. Accordingly, that is the standard we shall use in this essay.

This short discussion, while in a way a parenthesis, is crucial to all that will follow. If we could accept Pareto optimality as the norm by which policy is to be judged, and if this could give us answers in the areas with which we are concerned, then fundamental conflicts of value could not exist and hence neither could tragic choices. Potential Pareto superiority with tolerable distributional effects, instead, is a standard loose enough to admit of fundamental conflicts and of tragic choices. Furthermore, this discussion will help us to see why we hesitate to employ the pure market fully in a tragic situation. To illustrate the difficulties of market methods in such roles, we will discuss two problems.

A market-made first-order determination depends on premises of the kind, for example, that the social desirability of artificial lungs can be measured by the sum of what individuals acting atomistically will forgo in order to build and operate such machines. If, however, there are other factors which should in part determine the number of artificial lungs, then the sum of individual willingnesses will not give the proper result. All such other factors, whether they are moralisms like the cost to the rest of us of seeing you die because you will not buy a machine, or more traditional external costs and benefits, like the benefit to society (as against that to Keats himself) of Keats' willingness to live with a lung machine, could in theory be made part of individual second-order decisions and hence affect the first-order determination. But the cost of individuals atomistically evaluating these external costs and benefits, and then acting through the market to influence the appropriate individual deciders is such that it is very often more efficient to arrive at a first-order determination by a nonmarket mechanism.

To recapitulate for a moment, the only guide which a simple Pareto standard would give us to determine whether these costs and benefits should be internalized is whether the market in fact does so, that is, whether a market to internalize them has been created. We will often find, however, that other arrangements can be worked out, though only through nonmarket allocations, in which we believe that the winners will gain far more than the losers will lose without intolerable distributional effects.[5]

To return to the problem of first-order determinations, consider the external costs of having children. Individuals could perhaps seek fertile couples out and pay them not to have children. If, however, the cost of entering into such transactions were too great, we are presented with three possibilities:

(1) We can say, fine, that is the best we can do. Every other solution involves some coercion and hence cannot be shown to be Pareto superior to staying where we are.[6] But we had better realize that this result will harm those who in the next two possibilities would have been better off and that these first-result losers are not compensated for their losses. Staying where we are, therefore, cannot be shown to be a Pareto superior decision, either.

(2) We can attempt to value the costs and benefits collectively and allocate them to the best deciders, recognizing that this approach[7] involves spending the money to evaluate the costs and allocating these costs to the best deciders—money the market has refused to spend—and hence involves coercion, and cannot be shown to be a Pareto superior move.

(3) We can simply make the first-order determination in a nonmarket way.

Once we have decided that (1) is unsatisfactory, because we are able to better the lot of some people by going beyond the pure market, simple Pareto standards can no longer give us guidance. If we are to be concerned with efficiency at all, we must try to make the choice between (1), (2), and (3) on the basis of which is preferable, applying a standard of potential Pareto superiority with tolerable distributional effects. In other words, once we abandon the notion that the market can never be improved upon, the question of whether we stay with an untouched market despite its imperfections, or move to a fully nonmarket decision or to a semimarket decision, must be based on guesses as to the relative gains of winners and losers and, inevitably, guesses as to the distributional effects of the uncertain compensation of losers which each of the possibilities implies.[8]

At that point, the fact that tragic allocations made through (2) would involve the direct collective costing of human lives becomes highly significant. For if collective determination of that cost is itself highly demoralizing and destructive of basic social values,[9] then it may well be that we are best off either sticking with an imperfect but untouched market, or making the first-order determination in a purely political way.[10]

We must decide whether it is less harmful (a) to decide collectively, in a nonmarket way, how many children, for example, the society can afford to have, and then decide by a variety of means, including market methods, who will get to have them; or (b) to put a collectively determined price on children and let the first-order determination result thereafter from a series of market second-order decisions;[11] or (c) to use a full market to decide the whole matter, knowing that such a market will take into account neither the special value society gives to, say, Jonathan Edwards's children nor the extra costs atomistic decisions on childbearing impose on society as a whole. None of the three options satisfies the standards of avoiding interpersonal comparisons for any given distribution of wealth. We have suggested that one advantage of using the directly collective approach is that it avoids an explicit costing that the second, or liability-rule approach, requires; we have seen, however, that such avoidance creates its own problems.[12]

Before we turn to a less general analysis of the stresses produced by a market approach to a tragic situation, we should like to turn to the second reason which makes us unwilling to employ the pure market fully in tragic situations. This reason reflects our unwillingness to allow the allocation of certain goods and bads to be made on the basis of a market which depends on the prevailing distribution of wealth in society.

On the whole, the discussion of merit wants has not been satisfactorily dealt with in economics. Even the best treatments of it[13] leave many unanswered questions, most pointedly the relation of merit wants to the distribution of wealth. In fact, one cannot make sense out of the concept of merit wants unless one believes that there are some goods or bads whose allocation on the basis of the existing wealth distribution engenders external costs which would not occur were the allocation based on a different distribution.[14] These externalities may take the form of moralisms (one's horror, for example, that another will willingly take perilous risks or suffer degrading employment—one thinks of the prostitutes' cages in Calcutta—simply because the other is poor); they may take the form of social instability and unrest (it is not surprising that Civil War draft riots accompanied the proletariat's increasing disenchantment with the Great Cause as their youth sold themselves to take the place of wealthy draftees—or how frequently riots follow coal mine disasters even though the victims allegedly assumed the risk);[15] they take the conventional form of economic externalities (for instance, the fire and crime costs attendant on tumble-down housing—tenements selected by families because the rents are low and the families are poor). Since these externalities are difficult to internalize through the market, it may be that a potential Pareto superiority policy would allocate these goods directly in a nonmarket way or through a market based on a different distribution of wealth.

If, instead of being based on external costs, merit wants are the result of precautionary notions, for oneself or for others, a similar link, now between the precautionary notions and the underlying wealth distribution, is appropriate. If one believes that one knows better than another whether the other person will subsequently regret having forgone bearing and raising children—and one believes this not because one thinks one knows better than another generally, but because one knows the other's decision, however voluntary, to have been skewed by lack of wealth—then a precautionary, paternalistic reason exists for allocating child rights according to some different distribution of wealth. Similarly and more consistently with traditional economic ideology, if one is afraid that one may regret certain choices one will make if one were someday poor and therefore wish to limit one's freedom, say, to volunteer as a paid subject of a dangerous but useful experiment, a good reason exists for one's view that that bad should be allocated either in a nonmarket way or through a market which sufficiently compensates for poverty to alleviate one's fears.[16]

An additional factor occasioning merit wants, apparently not discussed in economic journals, is germane to tragic situations. We mean the possibility and cost of futures markets. Let us assume that a population is offered a series of possible wealth distributions each corresponding to a total social product. Let us further assume that the choosers are ignorant of which particular wealth position they will each have after the choice. Since a lower total social product is correlated with a more equal wealth distribution, the choice will depend on, among other things, each individual's aversion to risks and the actual ratios of equal distribution to product.

It is possible that some of the choosers will say, "Must all goods and bads be allocated according to the single wealth distribution? For I am very averse to the risk of not being able to purchase child rights, but not to being unable to purchase caviar. If all goods and bads are allocated under one wealth distribution then I dare not opt for less equality even though it means a greater total social product." To this a traditional economist might answer, "But you are being absurd, since it is better for you to have the money with which you can buy the right to have children under the single wealth distribution, than to have child rights allocated separately. You are more likely to increase your chances to have the child rights you want by maximizing your chances for wealth than if you get rights to children." To which our child-loving chooser would reply, "Not so, at least unless a futures market in children exists. If one exists, then I am better off choosing that wealth distribution, covering the allocation of all goods, which maximizes my chance of being wealthy enough to permit me to buy futures in children and someone else futures in caviar. But if no such futures market exists, then to be reasonably sure that I will be able to buy the right to have children when I want them, in view of the uncertainty of what they will then cost, [17] I may have to demand a more equal general wealth distribution than I would were I given the right to have children in the first place, or were I assured that child rights would be allocated on the basis of a different wealth distribution. The futures market would perhaps be the best way, but if a futures market costs too much, a nonmarket way or a market based on a different wealth distribution may be the second best." [18]

We should add that tragic choices are pre-eminently choices as to goods and bads where high risk aversion is likely and where futures markets are especially costly. They are, for this reason as well, often choices which concern merit wants. Indeed, tragic choices implicate all the grounds for merit wants we have discussed, and hence almost always involve allocations of goods and bads which are properly called *merit goods*. We need only ask ourselves what was repugnant about our system of wartime service during the Civil War, by which draftees were allowed to hire substitutes, to sense this. Examples like these encourage our allocating such goods and bads according to wealth distributions different from the one prevailing. This, in turn, calls into question the advantage of using the market in such cases and suggests the use of nonmarket allocations which do not depend on the existing distribution of wealth at all.

With the conclusion of this survey of the defects of pure markets, we turn to a consideration of adaptations designed to cure these defects.

First Modification: Nonmoney and Mixed Markets

The classic example of a nonmoney market is the award of a nontransferable ticket to the person who is willing to wait in line longest. It is hard to see, at first glance, what advantages such nonmoney market rationing devices would have over ordinary markets in tragic contexts. And yet they have not been without their proponents. It has been suggested, for instance, that our needs for military personnel can be met by requiring all citizens between the ages of nineteen and twenty-three to spend some time in public service;[19] the amount of time required in each form of service would reflect the relative desirability of each to the conscripts, and the first-order determination of how many people were needed for each. Thus a market could be set up which offered draftees a choice among serving three years with the Peace Corps in, say, Kenya, two years with VISTA in Appalachia, eighteen months in a fairly dangerous police assignment, and six months in a wartime army at the front. The lengths of service would then be varied until relative prices (in terms of time) were found which would produce for each form of service the number needed.

The first thing to note about such a nonmoney market is that it is not necessarily any less inegalitarian than other markets. It has merely substituted differences in relative availability of the new medium of exchange, time, for differences in dollars. The person who greatly values his time and has, for other reasons, little of it to waste, is in the position of the poor person in the ordinary market while the one with nothing to do is in the position of the rich person. And it is no more an answer here than it was in an ordinary market to say that one is better off by his own lights having chosen six months in Vietnam than three years in the Peace Corps. Again there is no direct connection between the first- and second-order determinations, again we are attempting to measure relative desire, and again we are doing it with a biased yardstick. Of course, variances in wealth distribution may be more easily noticed than disequalities in time distribution, and, if this is the case, some of the demoralization which accompanies making a tragic choice on the basis of an unequal distribution may, for a while, be avoided. This will not last.

Indeed, each shortcoming of the traditional market has its exact analogue in the nonmoney market. Why then are nonmoney markets frequently proposed and occasionally used? The first and most important reason is simply that the biased yardstick used in a nonmoney market reflects a different bias from that of the traditional market. The very fact, for example, that wealth in terms of time is distributed differently from wealth in terms of money—though perhaps just as unequally—may make it more acceptable as a medium of exchange. Most goods go on the basis of one bias; accordingly, some may say let us allocate some goods on the basis of another bias. More important may be the assumptions that different people give roughly the same value to time (which they clearly do not to money, and might not even were it equally distributed), and that society values different people's time roughly equally. To the extent the first assumption is true, then a market using time as a medium of exchange would accurately gauge relative desires for the goods or bads being allocated; to the extent the second assumption is true, a market in time reduces the other external costs of using a market. Both assumptions are obviously false.[20]

Thus markets in time are seldom adequate solutions to tragic allocations. Other nonmoney markets using other media of exchange (such as, for example, that embodied in the suggestion that those citizens with over a certain number of children should lose their right to vote) share the shortcomings of the market in time.[21] The effect of the example given in the parenthesis would, of course, be to allocate children in greater numbers to those who care least for the vote. Quite apart from whether such an allocation is desirable, it is again an allocation based on an unequal distribution.

More generally, whenever one is tempted to suggest that a tragic good be allocated using a nonmoney medium of exchange, one must ask whether we are moved to depart from the traditional market on account of unequal distribution, or on account of the use of money as the medium of exchange. If we are motivated primarily by considerations of equality, then continuing to use money but modifying the traditional wealth distribution when allocating the particular good is likely to be more desirable than substituting a whole other medium of exchange. If, on the other hand, we perceive the use of a money medium to be the source of our discomfiture with the market, then we should weigh a move to another medium to see if that medium presents analogous defects.

It can be argued that money incentives to avoid procreating impose external costs because they impose poverty on the children of those who choose to have children rather than money and, therefore, the defect of that approach may be traced to the use of money rather than to the presence of inequality. From such arguments comes the rationale of the no-vote proposal, since absence of the vote would penalize parents and not children.[22] Unfortunately, of course, the no-vote proposal imposes its own set of external costs by rendering childless, or relatively so, those citizens who are most civic minded and value their suffrage most highly.

Or if we object to use of a market on the ground that its obvious monetization is destructive of fundamental values, then we may prefer a nonmoney market in which the medium of exchange assigns a far less obvious valuation to the fundamental rights being allocated. It would appear to be less obvious that we are valuing both lives and children when we require that a certain period be spend in public service in order to avoid wartime service or in order to obtain child rights, than when we put a money price on wartime service and the right to procreate. Whether this would continue to be the case were such methods used to allocate children and war duties over long periods of time is, of course, another matter.

One major advantage, then, of a nonmoney market is that it may obscure the valuation that takes place. This, and the tendency for nonmoney markets to play down the distribution of wealth on which they are based and the fact that that distribution of wealth may be different from the prevailing one, account for the occasional popularity of such markets as ways of making tragic choices. Like all approaches (including the pure market when it is used to make both first- and second-order determinations) which owe their popularity to the ameliorative effects of having obscured conflict, nonmoney markets inevitably diminish honesty and openness. As with the pure market, however, the degree to which honesty and openness are in fact diminished will depend on how many reasons—whose validity does not depend on eclipsing the conflict, for instance, the fact that the nonmoney medium of exchange is based on a compensatory, if unequal, wealth distribution—can be marshaled to support the use of the nonmoney market. On the strength of these will depend the legitimacy accorded to the approach.[23]

Yet honesty is not the predominant value in our society. And a useful veil can be even more useful if money and nonmoney markets interrelate to make tragic choices. The use of a bureaucracy in tragic contexts sometimes reflects such a combination. Of course, the use of a bureaucracy can represent modifications of many different approaches to tragic dilemmas as, for instance, that of the aresponsible, nonrepresentative approach in which the allocation lies within the arbitrary discretion of a bureaucrat. But when a bureaucracy serves not to make arbitrary choices, but simply to impose a time burden on all those who would apply for the resource, it represents allocation through a mixture of money and nonmoney markets.

Let us assume that a scarce resource is officially made

available to everyone who can meet certain standards and that these standards have been *responsibly* determined (as we have used that word throughout) and are generally acceptable to the community, that is, do not themselves provoke tragic conflict. Let us also assume that in order to show that one has met these standards, one must follow a complicated bureaucratic procedure involving submission of documents, appearances, affidavits, and so forth. Let us finally assume that the number of people who in fact would meet the standards, absent the procedural hurdles, is far greater than the number permitted by the first-order determination. Imposing a complicated procedure functions as a system for allocation, limiting the resource to only a fraction of those whom the society has said are entitled to it. The market that accomplishes this rationing is not simply a money market since those applicants with time on their hands can probably be successful even if they lack money; nor is the market simply a nonmoney market with time as the medium of exchange, since those with money can hire someone to spend time (to stand in line for them) or, let us assume, can qualify with a lesser expenditure of time because they can employ professionals to assay the procedures involved, present proof in an acceptable form, and so forth, even if at substantial expense. The medium of exchange is a continuum between enormous amounts of time and little money at one pole, and enormous amounts of money and little time at the other.

The advantages of this sort of market approach, an approach which is perhaps less rare than one would think, should be clear. By avoiding a simple time or money market, the precise inequalities which inhere in the use of the medium of exchange are made less obvious. Similarly, such a mixture makes it more difficult to identify the exact price which that society has in fact placed on the precious resource. Since nominally everyone who meets generally acceptable standards is entitled to have the resource, the society can claim that it puts no price on the resource at all, much in the way some societies make similar claims when they convert an allocation decision into a decision on absolute worthiness in order to use a jury. Of course a very definite allocation does take place, and the resource is given to those who value it most, but only as this is measured by the various possible time-money combinations which suffice to evoke bureaucratic approval.

Is such a mixed allocation method desirable? In part an answer must depend on the distribution of time-money combinations. One can imagine time-money combinations being more equally distributed than either time or money is distributed. Or one may imagine an unequal distribution which nevertheless reflects the way that society wants to bias the ultimate allocation. Neither case, of course, guarantees that such a market would test relative desire.[24] Relative desire is tested as well as can be only if one assumes (a) that the time-money combinations are more equally distributed than any other possible medium of exchange, and (b) that the utility of and desire for the time-money combination is also more equally distributed than the utility of, and desire for, other possible media of exchange. These heroic assumptions are made only a little less so by the fact that they compare relative equality of distribution with respect to other media of exchange, and not absolute equality of distribution. To the extent that better, though imperfect, distribution is brought about, relative desire is better, though imperfectly, tested.

Before one may conclude that such an allocation procedure would be desirable, even if the last set of assumptions were met, one would have to deal with those problems which arise not from inequalities, but from the tendency of markets to equate social utility with individual desire. The time-money continuum might, let us assume, do an excellent job of gauging Holmes's and Moriarty's relative desire to have children; but leaving it at that presumes a complete indifference as to which candidate society would prefer as parent. True, the factors which make one candidate intuitively preferable to another, to the extent that they are considered legitimate by the society, can be given significance in the responsible standards applied by the bureaucrat.[25] And, while this approach would entail all the difficulties of control, access, and privacy which we have already discussed, something reasonably acceptable might be feasible. The really tough problems arise when the differences the society wishes to recognize are ones to which it cannot openly admit without offending values basic to egalitarian conceptions. As a reaction to this unwillingness, pressure to rely on aresponsible agencies may develop; but the agency in this situation more likely would be an arbitrary bureaucracy than a parajury, because the former is better suited to applying the time-money continuum, or market part, of the complex, mixed system of allocations. If the aresponsible agent is to be a bureaucrat, then the problems which we feared with parajuries—arbitrariness, lack of control, venality, lack of representativeness, as well as the bitter price extracted by putting process costs on the losers—assume that much more significance.

Having said all this, and indicated our dislike for this kind of mixture, we must concede that it is often used precisely because it renders imperceptible the bases of both the market and collective elements of the allocation. The first is accomplished through the complexity of the medium of exchange; the second through the use of an aresponsible bureaucrat advertised as approving all who meet responsible standards but who in fact does not do so. This approach has a special appeal if there is no tradition of aresponsible representative agencies like the jury.[26] Whether such an approach can withstand the kind of criticism implicit in Kafka's *The Trial,* and *The Castle,* or in Menotti's *The Consul,* is another matter. The fact that these artistic forms are quite modern suggests that the approach is very much of our time.

Second Modification:
Wealth-Distribution-Neutral Markets

A different approach to the problems we have observed when markets are applied to tragic choices retains money as the medium of exchange, but modifies the market to counter the effects of relative wealth positions. Theoretically, a scarce resource can be distributed through a market for which money remains the medium of exchange and in which virtually any degree of equal distribution can be brought about. The practical difficulties with establishing such wealth-neutral markets, and the problems which such markets do not solve are topics to which the present discussion is devoted; first, it will be useful to describe in some detail just how a money market can be made relatively wealth neutral.

The simplest way of reducing the dependence of the allocation of a scarce resource on the pre-existing distribution of wealth is to move from a rule of entitlement—in which everyone must buy the good (and pay to avoid the bad)—to a rule in which everyone is given the good (and must be paid to accept the bad). The contrast between the Civil War system of conscription and the totally volunteer army illustrates this change, as does the move from a situation in which people must buy the right to have each child to that in which people have an unlimited right to have children but are paid by the state to refrain from having them. But the equality achieved is, as we shall see, of a rather limited nature.

Given initial positions of wealth, which include legal rights as well as money, if everyone is allotted an additional good in equal quantity, without our having had to raise the money to provide this good, and if the good is desired approximately equally by all wealth groups, then we will have moved to a more equal total distribution of wealth. This is so even if the good is more desirable to some individuals than to others; and it is true if the good costs us money so long as we raise that money in a way which does not alter the pre-existing distribution of wealth. By adding the same amount at each level of wealth a greater proportion of wealth will have been given to the poor than to the rich.

If we alter the assumptions, the outcome is more complex. Suppose that, by and large, the good is desired more intensely by the rich than by the poor; then it is possible that giving it to all may leave the pre-existing distribution unchanged or may even increase inequality. Conversely, the more the good is preferred by the poor, the greater the equalization effect of giving it away free. Moreover, the money needed to pay for the good (assuming that the good is not costless) may be raised in ways which diminish, increase, or overcome the equalizing effect of giving the good away free; this will depend on the taxes or other method used to raise revenue. Similarly, if the good were sold, the money raised thereby could be used to manipulate the effects of selling the good. Thus, while these modifications of initial entitlements have a prima-facie appeal because they appear to alter relative positions within the market, whether the desired effects are ultimately realized depends in great measure on broader fiscal and transfer payment policies (for example, how the money is spent that was raised by selling the good). Moreover, free-good approaches at best only slightly limit the wealth dependence of a tragic choice. If, therefore, we wish to use a money market which avoids the problems of wealth dependence, we must look well beyond minimalist modifications of the volunteer army or the Boulding Plan sort. [27]

We must consider systems which charge the rich more than the poor to get the good (or avoid the bad), or which pay the rich more than the poor to induce them to give up the good (or accept the bad). In the first instance, the money raised by these charges would have to be spent in a way which was wealth neutral, or at least not so regressive as to overbalance the change in wealth positions brought about by the charges. Under the payment system, the subsidy would have to be raised through taxes which were sufficiently progressive, in relation to the pre-existing wealth distribution, to overcome the regressive subsidy payment. Apart from the problems which the spending or raising of the money entail—problems which can be mitigated by judicious decisions as to when to charge a differential price for the good and when, instead, to pay people to give it up—there remains a more important difficulty with these progressive pricing approaches. We really do not know how much more to charge the rich than the poor for, say, child rights if our object is to isolate their choice from wealth considerations.

The best approach to this problem is to begin with the result we desire and work backward. Let us assume a first-order determination which permits an average of 2.1 children per family. In order to approach a neutral allocation of these children the society would divide people into categories representing roughly equal wealth and assign prices for child rights to each category, so that in each there would be an average of 2.1 children per family. In this way the very wealthiest would bid for children (as against other goods) only in competition with others of similar wealth, and so would middle-income people, and so would the poor. The categories would have to be large enough so that a meaningful market within each category existed, and this would produce some disequality between the richest and poorest within each category.[28]

Since the object of the scheme is to achieve a 2.1 general average, and to measure desire independently of wealth, there need be no price difference, within each category, between the right to the first and to the fifteenth child. Thus, if a family of Rothschilds was willing to pay more for a fifteenth child than a family of Rockefellers was willing to pay for a first child, the Rothschilds would get the child right. The prices in each category would necessarily vary from time to time to reflect changes in the relative desire for children, but the prices would always be set so that each wealth category maintained an average birthrate equal to the general average fixed by the first-order determination. On a purely technical basis, the same approach could as readily be employed for the allocation of wartime military service, artificial kidneys, and in other tragic situations.

In using such a scheme there is no need to set prices for every wealth category. Indeed, one expects that such an approach would, like most negative income tax proposals, fix positive prices for the right to have children in the wealthiest categories, and diminishing subsidies for each child not had at the lowest wealth categories. Somewhere in the continuum there would be a category in which no prices or subsidies would be needed because the existing, "unchosen" market incentives would bring about a result consistent with the average required by the first-order determination. A society can give away a right and pay people not to overuse it, or force people to buy the right, or do both varying the technique for different wealth categories to achieve neutrality most simply.

Unfortunately, however, the scheme described only assures us a true measure of relative desire for a particular good apart from wealth considerations if we assume that desire would be equal among different wealth groups but for the difference in wealth. To put it another way, the scheme assumes that whatever the tragic good being allocated, the average desire in wealth category A and wealth category C would be the same if individuals in the two categories were equally wealthy.[29] But if, for example, a great many of a group which, for cultural or other nonwealth-related reasons, preferred large families (Italians, say) were clustered in one wealth category, then the approach described would not be neutral with respect to the distribution of wealth. It would charge a higher price to the category in which Italians clustered than it would to, say, the small-family-loving French, were they clustered in that same wealth category. Or, what is the same thing, our scheme would bring about an equality of family size between the categories in which the French and the Italians cluster even though the two groups desire different size families for reasons other than those arising from differences in wealth.

Theoretically one could attempt to determine all nonwealth-dependent characteristics and correlate them with the number of children wanted and then seek to correct, for these nonwealth-related factors, the prices charged each wealth category. But this correction would be exceedingly difficult to compute in practice, the more so because there would be incentives to lie about one's desire for children. More important, even were such a procedure feasible, it would make the resulting price system for children sufficiently complex so that the mass of people would doubtless come to believe that the true purpose of the scheme was to favor particular groups.

We conclude that it would be difficult indeed to establish a market which was truly neutral vis-à-vis the distribution of wealth. A scheme of the sort described would approach neutrality about as well as could be done, and it would come especially close if the desire to avoid the bad or get the good (though very different among different individuals) did not differ significantly among highly visible, self-conscious groups which clustered in particular wealth categories. Obviously this implies that the relative wealth neutrality achieved by any such scheme would depend on the particular good or bad being allocated.

Criticisms of Wealth-Distribution-Neutral Markets

If such discontinuities were the only significant limitation of the scheme we have been discussing, it would still be a promising approach. Unfortunately, there are a host of other difficulties with it, ranging from the quite technical to the fundamental, which make its use, at least in an unmodified form, very unlikely.

The technical problems with the scheme can be illustrated by one example. Although childbearing occurs at a time when most people are relatively poor, expectations of wealth vary greatly among people at a childbearing age. Indeed, it is not unlikely that at the same childbearing age the untrained worker's family will be wealthier, in any measurable sense, than the family of the newly graduated medical student with substantial expectations of inheritance, future earnings, and so forth. A wealth-neutral scheme must deal with this; but, as with most technical problems, technical solutions are available. Something like the Yale tuition postponement option (in which what one pays for college depends on one's future income) could be applied, so that ultimately the price one pays for children would depend on one's lifetime earnings and capital.[30] This adjustment, however, requires a fairly sophisticated administrative apparatus, in addition to that required by the scheme itself. One may properly ask whether the greater degree of equality achieved by greater sophistication is worth its costs, especially since greater sophistication generally involves greater unintelligibility.

We have already mentioned the problem of intelligibility with respect to attempts to correct the scheme for different cultural factors. This problem attaches, in fact, to any modification which is likely to make the scheme more precise. Thus the more wealth categories there are, the more dubious will seem the difference in prices charged. There is no reason, *a priori*, why a higher wealth category must in every instance be charged a higher price per child in order to achieve the predetermined average. Cultural differences and costs not incorporated in the scheme may already affect different wealth groups differently. The wealth group for whom private schools have become, on the whole, imperative may already bear a substantial financial cost per child which a lower wealth category does not bear. As a result, the desire for children, though dependent on wealth, need not move as a nice continuous rising function of any given index of wealth distribution, such as taxable income. If we adjust the price charged to reflect such pre-existing costs we may find ourselves charging some categories of the poor more than some wealthier groups. To some extent this anomaly can be alleviated by granting a subsidy for not having children to the poorer category at the point of the anomaly and discarding the use of charges at that point. But the possibility still remains that people believed to be in a higher wealth category will achieve the desired average at a lower price per child right than people in a lower wealth category. Of course, one could argue that such prices were nevertheless fair given the existence of pre-existing financial incentives such as school costs; to explain this effectively however is a highly expensive business. One is tempted to collapse categories which display such anomalies into one another (even though operating through broader wealth groupings will accomplish less equality) so that fewer apparent paradoxes will have to be explained. In practice, we are sure that any attempt to create a wealth-neutral market would trade off a great deal of equality for simplicity of operation and intelligibility.

The desire for administrative simplicity and avoidance of paradox may be strong enough to cause a modification in the first-order determination.[31] Let us assume that at a 2.1 average all sorts of paradoxes arise, numerous wealth categories seem necessary, and only a very small wealth category reaches the average on the basis of pre-existing incentives. Let us also assume that at an average of 2.2 the situation is quite different. At this last figure a very large proportion of the population can be left to procreate in peace, uninterrupted by any planned incentives, while a relatively easy and intelligible price and subsidy system works for the remaining groups (as, for instance, if within those categories requiring intervention, expectations of future wealth are essentially homogeneous at childbearing time, obviating the need for deferred payment schemes). It is very likely that the society, if it wished to use a neutral market system of allocation, would move to the 2.2 figure. The cost of putting the second-order choice at 2.1 would not justify its first-order desirability.[32]

All this suggests that the technical problems with wealth-neutral market schemes, though real enough and costly, are likely to be solvable at the expense of some precision, some equality, and some modification of the first-order determination. Unfortunately, however, even when modified to achieve simplicity and the appearance of equality, a neutral market approach to allocation in tragic situations leaves many fundamental problems unresolved.[33]

One class of such problems, similar to traditional externalities, occurs when part of the burden of the market falls on people other than those who are making the choice. Thus a money market for children—whether wealth neutral or not—

can be criticized because the children suffer when a parent is required to give up other resources in order to be eligible to have the children. One may question whether—at least if a minimum wealth level is guaranteed—children suffer more from the absence of material goods or from having parents who happen to prefer material goods to children, but such skepticism must be directed to particular cases and does not serve as a general retort. A person who gives up all his worldly possessions to get an extra year of life on an artificial kidney, burdens his family as well as himself. Somehow these burdens, which fall beside the chooser, as it were, have to be made to influence the choosers if the market is to work well. Not peculiar to tragic choices, this issue is absorbed by a related externality which is especially significant in the tragic context.

The ordinary money market, whether wealth dependent or neutral, assumes that social utility in the allocation of the tragic resource is maximized when individual desires are maximized (within the constraints of the first-order determination).[34] Since a wealth-neutral market attempts to achieve a maximization of individual desire through egalitarian means, the conflict between egalitarian purposes and proper allocation seems to be resolved. But it is, in fact, resolved only if we assume that the satisfaction of individual desires is the sole goal of society's allocations. That is surely not the case. There are differences, external costs and benefits, if you wish—or, if you prefer, different conceptions of egalitarianism—which most societies wish to recognize, explicitly or not, in making tragic choices.

We do not let the halt and the blind volunteer for front-line service, however passionate their belligerency. Nor would we be inclined to let an individual buy a kidney machine (however much he would be willing to spend, measured in wealth-neutral terms) if we were convinced that whatever his hopes, the machine would fail him and thereafter be useless to others.[35] These distinctions are ones which the society may be able to recognize through responsible political devices. But there are, in addition, a second group of distinctions (not reflected in individual desire) equally required by the society which offend deep values when openly affirmed. Integrating the first group into the market presents a less difficult problem.

The problem of introducing responsibly determined standards into a money market, whether wealth netural or not, is not difficult if we are prepared to give complete precedence to the responsibly determined standards. We can exclude the lame from army service, regardless of their desires. In so doing we are simply saying that the collective decision is more important regardless of individual desire. It is only when we want to give some, or even great, weight to a collectively desired and recognized distinction, but not make that weight so decisive that it will overcome really large differences in individual desire, that the problem becomes a puzzle.

Suppose that in the allocation of organ transplants, we have a general, responsibly promulgated notion that some precedence should be given those whose immunological systems will not reject the organ. Suppose also that our knowledge of the likelihood of rejection is quite probabilistic. Suppose finally that we are committed to giving some weight to individual desire for the organ, as expressed in a wealth neutral market. Then we would have a very hard time combining the desire expressed in market terms with the nonmarket injunction to consider likelihood of success.

We could, of course, abandon the market and try to gauge individual desire collectively and, as we have already seen, confront grave problems. We could gather data simulating market expressions of desire and, with figures indicating probabilities of therapeutic success, hand them over to a collective decider or agency. This invites people to lie when they express their desires and—even assuming that those picked collectively would still be made to pay their willing market price— introduces gaming strategies which cast doubt on the validity of the expressions of desire. (For example, the person who believed he had substantial chances of medical success if he got a kidney and therefore a high collective priority, might understate his market bid, betting he would receive the good anyway, at a cheaper price).[36]

Another approach would require us to convert the collective preference into market terms and then modify the prices faced by applicants to take into account the chances of success. Where we are dealing with a single, relatively discrete set of collective preferences this may work well. If there is a collective preference for a family of not less than two children and not more than five, and a heightening disapproval as the family gets larger, a low price (within each wealth category) could be set for the first two children, a moderate price for the next three, and a progressively higher one for each child thereafter. Disregarding its intelligibility to the mass of citizens, this approach is at least technically feasible. When we are dealing with a very complex set of collective preferences, or ones to which values must be given on an individual basis, conversion of those preferences into monetized elements in the wealth-neutral market is virtually impossible. Consider, for example, the difficulties entailed by an attempt to create a wealth-neutral market in kidneys, if the market had to take into account collective preferences which modified the price to each recipient on the basis of a combination of age and success factors. Obviously, too, the less absolute these collective preferences are, the harder it is to monetize them and use them in the neutral market.

Conversion of such collective preferences into money figures introduces an additional difficulty. It is one thing to say that these preferences can be openly and responsibly recognized by the society without degrading basic values. It is quite another thing to say that this can be accomplished when the society must express its preferences in money terms. Thus a society may be able to say that some preference should be given to the candidate for delicate and expensive surgery when his chances of success are greater than another's. But can society say that the preference counts five points on an exam scale, or earns a discount of $1,000 in a surgery allocating market?[37]

Thus we are presented with an instance of a common issue

on which many have commented. When one aspect of a problem can be readily monetized (or expressed mathematically) and this cannot be done for other elements without great difficulty, it does not follow that we may achieve an optimal result through a quantitative approach to the whole problem, even if, were all elements readily quantifiable, we could agree that a total monetization would be the best approach. It may be better to forgo market information, even as to those elements for which it is available and accurate, than to try to monetize the whole affair. A simple, muddled, collective determination may be preferable.[38]

If integrating this first group of distinctions—ones for which a collective preference can be openly recognized, like a preference for a certain family size—raises problems, one can imagine the difficulties which face a market approach that would also take account of collective preferences which are very costly to promulgate openly. These distinctions comprise the second group, whose discussion we deferred. They pose questions of the sort, How does a society which badly needs research scientists, but will not admit that their lives are more useful than those of ordinary citizens, give effect to its preference when the society also wishes the desire to live, as expressed through the market, to influence the allocation of scarce medical resources? and If we prefer priority in childrearing to be accorded good parents yet find it hard to state criteria for preferences which are both lucid and inoffensive to all egalitarian beliefs, how might we integrate this preference with priorities which reflect individual desires to be parents?

Ordinary market techniques will not do—unless the scheme is sufficiently complicated so that introduction of discounts to engineers or geniuses passes virtually unnoticed. But any scheme which is so unintelligible has its own problems, as we have seen. Society can abandon the market and use devices like a responsible agencies that can to some degree reflect those collective preferences which are not openly admissible. A shadow market can be used to gauge desire but, again, such a market will serve as an uncertain guide because its reflexive, "shadow" nature will invite people to gamble and conceal their true desires. Or, we may pretend that all who express desire through the market and who meet certain standards can receive the resource, and then introduce a bureaucracy (or even a jury) which will parcel out the scarce resource on the basis of those unspoken preferences we wish to remain latent. In sum, genuine, complex collective preferences, whether openly admissible or not, when they must be factored with market-expressed desires, rather resemble those time-money markets to which arbitrary bureautic deciders have been appended. One may question whether in such situations the market is, after all, the appropriate vehicle for relaying expressions of desire. Where, instead, collective preferences are relatively simple and monetizable or can appropriately be expressed as absolutes (as with a total bar on allowing the very elderly to bid for artificial organs), a mixture which retains the market (even restructured to be neutral) is feasible.

It is possible that a less wealth-neutral market will achieve even unspeakable collective aims reasonably well, justifying its lack of neutrality on grounds of administrative simplicity, abstention, or custom. On certain assumptions one could defend present childbearing incentives and allocations of scarce medical resources in just these terms.[39] But we should recognize that this possibility is entirely a matter of chance, and that it must be scrutinized lest it be simply a disingenuous attempt on the part of beneficiaries of the existing system to retain unjustifiable advantages.

From the first two groups of distinctions which were the source of problems with neutral markets—that is, those based on the inability of the market to take into account external benefits and costs and social preferences not expressed in the market—we turn to a different kind of trouble arising from the deep structure of the wealth-distribution-neutral market, namely, its inability to measure accurately even individual desire for some tragically scarce resources. We shall discuss two manifestations of this inability. While both mirror important theoretical objections to the use of markets, their significance for tragic situations is quite different. The first seems to us to be trivial in practice; the second so occludes our view of the advantages of markets in a particular class of tragic choices as to present an important practical flaw.

Even if we can assume that each of the relevant wealth categories would desire the generality of goods, apart from wealth considerations, about equally, we cannot readily make that assumption about individuals. Take the extreme examples of two hypothetical contemporaries, the priestly ascetic and the wealthy, pleasure-loving sybarite. If the wealth-neutral market is to see that more children go to those who want them most, this cannot be accomplished between the ascetic and the sybarite because, wealth considerations aside, the sybarite may still desire both other goods and children more than does the ascetic, and yet the ascetic will be the highest bidder in the market for children because the ascetic has even less use for the other goods. And it does no good to say, "But we can simply give the sybarite the goods the ascetic forgoes, and make them both happier," since there is no assurance in the wealth-neutral scheme that the goods the ascetic forgoes are of equal value to what the sybarite would have been willing to pay in order to have children. After all, the goods forgone by the ascetic who is in a low wealth category are likely to be of far less value than those the sybarite would have had to give up to obtain children. He might accept the ascetic's pittance, and yet say truly that he would rather have had children.

The wealth-neutral scheme will test relative desire for the tragically scarce resource only to the extent that we can assume that individuals, though differing in their desires for the resource, would, at the same weath level, equally desire the generality of goods (that is, money). Economists have long balked at making this assumption because it is too obvious that the world does contain sybarites and ascetics.[40] As far as we are concerned, however, this is a relatively minor, if theoretically fundamental, problem; we are, after all, not making models for economists, we are trying to think about how to approach real situations. We are talking about potential Pareto superiority, not Pareto superiority *simpliciter*. The real issue is, given a world in which sybarites and ascetics coexist, do we do better making the generalized assumption that, on the whole, people at the same wealth level are more like each other in their desires for the generality of goods, or might we be better off making some other empirical assumption. It appears obvious that most people in the same society are quite similar in this respect, however much their individual tastes for child rights, fast cars, and fast horses may differ, and that an approach which makes this assumption is more likely to work well than is any other. If it is worth the costs of identifying the sybarites and ascetics of our society and correcting for them, we can do so; but we may well decide that what works all right for the mass of citizens is the best we should do.

The second imperfection applies to the wealth-neutral market as it operates in a limited class of tragic situations. The market values desire in terms of alternatives forgone, that is, other goods given up in order to get the one desired. This may be a meaningful measure when we allocate shoes; it may even be so when we allocate child rights. But should it have a similar role when we allocate insulin? Indeed, what does it tell us about an individual's desire to live that he will give up more goods in order to live than will another person—equally wealthy, equally fond of the generality of goods, equally diabetic?

One is inclined to say that it means very little since death will obviate the chooser's enjoyment of whatever goods he took instead of longer life. Yet this betrays too narrow an appreciation of what the shorter, happier life might be like, or how grim its lengthened alternative. Nevertheless, one's inclination reveals an important feature of that class of tragic choices to which death is a necessary option: One doubts whether the postulate necessary to make the market attractive—that choosers, however much in agreement on the general desirability of goods, are highly differentiated as to particular goods—truly holds. If this postulate does not appear valid, then the importance of having a retrospective test by which the success of the market, in the eyes of the choosers, can be measured against other systems of allocation, assumes great significance. But it is a concomitant of such death choices that just this check is necessarily unavailable.

In situations of choice we could typically ask choosers afterward, "Were you happy with your choice?" and "Would another person have chosen better for you than you did for yourself?" By this method we might test our confidence in the market as the best method for bringing about individual desires. And we might find that, although some choosers were not happy and would have done better had another person chosen for them or had some other method been used to measure their desire for the good, nevertheless most people believed that they did better on their own than they would have done with any feasible alternative. If we further assumed that those who gained gained more than the losers lost, and that the distributional effects among gainers and losers were acceptable, then we might say that the approach taken was desirable.[41]

The problem posed by the scarce life-sustaining drug, or the transplant of a vital organ, is that we cannot do the retrospective research which would be required to support even the modified market postulate that people by and large know best for themselves what they want and that they can express these judgments in terms of alternative goods forgone. We are completely at sea as to whether some other system might better give effect to individual preferences as, for example, the testimony of the impoverished elderly has convinced us that the forced saving of Social Security better implements their wishes than a free market in pensions. We could, of course, interview survivors who got the life-saving good and ask them whether it was worth it. We could also interview those who bid too low (while they survive) and ask them if they were still pleased with their decision. But such data omits what surely is the real issue: Was the extra time (for all ultimately die) worth the diminution of other goods during that time? If we assume that the benefit, or a great portion of it, derives from individuals having the choice, the right to choose for themselves, between goods and time, then the answer is "Of course it's worth it." If instead the benefit of the tragic choice includes—and it is a principal benefit in other allocation situations—a judgment by the chooser as to whether he has chosen well, then it is very hard to say with any degree of certainty that there is utility in a market in lives simply because it saves those who bid most for more time.

Even if we admit that we have no better measure of desire, this suggests that given the shortcomings of the only measure available, and the dubiety of the postulate of differentiation, social goals other than individual desire should take precedence. If individuals don't in a market way choose between more time on earth and material goods, to their own satisfaction, then perhaps the society should choose for them according to its own scales of utility and efficiency. A decision to give dialysis to the person for whom it is more likely to be successful, but who is willing to forgo little to get it, would, for example, find support in this agnostic view of markets in lives. So would the lottery.

But we should say that for reasons not altogether clear, we are not prepared to discount, in these situations, the importance of individual desire as it is expressed in terms of willingness to forgo alternatives. It may be that we put more weight on the benefits occurring from the right to choose itself, or it may be that we assume what we believe about ordinary choices to be the best guide in transcendental tragic situations, that is, that the postulates of differentiation and self-competence do apply.

As we read over these pages, we fear the reader will tire of endless lists of problems, endlessly enumerated, each solution breeding new problems without end. The analysis to which this book is devoted is necessarily schematic since it is our aim to present an over-all mapping—an architectural drawing, if you will—of approaches to tragic allocations. There is seldom an opportunity to break the line without distorting the picture thereby. But it is our hope that the reader who works through this extended essay will know, in the broadest sense of that word, how a society's approaches to tragic situations, in the broadest sense of that phrase, interrelate. With this apologia, we resume our discussion.

There are two more problems engendered by markets that are neutral with respect to the distribution of wealth when they are used to make tragic choices.[42] The first of these is the familiar dilemma associated with too clearly monetizing the tragically scarce resource. The second problem, a stalemate of the wealth-neutral market, arises as a result of the phenomenon of desperation bidding.

Any money market designed to allocate a scarce resource will result in a price being assigned to the resource. Even if the price accurately weighted wealth so that neither rich nor poor were advantaged, there remains the offense inherent in giving money values to sacred rights. We should realize, however, that since a wealth-neutral market would set a series of different prices for the same resource, some of even this affront might be mitigated. The more unintelligible the scheme, the less obvious is the pricing of the sacred resource. This was, in fact, the advantage of the mixed time-money bureaucratic approach we talked about earlier.[43] It is nevertheless true that any market in money which does not openly sacrifice honesty puts to people quite clearly what they must give up in material terms in order to gain a tragically scarce resource.[44]

One might reply that the very fact that some people would choose the other goods—would join the army or choose not to have another child—shows that sacred values are myths and that individuals do value other things more. But even if this were true, it would not alter the fact that the obvious destruction of myths, when these are myths of the sort properly termed *ideals*, is a costly business for any society.

The neutrality of the wealth-neutral scheme makes that scheme vulnerable to stalemate by desperation bidding. Consider, for instance, the possibility of a wealth-neutral market in scarce artificial lungs in which more people than could possibly be accommodated wanted so desperately to go on living that they were willing to bid all that they had. In this situation, the market would not serve to allocate the artificial lungs and would act merely to heighten pathos. A nonneutral market avoids this problem because in it the rich can, and do, outbid the poor. But in a wealth-neutral market everyone is as rich as everyone else and no one can outbid anyone else if all desire the resources equally; there is no guarantee at all that, ultimately, the demand will be matched to the supply available.

At first glance, one might conclude from the presence of desperation bidding that the first-order determination was incorrect. But, although the first-order limit may in retrospect appear inadequate, desperation bidding, in itself, will not suffice to increase sufficiently the total amount of scarce resources made available precisely because the market we are using is wealth neutral. Moreover, there is no reason to believe that the same people who are now bidding everything would have voted for more of the scarce resource at the first-order level when their own need for the resource was only a statistical probability. Such discontinuity simply reflects the underlying conflict: People are not generally prepared to treat life as a pearl without price except when faced with their own certain death.[45]

Whatever amount one may give up to save one's own life when its loss is otherwise certain—what one will bid at an auction of one's life and death—is not only unequal to the resources one would give up to avoid a statistical risk of losing one's life, it is also unequal even when we discount for probability. A wealthy man might pay $50,000,000 to avoid certain death, but not $25,000,000 to avoid one chance in two of dying, and much less than $1,000 to avoid a death chance of one in fifty thousand (indeed, any of us probably frequently rides in a car or an airplane at a risk much greater than one in fifty thousand for pay-offs that amount to no more than diversion).[46] The amount we would pay to avoid a gamble with a catastrophic result gets smaller and smaller at a faster rate than the odds of the gamble diminish. This may be thought of as, in part, the converse of the favorable gamble paradox, noted by Milton Friedman and L. J. Savage, that people will pay more for a chance with a large favorable pay-off than that chance is statistically worth when the chance is remote and the cost of the chance small.[47]

But the first-order determination, though inadequate, is not necessarily incorrect. Indeed, the fluidity of risk aversion precludes us from adjusting the first-order level to the quite plausible judgment that since individuals appear in retrospect to have been willing to throw in everything for their life-saving resource, enough of that resource should be made available to accommodate the number statistically likely to require it, irrespective of other economic consequences. We cannot decree that kidney machines enough for all who need dialysis should be produced even should this require that all society live in hovels, for at the first order, people may well prefer to take a chance of dying for want of dialysis, which they may never require, than to live without decent housing, the need for which they know with certainty.[48]

Desperation bidding is a phenomenon largely confined to those tragic choices in which the risk of loss entails certain death. A couple's forfeiture of child rights (the consequences of which are certain) and conscription (though it risks death) are tragic paradigms which do not display this phenomenon in its disabling form. A neutral market is feasible. But it would be an error to think that, when the phenomenon disables a neutral market, choosers are unwilling to value lives. Rather, that valuation is thwarted by the structure of the wealth-neutral market.

Markets in Risks: An Attempt to Mitigate Some Problems of Modified Markets

Some of the problems of money markets in tragic resources might be avoided if, instead of using the market to allocate the resource itself when it was needed, we made a market in risks which allowed an earlier decision by the choosers—that is, we let people insure themselves against the possibility that they might want the resource in the future. If we know that a certain proportion of people will require marrow transplants, we could, long before the collapse of their immunological systems, offer to them and all others the right to get marrow transplants should they need them. (Of course, the futures element of such markets raises the possibility that some crucial choices would have to be made during minority.) Such a market could be wealth neutral or not, as we wished. It is worthwhile to see which of the difficulties we observed in the operation of normal markets are alleviated by a market in risks, and which new problems arise.

It is pretty clear that a market in risks, by forcing purchases before the time of need, would avoid the technical problem of clearing the market in the face of desperation bidding. Even with respect to life-saving medical interventions, different individuals would, in all probability, bid different amounts to guarantee access to the kidney machine, or the marrow, or the rare surgical technique; a market could be established which matched demand at the time of bidding with the supply available when the need ultimately arose. If this were not possible, then it would be hard to understand, let alone justify, the first-order determinations fixing the perimeters of scarcity. We shall soon see, however, that this treatment of the desperation bidding phenomenon is more a papering over, a technical solution, than a true resolution of the underlying conflicts which the phenomenon dramatizes.

A market in risks might also obscure the state's role in valuing lives. Taking advantage of people's propensity to undervalue unlikely, unfavorable gambles, society might well act as if the first-order determination depended solely on second-order (perhaps wealth-neutral) decisions made in the risk market. In this way a result consistent with what would be acceptable in a true collective first-order determination might be reached, and one might plausibly say that individuals had chosen for themselves while the state had abstained from valuing lives.[49] This would be especially persuasive if it was rather difficult for individuals to extrapolate, in money terms, from the cost of insurance to a price for a life. It is less clear how a market in risks would affect problems of intelligibility and administrative costs. On the one hand, taking into account the probabilities that a certain proportion of the population would need artificial lungs, for example, complicates the decision on appropriate prices. On the other hand, it is at least possible that the demand for intelligibility would be less if only risks were involved.[50] It may be also that the demand for a scarce resource reflected in a risk market would present fewer discontinuities and anomalies, so that a market, even a wealth-neutral one, could be set up with fewer complications. One simply cannot say in the abstract whether this set of problems would be aggravated or eased in such a market.

A market in risks would do little if anything for the ascetic-sybarite problems. Alternatives forgone would be a pretty good measure of desire to avoid the risk, so that one aspect of the problem of whether a market tested desire would be eased; but nothing cures the fact that what the ascetic and the sybarite are being asked to forgo has greatly different values to each. We would still be measuring desire with a variable yardstick.

Similarly, a market in risks would not solve the problem that individual desire is not necessarily congruent with social utility. Indeed, the problem might be aggravated. It would be possible to vary the price of the insurance according to the external benefits and costs which would arise if a particular individual chose to insure. But now, to the problems of egalitarianism and administrative costs previously discussed, would be added the cost of the uncertainty of external costs and benefits at the time the insurance was taken. We would not know whether a twenty-five-year-old Holmes or a twenty-five-year-old Moriarty was being subsidized to guarantee the scarce resource's future availability to him. Yet at the time the resource comes to be needed, the external costs and benefits are real enough.

Of course, collective intervention could take place at the time of need. This would accentuate inegalitarian characteristics of the preference since, at the time of need, collective intervention would be employed to counter a prior choice. Intervention would not appear as simply a slight tilting of the balance, easily mistaken or overlooked in a complex pricing mechanism; it would be clear that some are being saved and others condemned, despite their own previous choices, because of their relative value to the rest of us. Even if we placed restrictions on the scope of such interventions—if, for example, we could not deprive an insured villain of his previously reserved resource (since we do not, after all, impose the death penalty for general villainy)—the discrimination would be manifest.

A market in risks presents three final issues—or perhaps three facets of the same phenomenon peculiar to such markets, namely, that the risks market detaches, or defers, the tragic allocation from the initial individual decision. First, the market in risks embodies an implicit collective judgment that the risk averse, the cautious, should receive scarce resources before gamblers. If there were no differences in risk preferences among people, then the same individuals could obtain the resource in a market in risks as in a market for the resource itself. But if there is a different pattern of demand, it must be either that some people have different data on the risks involved[51] or that some people are simply less willing to gamble than others. Aside from whether cautious citizens with reliable sources of information should be favored just because they are more cautious or better informed than others who desire the resource as much, a society that establishes a market in risks must confront this silent bias or be rightly accused of hiding a basic preference.

A second aspect of the same general phenomenon arises from the fact that, in a risks market, the resource being sold is not the scarce resource itself but a package deal, the scarce resource plus the willingness to gamble. Since the object of the market is to allocate the scarce resource, one may well ask whether, even from a purely individual point of view, this is best accomplished by an allocation according to willingness to buy the package deal. The recent moves toward compulsory accident insurance, compulsory health plans, compulsory retirement plans have many sources; but one of their justifications surely has been that however well individuals choose when they choose for current use, they do not do well for themselves (and know this later) when they choose a risk-resource package the actual need for which only becomes known sometime in the future.[52] To the extent that one is sympathetic to the precautionary motives which such moves toward compulsory insurance reflect, one should be wary of accepting the judgments made by markets in tragic risks.

The third facet can be seen clearly if one considers what may happen at the moment the need for the scarce resource strikes. Consider the tableau of the desperate man who failed to insure scarce medical treatment and now, though willing to throw in all he owns for it, must be turned away, or who lashes himself to a lamppost in front of the appropriate hospital with a large placard across his chest, "Give me another chance." What are the social costs? We doubt that society would bear them even if it knew. Think of the fascination Faust holds for us, when it appears that he may yet cheat the devil of his due.[53] The repentant sinner, the person who has changed his mind and who pleads for a second chance, appeals to something deep within us—however much he has enjoyed his sins—and can only be denied that chance at high cost, and at very high cost to a society which professes that life is sacred.

We conclude that markets in risks may serve to make possible market allocations in situations where other difficulties, such as those of costing and desperation bidding, would preclude a market. It is equally clear that markets in risks provide technical solutions; they cure merely the symptoms of conflicts. In addition, they add some new problems of their own. But they are an intriguing variation, whose use we should keep in mind as a possible modification since in tragic situations the least bad approach is the one we are forced to seek.

Fringe Markets

So far we have been acting as if one could simply choose to have a market or, without costs, to forbid one. We have spoken, for instance, as if, given a market in risks, a wealthy man who had failed to insure and later needed a kidney would plead or protest but would not try to buy the kidney on the black market or emigrate to a state where he could buy one openly. Such, of course, is not the case. In fact, the whole relationship between the traditional wealth-dependent market and any nonmarket, or wealth-neutral market system of allocation is sufficiently important and complex to deserve some direct attention. It is important because it indicates what we can and cannot do in nonmarket and modified market ways, and because it sheds light on market situations in which we are prepared to make allocations quite similar to tragic ones.

Every time a system of allocation other than a pure market is established in a society in which the market continues to operate in other areas, there is danger that the nonmarket allocations will be altered by market pressures. This is true whether the system of allocations is directly and responsibly political, works through aresponsible agencies, or through bureaucracies, uses a medium of exchange other than money, and even if it is a money market with prices set to create wealth neutrality. In each case, those with money are tempted to buy the resource by bribing the deciders or by paying the recipients of the resource to sell it. Costly measures may be taken to prevent such actions. Generally the best that can be done is to make the penalty for corruption so high that the price of the resource on the black market becomes prohibitive. This works well in many areas. In tragic situations, however, demand, at least among the few rich enough to pay, can be so great that corruption will remain worthwhile despite high penalties. In addition, there is something especially poignant and difficult in any attempt to enforce the law against a desperate, pathetic figure; suppose a man has succeeded in securing a life-saving device—will the state not only penalize him but also doom him by taking it away? The vividness of the decision to let some individuals die becomes heightened whenever the nonmarket allocation is defended by state enforcement rather than by self-enforcement.

But we should bear in mind that tragic resources are only traded with difficulty. A black market is harder to establish here than it would be for shoes. It is hard to imagine how a poor family who had been allocated the right to another child, could easily sell that right under the table, to a wealthier couple.[54] The tragic good is either sufficiently personal or, as with the artificial kidney, involves enough other people, so that a black market sale would be hard to hide. For this reason, the wealth neutral market—which otherwise would be the most subject to assault from the normal market, through resales from poor to rich—seems fairly secure. Tragic situations, the economist might say, are situations in which price discrimination is likely to work.

Rather, it is the system which depends on decisions by human agencies which is vulnerable to market pressures. This will be true regardless of whether the decisions are technical and responsible ones (like whether the kidney is likely to take) or aresponsible ones. The more the decision is discretionary or judgmental, the more likely is corruption to remain concealed. Since aresponsible decisions are bound to be judgmental, they are particularly exposed to market pressures, but even responsible decisions which require individual fact-finding or application, and decisionless approaches like lotteries or first-come-first-served are prone to corruption by the market.[55]

These vulnerabilities should be especially kept in mind in deciding between wealth-neutral markets and essentially political devices. Of course, if a society wants market pressures to win out but wishes to pretend otherwise, corruption can become an accepted way of life for such allocations. In societies where this is the case, the nonmarket allocation is typically so complex that it is hard to pin down the market pressures which, in fact, determine the results.[56]

Finally, any allocation system can be broken if the person who fails to receive the allocation can flee the jurisdiction and go to a land which allows him access to the resource. That land may be one which has no war or no controls on procreation, and so forth. For some people, Sweden's provision for abortions must have had the same significance as Switzerland's neutrality. What is somewhat more interesting is the case in which the other land offers a market rather than abundance. Suppose a small island sets up a fancy hospital which provides marrow transplants to those willing to pay for them. Are we willing, so that we may protect the integrity of our allocation scheme, to forbid the re-entry of those who go to this island for operations? Would we ban the migration of such people or try to prevent them from taking money out of this country? The recent, though admittedly different, history of abortion laws should give us pause.[57] Yet if we fail to do these things—if we fail to enforce the official allocation whatever its cost—the rich will have two chances—first, in the legal scheme, and then, by buying the resource elsewhere.

Migration, moreover, is available as a way around all nonmarket allocation devices. It works against customary systems, lotteries, and wealth neutral approaches as well as against political allocation systems. Indeed, its effect in the lottery situation is especially severe, since there the double-chance element stands out so. Although migration is effective against wealth neutral markets, it may be that penalties against migration have lesser side effects and are hence better deterrents in this context than in others. A man who is migrating to avoid allocation by a wealth neutral market may not be leaving because migration is the only way left him to survive; he may be going because he can get the lifesaving resource more cheaply abroad. Accordingly, penalties against him, at least should he try to return, are more feasible. The same is not the case if the emigrant has failed to insure in a wealth-neutral market in risks. True, had he been willing to pay the price early, he would not be in a jam now; and letting him migrate freely will mean that no rich man need bother to insure. At the time of his leaving, however, the choice the rich man faces is migration or death—and the acts by which the allocation system is enforced in that situation are monstrous.

As a practical matter, it is hard to imagine that, as a consequence of a tragic allocation, any great effort to prevent migration or to ban the expatriation of funds will be made in this society.[58] (Even if exile were a feasible penalty, some people—those who don't mind exile and are rich enough to buy the resource abroad—would still not be governed by the official allocation scheme.) This observation brings us to a second point. On the fringes of those allocations which we will not permit a pure market to make, are many allocations in which, rather surprisingly, we give the pure market free rein. Migration is one example, and a readily understandable one since the costs of banning it are, we should guess, greater than permitting some few to have a greater chance. But there are many other examples, of which we shall give two.

Our willingness to allow volunteers in wartime, within the context of an army whose soldiers are selected by nonmarket means, provides the first example. This approach permits a wealth-dependent market to induce the very poorest citizens to join up, since only they are attracted by the relatively low wages of army pay. Once these poor have joined up with those who enlisted out of patriotism or for a change of scenery or for adventure, the rest of the army is selected by nonmarket means, since, as a general method of securing war personnel, we reject the market.[59] What is grotesque about this approach is that in wartime it allows the poorest (in America, blacks, Chicanos, and rural whites) to sell their services but seems to reflect the view that such sales are intolerable when the market begins to bring in lower-middle-class people. What is more, by cutting off the market at this point, we deprive the poorest of their seller's surplus, that is, the excess they would have received had we had a fully volunteer or market-based army and were forced to pay enough to convince the marginal, middle-class citizen to serve. We do not assert that all this was our intention; doubtless the desire to allow patriots to volunteer was a reason for the system and not a subterfuge to disguise it.[60] Nor are we saying that the all-volunteer army is fair to the poor. We merely note that the system it replaced was not unacceptable on the grounds we have been discussing; what ultimately brought it down were, rather, criticisms concerning the manner in which the middle classes were being picked. It was not the fringe market which was unacceptable; instead, the faults which underlay the nonmarket system which chose among the middle classes destroyed the system.[61]

The second example deals with the categorical difference between transplants, artificial kidneys, and so forth, on the one hand, and sophisticated, supercostly standard operations and treatment on the other. Whatever the outcome of the various moves toward universal medical care now underway, many scarce, but not dramatic, medical resources have been allowed to be allocated in pretty much a pure market way.[62] With a few exceptions owing to charitable treatments, it has been, by and large, the few rich or richly insured who got complex non-transplant medical care. What difference between transplants or artificial kidneys and less-publicized care accounts for this? The latter, because it is less dramatic and less publicized, does not so obviously put life at the mercy of market strength. The actual cases in which a rich person has survived because of better treatment are hard to identify; most of the time, the wealthier patient has simply spent more for treatment that has left him no better off. Here, as in the context of war service, one has the feeling that the market has been allowed to work in so limited an area that its patent inequities could be tolerated. Such a market continues to exist in England despite full, universal medical assurance.[63]

Thus we are inclined to conclude—from these examples as well as from the guess that we would not enforce a collective allocation against would-be migrants—that wealth-dependent markets are not unacceptable when they allocate tragic resources to small fringe groups. The rich who can migrate, those occasional people who do benefit from really exceptional and expensive nondramatic medical care—as to these the inequality of the market does not seem sufficiently troublesome to justify the costs of complete nonmarket, or wealth netural market methods. Our tolerance for fringe markets is no doubt increased if our perception of market inequalities is dimmed by, for example, the presence of courageous patriots in the enlistment line together with the needy, or if the benefits of high-priced therapies are speculative or not widely known. Where such uncertainty exists side by side with the fact that the market operates only as to a quite limited group, the situation approximates that of the land where starvation is rampant and where, therefore, allocating transplants to those very few who can buy them is not, whatever else it may be, tragic.

5

THREE FEATURES OF
TRAGIC ALLOCATIONS

B‌EFORE WE TURN to a considera-
tion of mixtures of the various methods, pure and modified, we
have discussed, we should note three characteristics of tragic
allocations generally which deserve separate though brief
treatment. These are (1) that they involve process costs; (2) that
all seek the illusion of first-order sufficiency; and (3) that each,
in its various powers and shortcomings, is an analogue of the
other.

Process Costs

All methods of allocations entail a category of costs distinct
from the harm to some which stems from failure to obtain the
scarce resource itself. The method chosen to accomplish the
allocation is inevitably costly and the issue of who is to bear
these process costs must be faced quite apart from the question
of who wins and loses in the allocation. There are four ways of
assigning process costs: (1) they may be borne by all who seek
the scarce resource; (2) they may be removed from the participants and be met by the society as a whole; (3) they may be
attached to the scarce resource or in other ways imposed on its
recipients, that is, on the winners; and (4) they may, finally, be
an additional burden placed on the losers. The approaches to
the allocations of tragically scarce resources which we have
been discussing differ substantially in the process costs entailed, in who bears them in the first instance, and in how
amenable to shifting from the initial bearer they are. Moreover,
even within any single allocation approach these features of
process costs vary with the scarce resource being allocated,
rendering the issue more complex.

Deprivations of privacy are, for example, process costs
borne by all the applicants for a scarce resource—all candidates

in a contest for deferments on account of conscientious objection or homosexuality must lay bare intimate details in order to increase their chances of winning. This is a process cost which cannot be readily shifted—how can one restore to privacy a homosexual who unwillingly must characterize himself? Furthermore, it adheres primarily to collective allocation approaches. Yet the nature of the resource allocated remains crucial. The process cost to privacy is substantially less significant in the allocation of, for instance, scarce medical resources (where private details are frequently already known to doctors) than in the allocation of child rights (where previously private information must be released).

The cost of maintaining and staffing decision-making bodies typifies those process costs which fall in the first instance on society as a whole, but which can, if we wish, be shifted to the parties or even to winners or losers. Like costs of counsel—which are initially borne by the participants, disproportionately, one might add, by relatively poor participants—it is a process cost associated with collective approaches. Also like counsel fees it is a cost which lessens when the standards applied by the collective decision makers are clear, relatively simple, absolute—when standards for allocations can be responsible and also be rather mechanically applied. The greater the individuation attempted, the greater are likely to be these process costs.

Where standards are unclear and decisions are highly individualized or aresponsible, another set of costs becomes prominent. The Kafkaesque costs of being in a process without knowing how to help oneself are typical of all aresponsible decision-making processes. During the process these may seem to be borne by all the participants, but in the end they fall squarely on the losers. If all the participants have suffered privacy losses in trying to convey every bit of information which just might conceivably help, the frustration of not knowing why one lost and worrying about what one might have done better makes the loser's cup that much more bitter. A responsible process avoids this, but has its analogue in the bitterness one feels in being able, too clearly, to identify precisely why one was found wanting. This is likely to be especially severe whenever the loser feels that had he done something different he might—on the basis of the grounds given for the result— have won. If all of us have known, at least in minor affairs, the anguish of not knowing why we lost, all of us have also known the frustration and self-doubt of knowing all too well.

The most dramatic example of process costs inevitably borne by the losers arises in allocations based on criteria of absolute worthiness. Where—so that the appearance of a first-order determination creating scarcity can be avoided and true juries used at the second order—an allocation is treated as if it were an open grant of the resource to all who are fit to receive it, the losers not only lose the resource but also bear the onus of being found unworthy. While some approaches select losers because they are especially worthy—spotless sacrificial lambs—and thereby in part compensate them, here the losers are told that their demerits made them lose. Thus they lose twice.

The market is more charitable. It hides its process costs in the price of the resource and so leads us to think— incorrectly—that it entails no such costs. Since the resource is bought by the winner, the market automatically assesses the costs in the first instance to those who gain from the process. Unfortunately prices are regressive and therefore process costs made a part of price are regressive too. Such an approach charges poor winners relatively more than rich winners and serves to make it yet more difficult for the poor to win at all. By hiding the process costs in the price, moreover, the market impedes consideration of whether another approach would entail lesser process costs which, even if assigned to the same people, might be small enough to permit the relatively poor to win more often. Private adoptions in which those who are granted the child are expected to contribute a standard donation to the orphanage, which acts as the awarding agency, may come close to this, insofar as the contributions defray the costs of the adoption process (rather than those of raising the un-adopted children).

The process costs of lotteries are easily stated: The arbitrariness of the approach makes the losers feel helpless and depersonalized. The chance that lotteries give is a computer chance, not a human one.

The process costs of customary approaches cannot be categorized, since such approaches employ market, lottery, or collective devices and thus share the process costs of that device which happened to evolve. But unlike the other, nonprocess costs of these devices, which costs are lessened by the fact that the device was not chosen, process costs are likely to be as great whether the allocation device employed is the result of conscious choice or evolution. A pariah bears his stigma no less if an absolute worthiness approach evolves than if it was intentionally established.

The First-Order Sufficiency Paradox

It sometimes appears that the first-order determination has not set a tragically restricted range and therefore tragic second-order decisions can be avoided. In the case of complete sufficiency, it may appear that a life-validating determination will have been made; in the case of less than complete sufficiency, it may still be that the appearance of a life-negating determination can be avoided. These appearances are, of course, merely a kind of optical illusion since no matter how sufficient the first-order determination appears, it necessarily diverts resources from other tragic situations.

In this sense a first-order determination operates as a second-order decision at a higher level of generality.[1] And yet a first-order determination does not seem to us to be merely a broader second-order decision. A decision as to how many iron lungs will be built is simply not perceived as the same kind of decision as one which determines who will actually be granted the use of such a machine. This fact about how we perceive categories of goods as discrete, though perhaps it has no formal, that is, logical, basis, is a crucial element in the operation of what we shall call the first-order sufficiency paradox.

That paradox may be stated as follows: The illusion of sufficiency (a) permits some tragic first-order determinations to be seen as life-validating despite the fact that they necessarily entail first-order determinations in other tragic areas which take life; (b) permits some of these other life-taking first-order determinations to be perceived as not-life-negating; (c) permits a class of second-order determinations to be perceived as not-life-negating even though every such tragic second-order decision entails a decision to take life. The role played by the paradox seems to depend on the relationship between the sufficiency of the determination and the principal humanistic value, preservation of life.

Substantial advantages flow from the operation of the paradox and therefore there are tremendous pressures when attention is focused on a tragic choice to move to a situation of sufficiency, or apparent sufficiency, which will allow the paradox to operate. By doing so many costs of expensive second-order choices as to who should be saved are avoided and the pricelessness, or at least the very high price, of human life is reaffirmed. Since many other values depend on valuing life as an incommensurable and since these values are constantly being eroded by decisions which, in fact, place a low value on human life, substantial benefits accrue from any demonstration by society of its devotion to life's pricelessness.

These advantages justify (even in mere economic terms) a very high per life expense if by that expense a complete sufficiency can be achieved, thereby avoiding virtually all second-order decisions and allowing the publicization of the ideal of saving life at any cost, expressed in the life-validating first-order determination.[2] A less high per life expense is likely when the paradox operates only partially; then the result is a category level which cannot be publicized as involving a completely sufficient first-order determination, but one which at least allows the first-order determination and its consequent second-order decisions to appear as not-life-negating. A lowest per life expense is likely to persist where for any acceptable per life expense no sufficiency plateau can be achieved which allows the paradox to operate.

In the following three sections we shall discuss (1) how complete sufficiency renders some first-order determinations life-validating; (2) how transformations, by which life-taking decisions are made to appear not-life-negating, operate with respect to complete sufficiency and partial sufficiency first-order determinations; and (3) how this kind of transformation works as to some second-order determinations.

Life-Validating Decisions / A first-order decision will be viewed as life-validating only if it results in everyone in a definable category being saved. This presupposes that no tragic second-order judgments will be needed to allocate the resources permitted by the first-order determination. This in turn means that the class of good must appear severable from other scarce goods and that some reason must exist for preferring to channel resources into its production rather than theirs.

Some goods more easily than others permit a segregation: We are accustomed to differentiating between various physiopathic diseases, for example, but we tend to lump serious mental derangements together. The difficult criterion, however, is not severability but establishing a basis for preference. Of the many reasons which might support such preference, factors of risk differences and cultural drama are perhaps the most obvious. But there are a host of others; to take but one example, how a victim dies may arouse emotions which lead to a preference.[3] It is interesting to note that societies have refrained from giving a single, unitary value to life; this allows us to draw lines severing categories from others, and to lavish expenditures on some of these groups thereby allowing the sufficiency paradox to operate. Thus an initial justification for allowing preferences—though this does not tell us which preferences—is that without them we could not achieve sufficiency in any tragic category and the benefits of the paradox would be forgone.

Often the preference for one particular category over another may be justified by reference to the substantial differences in risk of death between those in the category favored and those in other categories. Thus artificial kidney recipients can be distinguished from those who need complex heart surgery because those with renal failure are sure to die in short order while those who need arterial shunts—though a definite number are certain to die within a relatively short period of time—present a more diverse risk pattern.[4] As we have observed, the value we accord to life is not an invariable function of the risk of losing it; a first-order determination to spend $1,000,000 on kidney machines and a sum equal to $1,000,000 divided by the chance of survival without cardiac shunts on such shunts would not make any special sense, but neither would any other figure. We cannot derive an appropriate cost per life expenditure for cardiac shunts from the amount spent on kidneys. Indeed, as we have seen, individual risk taking defies parity of expenditure since it bears no consistent relationship to cost per life.[5] Where no widely accepted rational ground exists for deriving a figure for the expenditures in one area from those in another, one has considerable latitude in what can be spent in each. This makes quantum jumps in expenditure possible within a single category. In contexts such as these, an approach which makes quantum jumps in expenditure so as to achieve sufficiency in the preferred category will be viewed as life-validating. The categories can readily be viewed by society as truly different since the risk-taking differences are apparent and understandable.

There are also some categories which may trace their preference to reasons solely of chance, since these have, by chance, become dramatized for the culture at large. Such categories— or rather the preferential treatment given to victims within these groups—often persist even after the dramatic event has subsided, although differences in risk would not alone support different treatment. The amounts once spent on poliomyelitis are hard to explain in terms of risks of equivalent harm. They are better accounted for as reflecting the drama of an imposing figure like Franklin D. Roosevelt being a victim. The cyclical, seasonal nature of the disease, which led us to anticipate that, each summer, children and young adults in some part of the country would be stricken, enhanced the drama. Lines which are drawn when a chance factor brings a category into dramatic attention may well be completely artificial. The publicity which accompanied the Seattle God Committee brought renal failure into the spotlight.[6] The response in such situations may be to save all those suffering in the glare and to ignore others on whom attention has not fallen. The cost per life saved may be absurd in a strict, statistical sense but permitting the sufficiency paradox to operate and thereby gaining the benefits of reaffirming eroded values may well make the bargain worthwhile.

The impression that a first-order determination is life-validating depends, as we shall see, on the existence of a correlative notion that decisions can be not-life-negating. But this latter concept operates in many other situations as well. To it we now turn.

Decisions That Are Not-Life-Negating / The impression that a decision is not-life-negating is, as the awkward construction implies, the result of a kind of transformation, that is, an impression transforming the fact that a choice was made to take lives. This transformation is crucial to the operation of the sufficiency paradox.

With respect to complete sufficiency, the transformation can enable the construction of a life-validating determination through a process in which stable not-life-negating second-order decisions to deny the good are aggregated and what remains, silhouetted as it were, defines the sufficient first-order determination. Thus above we first spoke of setting a determination of sufficiency for a category which was severable and justifiably preferable. But we might just as easily have arrived at this determination by counting up the results of those second-order decisions which (though obviously life-taking yet nevertheless perceived as not-life-negating and therefore stable) tell us who is not to receive the good: Sufficiency will be the number that is left. To take a common example, it may be that responsible political decisions not to give artificial kidneys to patients in whom they are not at all likely to work can be expressed as an amalgam of acceptable, nontragic, stable second-order choices and hence that a first-order determination to give dialysis to all other candidates will be seen as creating a life-validating sufficiency.

The most interesting roles played by the transformation, however, have to do with its use in situations of partial sufficiency. In the first place, it forms one basis for preferential first-order determinations which can be regarded as life-validating. Thus first-order decisions not to achieve complete sufficiency in cancer treatment and similar decisions with respect to genetic repairs and exotic inoculations, and so forth (if those decisions are by virtue of the transformation viewed as not-life-negating because, for instance, too little is known to justify the expense), may support a decision like "dialysis for all who need it." Similarly they permit what were initially considered to be life-validating determinations to retain that status even though the preferential nature of the first-order sufficiency line drawn could be criticized on the ground that it necessitates other life-taking decisions. Why, one may ask, save all kidney victims and not all victims of aplastic anemia or all risk-taking coal miners or all people injured at grade crossings? By working to reframe the way these latter, partial sufficiency decisions are perceived, the transformation enables us to see, and publicize, the life-validating decision as one in favor of life in the category saved and not one against life in other categories.

In the second place, the transformation makes the great mass of partial sufficiency, first-order decisions bearable and renders them less destructive to humanistic values by so depicting them that they are viewed as not-life-negating. We focus on stable second-order decisions reached through methods which disguise the fact that a first-order determination for only partial sufficiency has been made, and the transformation occurs.

To effect the transformation we require second-order decisions (the stability of which depends on their being themselves perceived as not-life-negating, and to the discussion of which we shall turn next) which are so decentralized and so depend on individual choices in those cases in which a tragic decision is made, as to enable it to be plausibly said that any first-order result is possible at any given time. (A lottery or a first-come-first-served customary approach to the allocation of life rafts, for example, though perhaps stable at the second order, could not be made to support a first-order transformation.) This way of looking at things may persist even if it is in fact the case that certain first-order results would immediately trigger collective intervention to alter the process because the first-order determination had become too expensive; often we do not know for sure whether individual changes in second-order decisions would bring about a collective intervention.[7]

For example, if a standard of fault or absolute worthiness is workable at the second order, its use may bring about the transformation in perceptions of the first-order determination from life-taking to not-life-negating precisely because at any given moment the first-order result, though statistically predictable, is not certain. It need only be plausible that everyone might be able to meet the standard of worthiness, or perhaps just that worthiness have a positive effect on the availability of the scarce resource, for the transformation, and therefore the paradox as applied to a situation of partial sufficiency, to operate.

It is possible that, for instance, a wealth-neutral market for subjects in medical experiments might be perceived as entirely consistent with the proposition that no life-negating first-order determination has been made. Second-order decisions other than as to who shall participate can be made on the basis of medical efficiency; and even if the state spends money to advertise and encourage subjects to come forward, it appears to have made no explicit first-order decision since only those who wish to be subjects actually volunteer. Similarly, a market system, if acceptable at the second order, may allow the society to benefit from the paradox. Since, for example, at any given moment people may change their minds or desires, and no one might actually volunteer for wartime service, one might conclude that the state did not decree any number of victims and made no first-order determination against life. Of course, the more finely tuned such systems are, the more there is collective intervention as soon as the number of volunteers alters. Then it can less plausibly be maintained that no life-negating first-order decision has been made. But so long as a tolerable fluctuation persists, the effects of the paradox are perpetuated.

Wealth-neutral markets are particularly vulnerable to the collapse of this illusion since, being self-consciously designed, they are subject to pressures for constant readjustment. The longer the customary second-order choices are left untouched or are modified obscurely, the less there will seem to have been any first-order determination at all, and the more the unsaved will seem the victims of fortune or their own desires, and not of society's choice. It is no accident, for instance, that many can continue to describe the system of population control in the United States as totally voluntaristic and as involving no first-order decisions for or against childbearing.

It should be clear that first-order determinations arrived at in this indirect manner can at best be not-life-negating and cannot be life-validating. A life-validating, like a not-life-negating, decision requires a surrounding mass of not-life-negating decisions against which it is set off; but it requires more. Since it must be publicizable as a decision which saves all lives in the preferred category, it cannot merely evolve unchosen from the surrounding mass of not-life-negating choices. A clear, conscious, collective action is needed. As we have seen, such an action may be rendered possible because the category to be preferred becomes roughly outlined as a result of these surrounding decisions or it may be possible on other grounds. But either way, life-validating decisions require the very kind of conscious, collective choice which voluntaristic or evolutionary schemes abjure.

Not-Life-Negating Second-Order Determinations / The transformation at the first order depends on there being stable second-order decisions which the allocation approaches can aggregate. Many tragic, second-order choices are, of course, violently unstable. To be stable, at a minimum, somehow second-order decisions themselves must be able to be perceived as not-life-negating.

We have elsewhere discussed how some second-order choices can be made stable.[8] Here we are interested in the much smaller class of such stable choices which owe their perception in the public eye as not-life-negating to the operation of the same kind of partial sufficiency paradox as acted with respect to first-order determinations.

As with the first order, the factor of risk differences is probably the principal way by which one can account for transformation at the level of the second-order. If there is an unbroken continuum in probability of success, then it is unlikely that a stable second-order decision can be made to separate out some victims and refuse treatment to the rest. Any life-risk combination must look very like the next life-risk combination when the chances of success do not greatly vary. As a result, there is inevitably an extrapolation of what is an appropriate expense to save additional lives as the chance of success diminishes. The presence of such a calculus shatters the effect of the paradox.

If instead there is a break, either at the level of sure successes (as was once the case in renal transplants between identical twins and all others) or at the level of substantial failure, then the appearance of sufficiency can enter and be used.

A change in the ways in which groups along the continuum are perceived (even just by the chance dramatization of a particular group) or in the cost of reaching the next stable level suffices to bring about a discrete or quantum jump in expense per life actually permitted. If the jump brings us to a level where real differences exist, then the difference in per life expense is likely to persist until another change in costs or in risks occurs. If, instead, the jump occurs simply in response to a dramatic situation, then instability is likely. Sooner or later, as people not equally favored attempt to dramatize the choice against life involved in their cases, the hitherto stable second-order criteria become unsupportable. Indeed, one can imagine situations in which it would be better to fail to respond in the first, dramatic case because a response would simply serve to dramatize all the other cases to which we do not respond, and in which, tragically, we would not be prepared to respond. They would cost too much to accommodate and we would not spend it even if they were all dramatized.[9] The fact that we tend to respond in single, dramatic instances suggests that our ability to detect distinctions is well developed, while the ability of disfavored individuals to dramatize their similar cases is, on the whole, limited.[10]

In conclusion, we have noted how the stability of second-order determinations plays a significant role in the operation of the sufficiency paradox. One must be aware, however, that such stability, or more precisely acceptability of nontragic criteria on which stability depends, will vary with the history of past allocations, from society to society, and with the good being allocated.

For a long time we permitted poor volunteers to fill out enlistment drives, and this practice seemed completely acceptable. Other societies more hierarchic or more market-oriented than ours may well find second-order criteria which enable the sufficiency paradox to operate even though, in similar contexts in our own country, the paradox would fail.

Shortcomings and Powers

The patterns of allocation approaches we have discussed present a symmetry of variations. Because allocation is, by its very nature, an act signifying inequality, because it relies on

putting a value on things, and because the allocation of important goods has significance for society generally as well as for the
actual recipients, any approach to allocation will display flaws
which reflect these ambivalent necessities. When any approach
is applied to a particular tragic choice in a particular cultural and
historical setting, the manifestations of those underlying failings and strengths specific to that approach become more or
less significant. The strategy of using mixtures of approaches at
any given time and over time—which is the subject of the next
and last chapters of this essay—arises from an effort to offset the
flaws of one approach by resort to another. In this section we
should like very briefly to outline the symmetrical relationship
of the shortcomings and powers of each of the approaches.

The pure market's principal shortcoming is that it depends
on the prevailing distribution of wealth. While this dependence
serves a laissez-faire egalitarianism, the equality of opportunity
exemplified in the law's majestically forbidding rich and poor
alike to sleep under the bridges of Paris, it offends other notions
of equality to which most societies are committed. The second
important shortcoming of the pure market is its indifference
to societal preferences. The market determines what society
thinks is best for itself by simply taking the sum of those
atomistic individual desires which can be manifested in the
market place. As discussed in Chapter 2, it treats Madame
Defarge and Madame Curie equally, as if the social utility of
either obtaining a tragically scarce good depended simply on
their individual desire for it. Thus, while the market may be, on
the whole, successful at gauging such individual desires, it fails
at giving weight to the harms and benefits external to them.
Finally, the market entails external effects that we have called
the costs of costing. The market allocation of tragically scarce
resources requires that a price be set on the resources to be
allocated. This requirement, that we put a price on things we
desperately would like to treat as priceless, makes markets and
the societies which use them appear contemptible when tragic
resources are being allocated.

The shortcomings of responsible political approaches are quite analogous. Accountable decisions to give a scarce good to one person rather than to another fail to treat both in the same way. Because they treat alike what the responsible decision maker has defined as like cases, they serve a formal egalitarianism—they treat people equally but not as equals. This affronts other conceptions of egalitarianism and no one conception is likely to be absolutely held by any society. At best the results of formal egalitarianism discriminate against groups disfavored in the society generally since the standards it applies originate in social life. This "fair" oppression offends us. On the whole, responsible political processes are successful in coping with the first set of externalities with respect to which the market fails: Political processes can take into account social desire. But they do so at the cost of being substantially unable to distinguish, and give effect to, individual desires. Thus anomie is the disease of modern bureaucratic societies. Accountable collective approaches do avoid the costs of costing, but only by creating an analogous cost. A clear determination by the state that some people are not equal to others, or that some lives are not worth saving, while it does not price some incommensurables, vitiates those values which depend on certain rights being perceived as absolute. It makes the state itself become involved in the killing.

Lotteries do not avoid the first two kinds of problems, they simply restate them. By treating as equal all candidates, lotteries embody the naïve or simple conception of equality, which is anathema to other conceptions. Moreover, in their pure form, lotteries give no weight to either individual or societal desires—except the societal desire to treat everyone in precisely the same way, regardless of the consequences. Nor do lotteries entirely avoid the costs of costing. True, they do not price tragic goods nor do they nakedly involve the state in the selection of victim-losers. But they do something just as costly. The pure lottery inevitably spotlights the first-order determination which created the scarcity. This has the same effect as pricing lives, for example, since it emphasizes our inability to maintain that the right to the scarce resource, life in this instance, is absolute.

Modifications in each of the basic approaches are efforts to mitigate these three symmetrical flaws. But since these kinds of flaws are endemic to allocation itself, a modification can merely introduce the analogous shortcoming of another approach, or must try to conceal what is being done so that the effects of the flaw are not perceived. Indeed, each modification we have discussed in the two preceding chapters can be analyzed as an attempt to introduce a plausible subterfuge into a basic approach or as a compromise between basic approaches usually entailing in modified versions some of the shortcomings (and concomitant powers) of each.

Customary approaches, as we noted when discussing process costs, cannot be categorized in the same way since they result in allocations which take their features wholly from one of the basic or modified approaches. Customary approaches, therefore, simply display the shortcomings of those approaches which have evolved in the particular tragic situation: At times they will allocate goods without taking into account individual desire, at other times they will slight societal needs. Customary approaches will violate varying conceptions of equality and serve others. But because they will do all these things unselfconsciously—because the approach has evolved—they are likely to reduce and even avoid the costs of costing. Of course this is accomplished by sacrificing honesty and candor. Evolutionary approaches epitomize the fact that subterfuges do not extinguish costs of costing, but rather transform them into costs in honesty.

We should not conclude from the symmetry of variations that a mixture of approaches cannot add to the power of the allocation or lessen its shortcomings. Some subterfuges are relatively harmless, some are noxious; some situations justify emphasis on individual desire, some on social desire, and some on naïve egalitarianism. Mixtures of approaches are no more than methods to take all this into account.

6

THE TRAGIC DILEMMA:
MIXTURES OF APPROACHES

W<small>E HAVE NOT STUDIED</small> the methods of Chapters 2, 3, and 4 only to draw the attractive, erroneous conclusion that the limitations and promise of various approaches are merely functions of their own structures. Some, of course, are. But it would be a delusion if we were to believe that by mastering the nice ontologies of such decision structures as we have sketched, one could devise, without more, an appropriate way for coping with particular choices. That coalition of modified and pure approaches which proves most successful in a single situation will depend not only on the power of the approach taken, but on the nature of the precise good being distributed, the society by which the distribution is to be made, and the period in that society's history during which the dilemma is confronted and to which a single array of approaches is committed. We do not wish to contribute to a mood of impotent perplexity by emphasizing, as we must, that even the most accurate assessment of these contours of the tragic situation coupled with the most sensitive application of allocation approaches will not eliminate tragedy from the situation. Our task is to limit the spreading stain; that is the best for which we can hope. But this makes ever more necessary an appreciation of the situational nuances within which mixtures of modified techniques must work.

The object of public policy must be, therefore, to define, with respect to each particular tragic choice, that combination of approaches which most limits tragedy and which deals with that irreducible minimum in the least offensive way.[1] Of course, that combination will vary, not only over time—as we shall see—but also from society to society, since the object is to find the approach which is least destructive of values fundamentally held in each society. This will vary with, among other things, the faith each society has in decision-making approaches, like the jury or administrative agencies (as revealed, for instance, in that society's legal tradition); the relationship of the choices to other realities of the human condition in that society (for instance, the general economic level); the social structure of the society and the degree and kind of stratification it professes to prefer. On all these counts, we are not likely to find that countries as different as, say, England, Italy, and the United States will find all the same choices tragic or will approach the same tragic choices in the same way.

This final chapter is devoted to a brief survey of those factual contours which are not, categorically speaking, part of the approaches themselves but which will in great measure determine the appropriateness of any particular set of approaches to a tragic choice.

The Particular Scarce Resource:
The Good to Be Distributed

Principal among the factual contours which impose greater or lesser stress on both the first- and second-order determinations is the nature of the scarce resource to be distributed. Although this observation should serve to underscore the idiosyncrasy of every tragic situation—since no general discussion can anticipate the various associations, connotative and emotive, which the members of a society may attach to a particular good; hearts are different from livers—some rough guidelines may be given which relate aspects of the scarce resource to the mechanics of the decision.

First-Order Determinations / It is crucial to consider whether the nature of the scarce resource admits of an open first-order decision.

This depends in large part on how the good came to be scarce and whether dramatic attention is focused on the first order. We must determine where—if at all—in the history of a society's approach to the particular scarce resource a decision substantially within the control of that society was made as a result of which the resource was permitted to remain scarce. Only by placing the first-order determination in the stream of events can we properly define the good to be allocated and identify on what, and at what point, public attention will be focused.[2] Scarcity cannot simply be assumed as a given.

Thus in a famine it may make a great difference whether scarcity arose from a natural pestilence or drought and whether that pestilence or drought itself could be perceived as resulting from prior societal decisions, or whether scarcity is traced to deliberate or casual decisions to channel labor toward nonagricultural activities. In all these cases the scarce resource is food; but the nature of the good, which in part depends on how it is perceived to have become tragically scarce, varies enormously. This in turn shapes the kinds of first-order determinations the society can now make in response to that scarcity. An appreciation of the nature of the good, in this context, therefore requires both a retrospective assessment of the series of preceeding determinations and a prospective judgment as to how the making of the present first-order determination will define the good in the eyes of the public. For example, when a drought is not traced to proximate decisions of the society, a first-order determination to drain reservoirs, but not to conscript labor to dig emergency wells—in other words, to alleviate the drought in part—has a good chance of being taken as a not-life-negating response rather than as a life-destroying unwillingness to do all that can be done.[3] As such, it can be made openly. If the first-order determination is taken to be the number of soldiers required to fight a war and not the decision whether to enter the war itself, if, for example, engagement in conflict is perceived to be a matter of necessity upon which depends the actual or cultural survival of the society, then as we have seen, much of the controversy which would otherwise attend a first-order tragic determination is averted.

There are other features, however, of the scarce resource, besides the perceived cause of scarcity, which affect the scope of the first-order decision. A wartime draft does not allocate certain death, assigning instead mere statistical chances, risks, of death; it has the paradoxical quality that the more citizens who receive the bad—a chance to die—the less bad it is. This is almost a certainty in a statistical sense and may turn out to be true in gross terms as well, if the mere size of a nation's army deflects attack, or overwhelms opponents on the battlefield. This paradoxical quality leaves the first-order determination relatively unrestricted; attention focuses on the causes of the war and on who is conscripted rather than on the size of the army. Consider, by contrast, the situation of a quarantine. The decision to include citizens in the quarantined group shares with the conscription case the claim that necessity has made the initial determination, as well as the fact that only risks of death are being allocated. Furthermore, it is likely to be true that an increase in the number of persons quarantined reduces the statistical chance of death for each individual in the quarantined group. But because such inclusion does not also operate to reduce the total number of deaths within the group—because there are not contagious immunities, as it were—one would expect considerable passion to find its target on the first-order determination of the number to be quarantined. The effects of controversy and inflamed scrutiny are to restrict the role of efficiency factors, such as how many persons were exposed to the disease carrier.

It also restricts the role of other factors. Suppose that the most efficient, however defined, small army consisted almost exclusively of blacks. It is unthinkable that we would fail to double, say, the size of the army to avoid so grotesque an allocation of risk. It would by no means be as easy to double or triple the number of persons quarantined when the most efficient control of the disease could be achieved by segregating a group almost wholly of a single ethnic origin.

The passion with which the quarantine determination was scrutinized is still comparatively limited to that aroused by first-order determinations involving resources whose natures are only slightly, but crucially, different. Suppose, for example, that one is not drafted to serve in an army but instead is chosen as a hostage when the only way to halt the aggressor is by giving him a set number of people to sacrifice. Then the initial decision to resist aggression becomes intensely more controversial. In part, this is because we are uncertain whether the bribe will work or whether the demand will be constantly repeated. But even if we were confident that the bribe would work, we would face a completely different sort of determination, since the lives taken are not statistical lives and there is no hope that by some wild chance no one will actually die. The first-order determination would be even more complex and constricted if the aggressor offered to trade a decrease in aggression for increasing numbers of victims. We would then face a first-order determination which ineluctably paired each individual victim to a benefit gained.

For similar reasons wars begun out of purely economic motives, even though the first-order determination sacrifices only statistical lives, are much harder to carry on because they are much harder to sell. When attention focuses on the first-order decision to enter war, such wars have commonly been defended by resort to other, noneconomic goals.

If, finally, we should be faced with the alternative between a tremendous monetary tribute which diminishes to zero in exchange for an increasing number of people to be sacrificed, then the first-order determination becomes an arena of crisis. Such decisions may have been made in the past and may be made again, but if such were the case one would expect attempts to disguise the first-order decision; honesty, at least in the short run, seems to become the most immediately dispensable value.

These few examples should suffice to give some notion of the vast universe of discrete but related ways in which a change in the nature of the good itself affects the decison-making apparatus at the first-order level. The first-order decision determining how much will be spent to produce artificial, life-saving organs presents perhaps the most obvious example of attention riveting on, and altering, the first order. Tragically, while this alteration may result in artificial organs being made available to all, it frequently causes fewer people to be aided. The subterfuges by which the society avoids pricing lives (for instance, the assertion that anyone for whom an implant will be successful will be allotted one) dictate guidelines at the first order which may diminish the resources devoted to the production of such organs. The spectrum extends from these highly vulnerable first-order configurations to the relatively secure ones of the simple conscription case with which we began.

Second-Order Determinations / We must now concern ourselves with those characteristics of each individual tragic good which determine what adaptations in approaches are necessary to facilitate second-order allocations. These characteristics control the degree to which we can in fact use any factor on the basis of which we wish to make second-order distinctions. The particular tragic good affects this in three important ways. It determines (1) the extent to which each factor can permissibly be taken into account (color of the factor); (2) the amenability of the factor to accurate, usable expression (its expressive power); and (3) the costs of identifying, gathering, and organizing the data necessary to give content to the factor (its accessibility).

By the term *color* we mean the capacity of the factor to arouse emotion. This quality does not inhere in the factor itself, but depends rather on each society's perception of it; it varies over time with the prevailing conceptions of justice, equality, and so forth. It is color which determines whether a factor can permissibly be openly used. In some situations, such as the award of child custody, the sex of the competing applicants may be an arguably relevant factor but it is one which today is becoming so highly colored that the decider may soon dare not explicitly include it among those factors which determine his decision. In the allocation of places in a lifeboat the same factor may still be entirely colorless. There may be some factors which are in every instance so highly colored that their open consideration inevitably produces an outraged reaction in the culture. We hope race is,[4] perhaps sex may become so. It may also be that a highly colored factor, if used openly, will be given a weight out of proportion to that the society wants it to bear. Thus the rules of evidence, for example, often exclude as irrelevant clearly relevant testimony when, through its color, it is likely to affect the result unduly.[5]

Similarly the particular tragic resource itself will determine whether there exist factors of sufficient expressive power to be of use in the second-order decision process. If the individual desire of participants to obtain a tragic resource cannot be discerned and formulated in ways which can be used in the process, we may be forced to act as if the factor were of no significance.[6] That is all too often the fate of nonquantifiable or soft variables. Where no factors of sufficient expressive power are available we may be reduced to deciding by lot much as the ancients resorted to witchcraft or entrail reading.[7]

Finally, the costs—not merely in money but to privacy, self respect, and fair play[8]—of gathering and presenting the information required to give that substance to the factor which enables it to be used, will vary according to what we have called the factual contours of the particular tragic situation. Revealing one's mental illness is of limited cost when the allocation of scarce psychoactive drugs is at stake and trained investigators are interpreting the data; but it would entail considerable privacy cost in a competition for a scholarship.

A single example—the situation presented by the allocation of child rights—should display all of the above characteristics which determine the use of factors on which second-order allocations depend.

Virtually any distinction in rights to have some children which is derived from factors based on social efficiency—eliminating hemophilia, for example, by not allowing women carrying the triggering gene to bear children—offends some conceptions of egalitarianism, since such factors in the context of child rights almost always reflect general status, that is, society's preference for one individual over another. In the past, marital status has been an exception. Because the same person could, by marrying, gain the rights previously denied, the statement of hierarchic preference was muted. Perhaps for this reason or by reason of historic social convention, marital status in this context was colorless. This is no longer obviously the case. It may be that when biotechnology makes cloning possible, the requirement that all children be the product of a bisexual fertilization will be deemed a similar, colorless factor.[9] Even age might become such a factor, were it quite clear that children conceived by couples above or below certain age limits were much less well endowed genetically, or were less likely to be well raised and well treated. But the derivation of usable factors from such considerations implies criticism of the children of such pairings, if not of the couples themselves, and is therefore likely to be highly colored on this account.

This does not mean that accountable collective second-order decisions have had no place in the area of childbearing. They have, in fact, rather stupidly and pathetically been made with respect to epileptics and others.[10] It means instead that a full array of factors, such as one might encounter in the selection of astronauts or judges or racehorses—age, background, health, intelligence, experience, and so forth—are not likely to be introduced and smoothly applied without protest.

True, color will not prevent responsible decisions with respect to maximum numbers of children permitted for anyone. But this brings us to the second way in which the particular tragic good affects the second order, namely, by circumscribing the expressive power of the factors we wish to apply. Individual desire varies widely for child rights. Unless individual wants can be factored in, a flat maximum will result in some parents feeling seriously deprived while other couples receive a good they little value. In contrast to cases of desperation bidding when life and death are at stake, individual desire for child rights need not be a soft variable; indeed, it can be effectively discerned and quantified.

The inclusion of individual desire, however, would involve either wealth-neutral markets—pure markets would surely be too highly colored—or substantial privacy and equal access costs. This is the third way—accessibility—in which the tragic situation affects second-order allocations. Wealth-neutral markets are costly, even in money terms. If individuals, instead, were required to plead their desire for children before agencies or boards, great sacrifices to privacy will occur, to say nothing of the costs of affording the applicants reasonably equal access. This, coupled with the color which attaches to any assessment of relative social utility by such boards, suggests that these agencies are not acceptable devices for assigning child rights.

The factual contours of the particular problem of child rights more than anything else explain the dominance of the complex and curious combination of custom, unorganized moral suasion, and *ad hoc* market incentives in the United States today. In this way the pattern of childbearing has come to reflect unspoken and unspeakable social desires, while accommodating individual wants.

Historical Perspectives and the Tragic Choice

Beyond the requirements of the particular scarce good are the restrictions imposed by the background of the tragic choice, the landscape against which the tragic events unfold. This background is composed of those historical antecedent choices which prefigured the present tragic dilemma and that collection of mores, biases, and attitudes which differentiate one society from another. With the latter we shall deal in a later part of this chapter. The former may be studied from what is commonly regarded as a historical perspective, although it is obvious that social history and social character are inextricably bound together.

A historical perspective presents a mapping of society's confrontation with a tragic choice—by showing how a society has dealt with the dilemma previously, we are made aware of the perimeters of future choices, most especially those adaptations which are necessary just because other attempts have preceded. There is a recent tendency among social philosophers,[11] indeed, almost a vogue, to treat social issues as if they existed outside of history. Perhaps this is a natural reaction to a doctrinaire determinism that would have us believe that because something is, so it had to be, or possibly a reaction to the sheer complexity of events and choices by which society arrives at its decisive junctures. At any rate, it is error. How tragic choices are made, how they can be made, is necessarily governed, in some measure, by earlier attempts at resolution.

We shall consider one instance, the present method of conscription in the United States. A historical perspective on this tragic choice serves to reinforce the conviction that to engage the tragic situation is to beat against a current whose pull and undertow can be discerned by the study of previous journeys, the wreckages of which are significant barriers to contemporary passage.

Prior to 1776, the American colonies passed literally hundreds of statutes and ordinances providing for the raising of militias; typically these empowered authorities to recruit and pay men under arms rather than draft them into service.[12] One commentator has observed that, during that period, the colonies "required all able-bodied men between the ages of 16 and 50 to compose the militia. . . . A fine was generally imposed upon those unable to attend [drill]."[13] These were the colonial soldiers who fought the Indians and the French.

With the dawning of the Revolution the Continental Congress recommended, but was not empowered to direct, that the states furnish troops to the Continental Army.[14]

In 1780 the Congress asked for 41,760 men from the states but received only 21,015. When combined with the various militias then in uniform, this represented a total force of only about half the number which had been serving in 1776. Not only the increasing difficulty of raising forces, but the short duration of their service when they could be inducted, doubtless prompted George Washington to propose, upon being

elected President, that a national force be raised and maintained by the compulsory draft of men between eighteen and
twenty-five years of age. The new Congress rejected this
scheme.[15]

The wars with Britain in 1812 and Mexico in 1845 were
fought with state militias and volunteers.[16] Not until the Civil
War did the United States face a struggle which moved its
Congress to institute a form of compulsory conscription.

When hostilities began, the Northern armies totaled
slightly more than 15,000 men. President Abraham Lincoln's
call for 75,000 volunteers to serve for ninety days was met by
more than 90,000 men. When it became clear that a more
protracted struggle was to take place, Congress authorized the
President to accept a million volunteers for three years; this was
followed, a year later in 1862, by a similar authorization for
300,000 men. The tepid response to this last call made clear that
the initial enlistments represented about the full, hard core of
enthusiastic sentiment. Although the forthcoming recruitment
eventually produced more than 400,000 volunteers, a panicky
Congress passed, scarcely two weeks after its 1862 call, the
Militia Act of 1862[17] which empowered the President to direct
the states to levy drafts upon the state militias, thereby to fulfill
quotas for the national army.[18]

The Militia Act was the first draft act in the United States;
reaction to it was said to have been "immediate and unfavorable."[19] It was argued that the draft was insulting to citizens who
would otherwise have volunteered; that it was timed seriously
to impede that year's harvest; that it was unnecessary. But the
most violent objection centered on the bill's provision that
enabled a drafted citizen to hire a substitute in his place. The
effect of this provision was to stop all voluntary enlistment. This
in turn increased the demand for draftees and thus the cost of
hiring a substitute; a lucrative arbitrage in service conducted by
brokers arose and desertion increased.[20]

In part to respond to the criticism which accompanied this
ill-conceived measure, Congress passed a superseding statute

in 1863. The new act granted to the War Department the power to induct draftees directly into the federal force, and set a flat fee of $300 for exemption from induction. This latter provision was thought to remedy the trade in substitutes (the price for which had risen to $1,500 in some places) and thereby to provide a pool of eligible men as well as a sum of money which could be used for bounties to encourage enlistment and re-enlistment. In this way it was hoped that any gap in induction and deployment could be closed.[21]

As might have been expected, the open pricing of service by the Congress—even though it brought exemption within the range of relatively less well-off people, it was still close to a year's wages for the average workingman—evoked furious and sustained outrage. In Ohio, draft resisters were fired on by federal infantry, in Indiana and Illinois, the officers conducting the draft were murdered and their records destroyed. A single draft riot, in July 1863 in New York City, took the lives of more than 1,000.[22] A year later, President Lincoln issued a new call for volunteers, and signed into law a statute eliminating the $300 avoidance option.[23] At war's end, local enlistment efforts produced the vast majority of soldiers in the Northern ranks.

The first draft was something less than a success.[24] Of the 292,441 names drawn, only 9,881 were held to service: 164,395 men were exempted for physical or other reasons; 26,002 furnished substitutes; 52,288 registrants paid the $300 commutation fee.[25]

In 1866, the difficulties with Civil War conscription were the subject of a study commissioned to review draft procedures. Every one of its major suggestions was adopted more than fifty years later when forced conscription was next employed. The author recommended, in part, "that the military be relieved, as far as possible, of any local administration in any future draft; that a personal registration at some designated spot be held rather than a house-to-house canvass; and that there be no bounties or purchases of substitutes."[26]

American military manpower needs in the Cuban, Philippine, and border conflicts did not require a resumption of the draft, in part because of the enthusiasm with which public opinion greeted these conflicts and the mode of warfare then prevailing. The staggering British and French losses during 1914–16 apparently disabused the American administration of any thought that similar conscription measures would suffice in the European theater. In February 1917, the day following the United States rupture of diplomatic relations with Germany, President Woodrow Wilson directed his Secretary of War to prepare a program which would institute a draft as the exclusive means of recruiting and maintaining a national army.[27] The Act passed by Congress in May of that year embodied this concept; the national army was to be composed entirely of draftees.[28] Regulars and a National Guard were to be volunteers where possible but authority was granted to use forced conscription to bring even those forces to designated levels; bounties and substitutes were forbidden. Liability to the draft covered all male citizens, though conscription was authorized only for those twenty-one to thirty-one years old. Ministers and divinity students, some public officials, those men with dependents, and those serving in certain occupations were exempted; conscientious objectors were exempted from combat service.

In the three months from the Act's passage to the first lottery which determined the order of induction, 10 million men registered. In two more months, another 14 million were enrolled. Of these, 2,810,296 were drafted before the end of the war in 1918. The administrator in charge of this logistical triumph seems to have been convinced that "scrupulous fairness" was the essential factor to success and commentators concede that "hardly a charge of unfairness or discrimination" was made at the time. Be that as it may, by August 1918, 16,000 men were being held in New York City for failure to register or appear when drafted. During this period a move to adopt a permanent system of universal military training failed to pass the Senate. At the end of the war, the draft lapsed and the United States returned to a voluntary system.[29]

Many persons today recall the sickening rapidity with which France fell in 1939 and Europe was again the locus of international conflict. But it is hard even for them to remember the impassioned debates occasioned by the proposal, in the summer of 1940, of the Selective Training and Service Act.[30] The United States was not at war and the advisability of our entry into war was itself sharply disputed. It was the conviction of many that a peacetime draft was a measure designed by the Roosevelt administration to take the country into war. When it passed, service was limited to one year.[31] The Act authorized a national draft using a lottery method much the same as that used in 1917. Service was limited to one year; no more than 900,000 men were to be inducted; and their service was limited to actions in the Western Hemisphere. Again, bounties and substitutes were prohibited.

The Act was unpopular, and thus, when in August 1941 Congress voted on an extension of service, passage came by one vote in the House.[32] By this slender margin, the Act was renewed for eighteen months; four months later Pearl Harbor was attacked.

With the declarations of war against Japan, Germany, and Italy, Congress removed the territorial restrictions on service and extended its duration to the life of the conflict.[33] By mid-1942 various modifications were introduced: All males between eighteen and sixty-five were required to be registered; the lottery was discarded and registrants were called by order of date of birth; voluntary enlistments were severely restricted, apparently so that first-order determinations with respect to the production of war materiel, which underlay the system of exemptions or channeling, could be more easily fulfilled. By August 1945, more than 9.5 million men had been inducted.[34]

The 1940 Act, in its subsequent incarnations, continued until March 31, 1947. But less than a year after that President Harry Truman requested draft legislation; the subsequent statute, the Selective Service Act of 1948,[35] remained the basic method for conscription until its repeal at the close of American ground action in Vietnam. For most of those years, call-ups were small and "the chief problem in the administration of the draft [was] to manage a deferment system that could success-fully reduce the overabundant supply of potential draftees."[36]

During the Korean and Vietnam conflicts, vigorous con-troversy focused on the winnowing methods by which second-order allocations were made by the 1948 Act. Under that Act, all eighteen-year-old males were required to register for induc-tion with a local draft board. Liability for induction continued until age twenty-six, or age thirty-five if initial liability had been deferred.[37] The local board classified the registrant according to various categories which reflected his order, vis-à-vis other registrants, as to priority of induction. Information by which these categories were actuated was provided by the registrants. First-order determinations by the Department of Defense were prorated among the states and then, by state administra-tion, among the local boards. Among that category deemed eligible for service, the local boards exercised broad discretion within guidelines which preferred, that is, drafted first, older registrants and delinquents and drafted last young nonvolun-teers. (Volunteers counted toward meeting the local quota, thus heightening even further geographical disparities.) All sorts of appeals were available to the registrant dissatisfied with his classification; and a new classification was, of course, re-quired by each relevant change in the registrant's status.

A good lawyer became extremely useful to the reluctant soldier. A complicated system of deferments operated among the categories whereby some registrants were moved to the bottom of the call-up list. This was the case, at various periods during the many revisions to the regulations promulgated bureaucratically under the statute, for those physically or men-tally unfit for combat service, college students, graduate stu-dents, fathers with a dependent child, farmers employed in the production of "substantial" quantities of agricultural com-modities, Peace Corps and VISTA volunteers, medical stu-dents, those conscientious objectors willing to perform noncombat service. The deferment applied over two dimensions, that is, for the life of the condition by virtue of which it was created, and across that period, not designated a "national emergency" by the President, as provided by the statute, when manpower needs could be satisfied by the call-up of nonde-ferred registrants. Often the application for deferment, if suc-cessful (though not, paradoxically, its grant absent a request by the registrant), acted to extend the limit of liability, although, with the exception of physicians, the relatively short duration of high manpower needs and, recently, the preference for younger men, mooted this provision. Deferments are, nevertheless, to be distinguished from exemptions, for in-stance, those granted to ministers and divinity students, con-scientious objectors to any participation, aliens, veterans and the orphans of veterans, which removed such categories from the liability pool together.

This system—of broad liability and broad, though vague, deferments—operated with various modifications during the period when draft calls went from 108,000 in 1964 to 299,000 in 1968. Even the latter figure fails to convey the omnipresent nature of the draft in these years; to it one must add the further statistic that more than half the voluntary enlistments during this period occurred as a result of individual efforts to avoid compulsory conscription.[38] (At various times bounties, choice of branch and duration of service were offered as inducements to volunteer.) The controversy surrounding the draft during these years is too fresh in our memories to require repetition. On campuses in every part of the country there prevailed a reckless irritability among students that was at once the product of anxiety at the prospect of being called and guilt in the knowledge that one's contemporaries without academic refuge were being sent to war.

In November 1969 the Nixon administration signed into law a proposal which permitted it to reduce the period of liability from seven years (eighteen to twenty-six) to one year, the latter being the calendar year following a registrant's nineteenth birthday.[39] Also, draft selection was to be determined by lot, preference being paired with birth dates drawn at random, and not, as previously, by age. Deferment for graduate students (except medical and dental students) had somewhat before been curtailed by regulation; those then in graduate schools were allowed a set time in which to finish.[40] In April of the following year, an Executive Order provided that occupational and paternity deferments be phased out.[41] Then, in September 1971, the Draft Extension and Military Pay Bill[42] was enacted, eliminating undergraduate student deferments for those thereafter entering college and establishing a uniform national call to insure that registrants throughout the country with the same lottery number would be equally liable to induction, despite the fact that some local boards had larger pools of nondeferred from which to draw. At about the same time demands for military forces began to diminish significantly, thus reducing the likelihood of an unlucky draw.[43]

All of the underlying statutes providing for compulsory conscription were in form extensions of the 1948 Act. By 1973 only about 50,000 registrants were being drafted and in July of that year the statute was allowed to lapse. An all-volunteer combat force, with a small draft for physicians and added reliance on civilians for some support tasks, replaced the mixed military of draftees and coerced, and noncoerced, volunteers. "The key element," the Secretary of Defense wrote at the time, in the change-over, "was a substantial and costly increase in pay and allowances for personnel in the lower enlisted grades."[44] Thus are we brought full circle to the system of bounties and substitutes, though one considerably more concealed than that which operated during the Civil War.

From the preceding discussion it should be apparent that a mixture of approaches has been used in allocating wartime service or, what is the same, exemption from that service and its deathly risks. Mixtures over time no less than mixtures at any given time have varied in part in reaction to approaches previously used.

In the case of a wartime army, it is clear that the first-order determination of how many soldiers are needed will be made collectively and relatively openly and responsibly. This has been the role of the executive requests for, and the congressional passage of, the statutes authorizing calls. In addition, a fair number of accountable second-order decisions will also be made. Some, like age, will be made in a highly centralized way; others, though made responsibly and at a centralized level, will rely on their application being made at a local level where the decision may or may not be responsible. These second-order determinations may be based on either contemporary views of societal efficiency or on a recognition of individual desire. Typical of the first are health and perhaps age and of the second, conscientious objection.[45] The degree to which these local decisions are made by applying open guidelines openly will, in part, depend on how strongly the society wishes to enforce still other rankings which cannot be made accountably. The existence of acceptable, vague categories like health and conscience permit other, unspoken grounds for allocation to be introduced, *sub silentio.*

We have observed, of course, many other grounds for second-order allocations which have served as bases of accountable, political allocations. Occupational exemptions and deferments (including student deferments) are typical of these. We have oscillated between recognizing these responsibly, or recognizing them in part and aresponsibly on the one hand (as when deferments have been granted with considerable local draft board discretion in situations in which the life of the deferment long outlasts the war or the appropriate age of service), to denying them altogether, on the other.

Finally, we have seen that the market has always had a place, at least at the fringe, since volunteering has almost always been permitted. Indeed, the draft seems to have been initially used, in this country, primarily as a stimulus to enlistment. Volunteers need have met minimal efficiency criteria often less stringent than those which would exclude nonvolun-teers; for instance, a person somewhat below or above draft age could nonetheless volunteer or re-enlist.[46] This represents a tacit recognition that efficiency was never the sole criterion by which men have been chosen to fight; ever-present has been a place, neither dominant nor subservient, accorded to the desire to serve or, what may sometimes have been the same thing, a willingness to sell oneself.[47]

Despite the use of all these approaches, there has remained a core of necessary second-order decison making which was not comfortably assimilated to any of the relatively acceptable second-order choices just described. How the remaining soldiers—those still required by the first-order determination when voluntary enlistment and acceptable second-order choices have been exhausted—were selected or excluded has been a strange story, for every possible device—from pure market to pure lottery—has been used. Wartime armies in America have been selected (a) by a complex mixture of approaches, each of which, while expanding and contracting at different times, has adequately dealt with a definable part of the second-order decision, and (b) by an unstable succession of approaches, tolerated for only a relatively short period of time, dealing with the remaining part.

The Nature of The Society Making the Tragic Choice

Tragedy is a cultural phenomenon. Societies differ as to what is, for them, tragic and as to what are deemed appropriate ameliorative methods. It is difficult to show the precise ways in which a culture influences the tragic situation; the threads which make up a culture are too intricate, and the authors of any study being, obviously, the product of particular cultures, cannot extricate their perceptions from the pattern of the fabric. Nevertheless, two narrative perspectives may serve to limn the cultural outline of the tragic choice: We can discuss a single problem as it is presently being treated within the American culture, trying to derive from aspects of American cultural

history related to a particular tragic good—as distinguished
from the history of how the good itself has been allocated in
America—factors having a significant influence on present-day
allocations; and we can look at different treatments, by different
societies, of the same tragic problem. Perhaps by these indirec-
tions the important but elusive effect of national culture can be
suggested.

American Population Policy / At the end of a preceding
section, we wrote, "The factual contours of the particular problem of child rights more than anything else explain the dominance of the complex and curious combination of custom, unorganized moral suasion, and *ad hoc* market incentives [which
determine the pattern of childbearing] in the United States
today."

By this we meant to put emphasis on the decisive role of the
nature of the good, in the ultimate allocation of that good in this
country. It should be equally clear that the historical allocations
of that good—our past population policies, unconsciously chosen as some of them were—have in great measure set the terms
of the choices we face today. Indeed, unlike the allocation of
other goods, past population policies here and in other countries set the perimeters of numbers which bound the present
situation. But there is much else. The people we are, the
people we have become, will direct the terms of future discussions, even as these in turn shape us.

This is obvious in a trivial way; that is, were we another
society, our first-order population determinations would likely
reflect a completely different policy direction. Demographers
assert that the United States is one of few among developed
nations seriously seeking to slow population growth and eventually stabilize size.[48] Rarer still, the United States, unlike the
Netherlands and, cyclically, Japan, is not motivated by considerations of high density.[49] In most developed states, pressures
which have their origins in the cultural history of each state
have acted to encourage population growth. Commentators

have explained high birth policies in developed societies such as France, Israel, Argentina, Poland, Hungary, and various other Eastern European countries in terms of more or less plausible cultural and political sources specific to each—for instance, Israel's solitary geopolitical position.[50] A summarizing chapter in a current review of population policies in developed countries, by the Population Council, begins, "If one thing is clearer than any other in this array of policy discussion, it is the close relationship of the matter to the national circumstance. Each country reviews its own situation in the light of its own history and tradition, its own values and operating procedures, and determines its position accordingly."[51]

But the role of culture is influential in a nontrivial, nonobvious way, also. Even if the first-order direction is set, the proper scope and sort of second-order allocations will reflect national preoccupations, self-assumptions, values. We have been committed, since before our society organized itself as a nation, to a customary system of population allocation with market cues. A brief review of past population policies, as an analysis of current ones, will confirm this. Here there has been no historical dialectic of the kind we discussed with respect to the draft in the previous section since this country has never, in the past, confronted a tragic child rights situation. Past allocation practices, when they manage to avoid the trauma of tragic choice, may easily be translated into cultural preferences, thereby coming to seem the appropriate, proper means by which similar issues are to be treated, even if these latter do pose tragic dilemmas. The approaches become, as they say, as American as apple pie.

Early American population policies were typical of a youthful nation with a vast frontier, an expanding industrial base which required cheap labor, and a labor-intensive plantation network.[52] They were expressed in three explicitly demographic strategies which formed the basis of the development of population here: We mean, of course, the American policies

toward land, slavery, and immigration. Of these, land policy set
the general pattern of indirectly bringing about population
goals.

Scarcely four years after the Revolution and four years
before the ratification of the Constitution, the nation inaugu-
rated the first of the great land statutes: The Ordinance of 1785
provided for the sale of land at government auction to the
highest bidder, the land passing in fee simple absolute at a
minimum of $1 per acre.[53] Unlike the statutes which followed
it, the Ordinance relied on a pure market. Millions of acres
were distributed.[54] This statute was superseded by the Pre-
emption Act of 1841 which recognized rather different
principles—settlement was to have priority over raising revenue; small farms and bidders without landholdings were to
be preferred, and the latter were allowed reasonable periods in
which to pay off their purchase prices.[55] This statute introduced, into the indirect, customary population policy, nonmarket methods and the notion of using market cues in a
context which sought to compensate for uneven wealth distribution. Both this Act and the Homestead Act of 1862,[56]
which opened vast tracts of virgin land in the West, were
responses to the concentration of desperately poor, unemployed families in Eastern cities.[57] Reflecting the third important characteristic feature of American land policy, these
statutes gauged their allocation to the individual family unit,
ignoring other land-based interests—mining, cattle raising,
timber harvesting, railroad development, as well as state
needs—which required more space than the 160 acres allotted
to homesteaders. Land policy affected population allocation by
using those approaches which have ever since characterized
American population policy—a customary, indirect system of
apportioning births prevailed; the family unit was the matrix of
distribution; wealth-compensating market and nonmarket
methods were mixed.

An overlay on this general pattern is the direct method of
statutory immigration rules by which both first- and second-

order population considerations have been given effect. With respect to the first order, Americans being almost all the descendants of immigrants have refused to accept complete immigration bans. This necessarily affects what is deemed an acceptable total of births within the United States. During the past decade, because of the sharp decline in the birth rate, the significance of immigration has greatly increased, currently accounting for about a quarter of annual growth.[58] It would be surprising if our attitudes toward immigration were not in part responsible for America's almost unique preoccupation, among developed low-density nations, with the limitation of births as the locus of first-order population policy.

But it is the second-order allocations made by immigration statutes which primarily concern us because they represent exceptions to the general method of affecting population policy through indirect means. Indeed, in these, our culture brushed against tragic choices, and the dialectical effects noted in the previous section can be discerned in the succession of statutory schemes by which efficiency criteria and ethnic quotas operated to exclude some and admit others.

We began with immigration approaches very much like early land policies—the price was the cost of the ticket. It was not until 1875 that the first American immigration law which contained some general restrictions on immigrants was passed.[59] In addition to adding new prohibitions on the importation of "any subject of China, Japan or any Oriental country" under a contract for a term of service in the United States, it introduced various "acceptable" efficiency criteria by excluding convicted criminals and women imported for prostitution. Even this was hardly enforced. The immigration of great numbers of Chinese laborers prompted the initial restrictions on the free migration of any ethnic group as such, embodied in the Immigration Act of 1882.[60] By 1920 immigration since the passage of the first Act totaled 23.5 million, mainly from Southern and Eastern Europe.[61] Beginning in 1922, Congress reacted with a series of quota laws based on estimates of ethnic composition of the population prior to the period of very high non-English-speaking immigration.[62] More recently, quotas were drastically altered to reflect America's ethnic composition during the years of the melting pot.[63] But the principle of a direct second-order approach remains. Ethnic immigration quotas—accepted but not perhaps fully acceptable—apply to outsiders explicit criteria which have their source in the same relative preferences that might structure, for example, ethnic quotas for birth rates.[64] Immigration policy thus stands in arresting contrast to customary population allocation, operating as if entirely detached from the general pattern but presenting an implicit, insidious challenge to that system.

An even more profound overlay on the customary system is the special attitude of, and toward, blacks. Within that racial sector, a pure market operated from the beginning. This is a function of the American culture that no reference to the good itself—children and parenthood—or to past tragic allocations of that good—there was no widespread desire to restrict black births—can account for. Slavery entailed many tragic consequences. And certainly slave population policies, such as sales as well as emancipations, both of which sometimes destroyed families, evoked tragic choices.[65] But the allocation of *births* within the slavery system did not present a tragic dilemma to the dominant American society.

In the North American English colonies, black slavery first appeared in 1619, in Virginia. It developed rather slowly at first, so that in 1671 there were only about 2,000 black slaves; they were greatly outnumbered by indentured servants of European origin. But in the middle of the eighteenth century, Southern colonists began to generate profits from tobacco cultivation that could support the capital investments required by slave purchases. By the time of the Revolution, the slave population in Virginia had increased to about 200,000. In South Carolina there were said to be 2,444 blacks in 1700; by 1770 the figure was 75,178. With the introduction of cotton, and the invention in 1793 of the cotton gin, the trade in slaves became

more profitable than ever.[66] Despite the passage of a statute in
1807 barring the importation of slaves into the United States,[67]
illegal traffic and natural increase kept the black population
growing at high rates. On the eve of the Civil War there were
3,953,760 slaves in this country. For generations they had been
bred for profit.[68]

Though by no means the only elements in American cultural attitudes toward population policy—one need only think
of the role played by Catholicism and anti-Catholicism—these
three demographic approaches embody feelings of diffidence,
and an ambivalence toward racial and ethnic classes which help
to explain the fact that the United States does not have an
explicit population policy. Indeed, population control has represented an almost prototypical use of a customary approach to
achieve an acceptable first-order result and to avoid offensive
second-order decisions. This approach has relied on unseen
financial incentives, considerable moral suasion based on both
responsible and aresponsible societal judgments, and an appeal
to the worthier to sacrifice for the general good. Thus explicit
collective and responsible decisions have long been avoided.

In contrast it might be possible to view the first-order
population result not as a customary, nonmarket choice, but
rather as a pure market result of second-order market choices.
If the existing pro- and antinatalist incentives written into our
laws—and we mean not only laws having to do with marriage,
divorce, contraception, and abortion, but also health, housing,
taxes, sex discrimination, day-care legislation, and the like[69]—
could be taken more or less precisely to put all the social costs of
childbearing on the parents, then it could be said that the
first-order decision which accreted in response to those incentives was not customary, but pure market.

We think such a reading is implausible. In the first place,
this would imply that all the social costs of childbearing were
currently put on families who were choosing whether to have
children, not only correctly in the aggregate, but also correctly
by category of family. This seems most unlikely in view of the

haphazard nature of our unseen pro- and antinatalist incentives and moral suasions. More important, such a view would require that, were the number of children born in the United States today suddenly to increase or decrease dramatically, we would still be content with the result, so long as it continued successfully to internalize the social cost of having children. This is implicit in accepting a first-order market decision based on an appropriate internalization of costs. If, instead, as is clearly the case, a drastic change in birth rate would be met by a demand that the underlying incentives be adjusted, quite apart from any change in the social costs caused by children, then by that demand we would be conceding that previously a customary, nonmarket first-order determination had been at work, and that only the particular rate or range of births had been acceptable.[70] Financial and moral incentives would then be properly viewed as having been simply ways of rationing the children which the first-order determination permitted us to have.

The results of this method in the United States have been roughly as follows. Very high mortality and fertility rates prevailed during the eighteenth and early nineteenth centuries. In 1800, the fertility rates remained at about 8 births per woman. By 1900, this rate had dropped to between 3 and 4; today it is less than 2. In contrast to many ancient societies, the prevention of infant mortality was always a goal, as was the perpetuation of life at all age levels. In this aim, the United States has been relatively successful: In 1900, average life expectancy was 47; today it is 70. The death rate in this interval has dropped from 17 per thousand to 9, while the birth rate has similarly dropped from 32 to less than 16. Thus our present rate of growth, including immigration at the rate of about 2 per 1,000, is presently below 1 percent per year. Since our total population has, during the same 100-year period, gone from 76 million to 215 million, even this rather low growth rate adds substantially to the total number.[71]

The nonwhite population (of which 92 percent is black) is growing much faster than the population as a whole. The rapid increase in the nonwhite population in recent years results from higher fertility rates. In 1960 this was 27 per 1,000 among nonwhites and 18 among whites; the gap has increased since then. In 1966 the death rate among nonwhites was 9.8 per 1,000; it is projected to decrease to 8.1 by 1990, a significantly lower figure than for whites since nonwhites will be, as a group, younger.[72]

The current trends in population, and the customary choices by which they have been brought about, have evoked a two-pronged criticism. It has been argued that a responsible first-order determination is needed since the customary approach has been allowing too many births, for too long. And second-order decisions accomplished by existing unseen incentives have been criticized as allocating too many births to some sectors of society and too few to others.[73] These arguments have led to two movements.

One has been a more or less conscious attempt to alter the incentives among one group which is deemed to be procreating too much—the poor.[74] (Attempts to manipulate Aid to Dependent Children payments by making them contingent on receiving birth control advice, or even on employing birth control methods, reflect this movement.) Such attempts would retain the customary approach, if some additional market or nonmarket controls could be imposed on the poor.

The second movement has sought to devise plans to avoid the haphazard results of a customary approach. Both market and nonmarket methods have been suggested.[75] The difficulties with nonmarket approaches have seemed, as expected, most severe. The only ones seriously suggested have been lotteries or methods which, like lotteries, display a simple egalitarianism. Here they take the form of giving everyone a predetermined number of children; this does no little violence to individual desires.[76] When market approaches have been suggested, the problem of wealth distribution rears its formidable head. Rather unsophisticated attempts to decapitate it have been proposed.[77] Most market proposals have suffered, moreover, from an uneasy doubt as to whether measures of individual desire to procreate, even if achieved, would bring about an acceptable second-order mix of children; and it has been felt that while introduction of some collective efficiency factors might be desirable, this was very hard to do (with the possible exception of maximum family sizes) because of the patent inegalitarianism the introduction of such factors would imply.

Complex partially wealth-neutral systems of the sort we have discussed and criticized earlier might mend such flaws.[78] But in the absence of sufficiently sophisticated proposals of this sort, these movements have tended to reduce themselves to tinkering with the customary system. Tinkering, however, works increasingly less well as more of it is tried because the more the existing system of allocation is altered, the more obviously chosen and less customary it becomes.

One can describe the mixture that has prevailed in American methods of allocating procreation in the following way. Responsible first- and second-order determinations have been avoided by use of a customary approach. This is prefigured by, and consistent with, the progrowth land, slavery, and immigration policies discussed above. It has the virtue of being attractive to the attitudes fostered by those policies, yet it can be used to achieve a slow-growth goal. This approach uses a mixture of (a) market incentives which show an unusual relation to wealth, cutting most sharply into allocations to middle-income groups, and (b) moral suasion, which seems to be most effective with the same group. At the fringes some, very minor, absolute worthiness responsible decisions have existed, but perhaps in part because of deep fears engendered by memories of ethnically-based immigration restrictions, there has been little tendency to expand these highly colored methods.[79] In any event, curing the existing dissatisfaction at the middle-income level would require more than simply placing birth limitations on such "unworthy" groups. In general, individual desire has seemed very important; conversely, responsible and aresponsible second-order decisions have been perceived as very costly.

One need only consider, for a moment, the legislation introduced and almost enacted in Maharashtra which would have imposed jail sentences on couples if both partners remained unsterilized after the birth of their third child, to realize how crucial it is which society is making the procreation decision.[80] Most societies do not—certainly this society doesn't—face population pressures anywhere close to this magnitude. But we trust that this contrast also makes evident the social attitudes which, varying from culture to culture, make some methods plausible and others unthinkable. Perhaps a more thoroughgoing comparativism will further display this thesis.

A Comparative View / The proposition that the existence and nature of a tragic choice depends on which society confronts the choice is a truism—after all, whether a value is regarded as fundamental, to say nothing of the facts of scarcity, will vary from society to society—and one may justifiably balk at an extended discussion that professes to support that proposition. What may prove more interesting, however, are examples of societies which present rough concurrences with regard to the status given to values of life and equal treatment, and approximate equivalences of economic conditions, but which seem to display quite different approaches to a problem all regard as tragic. Such an exercise should act to show the incandescent role of a society's own conception of the values at stake and of the legal tradition which must cope with the conflict.

We will discuss very briefly three societies—Italy, England, and the United States—and their treatments of the problem of allocation of renal dialysis units, a paradigmatic tragic choice. Enough has already been said about subterfuges in tragic situations so that the reader will understand why no completely limpid or scientific description of the allocation process in these societies can be given. One must intuit from what is written, or even just said, to what in fact took place, and

that process can readily lead to error, or more likely to caricature. No matter . . . our object here is not to describe how
renal dialysis allocations were made in three societies at certain
moments in their history. Rather, it is to suggest how different
conceptions of equality interplay with different institutional
and legal traditions to make some approaches to tragic choices
plausible for a society while excluding others.

We will focus on three conceptions of equality: absolute or
simple egalitarianism, formal egalitarianism designed to
achieve a result which can be termed efficient, and qualified
egalitarianism which strives for efficiency but corrects the efficient result to mitigate socioeconomic disadvantages. There
are, in fact, many other conceptions of equality held in tension
with these in the three societies we are considering. And in
none of them is one conception dominant; therein lies the rub.
Yet it seems to us that each of the societies has a peculiar affinity
for one of the conceptions mentioned, and that this affinity
played a significant role, together with each society's view of
allocative institutions, in determining which approaches could
be tried, or at least defended, and which could not be seriously
considered.

EGALITARIANISM IN ITALY[81] / One might well describe Italy as
being as egalitarian a society as is the United States. The Italian
Constitution declares equality in lines as universal as those of
our Declaration of Independence.[82] The heritage of the French
Revolution, which changed utterly Italian legal structures,[83]
acts in concert with the Italian Constitution to make official
inegalitarianism more odious than in the United States. Universal military training is the rule, even in peacetime. The right
to public education, through the university, is guaranteed to
all, albeit in a special way we shall discuss.[84] Indeed, whenever
one looks for an official rule, one is apt to find a statement that
sounds like absolute or simple egalitarianism.

And yet equality of status and treatment are far from a
reality. Wealth differences, especially after taxes, are very

great. One's family and all that means—background, manners, connections—are very important. Many goods, the allocation of which is said to be based on egalitarian premises, are in fact given to preferred groups to a degree much greater than in America. Take education, for example: Public school examinations for promotion were, for many years, so demanding that only a very few could pass without special preparation. This extracurricular tutoring was expensive and effective. As a result, the children of the *borghesia*—the good middle class—and the intelligentsia—the latter who could be prepped by their parents—survived the paring process. Children who were not from *buone famiglie* did not last in the system very long. When they did, they found that the allocation of jobs, even to those with university educations, was very much a matter of connections.

As egalitarian pressures have grown stronger, universities have become so crowded that it is almost impossible to obtain an adequate education simply by being enrolled. Some few students are selected by professors for special attention; these receive excellent educations and jobs. The others, all too frequently, get neither. The net result is inegalitarian by almost any standards. In contrast, the American system, many parts of which overtly abandon simple egalitarianism in favor of approaches which select for advanced or special training those who would gain, and return to society, most from it, mitigates the effects of different backgrounds by financing remedial work, awarding scholarships on the basis of need rather than pure academic promise, recruiting university students from intellectually and economically deprived backgrounds (even when students' scores on standardized tests fall below those of the average student admitted), and thereby achieves a degree of egalitarianism much greater than its formal structure would suggest.

Italian society accepts outcomes that contradict a simple egalitarian ideology—outcomes that would arouse much criticism in the United States—because the content of laws and rules is viewed as expressing ideal goals and not programmatic guidelines. Italians commonly joke that many laws, at least those that are *regolamenti* (administrative regulations), are made to be broken. It is taken for granted that specific allocations will not implement the naïve or simple egalitarianism of a general statute or, for that matter, of the Constitution. Arguments of the kind, "If everyone followed a law to the letter, it might be best and surely it is right for the law to state the ideal rule. But since it is not followed, it would be absurd for me to follow it; I would be the only one, I would even have to do more because everyone else is doing so much less, and so forth," stand for a general awareness—that is quite separate from cynicism—that legal norms, as it were, need not be used as rules but may instead have a proper heuristic role not detached from, but certainly not determinative of, actual outcomes.[85] One might hear an analysis very like the one paraphrased above even in church sermons or newspaper editorials offered to explain why cheating on one's taxes is not robbery.[86]

Simple egalitarianism does permit the use of some distinctions among candidates. Interestingly, these tend not to be of the efficiency sort (indeed, *utilitarianism* is a pejorative in Italy, connoting a certain crassness), but of a kind reflecting past sacrifices. Preferences in civil service hiring are responsibly— as that term has been used in this text—given to disabled veterans, those handicapped by work-related injuries, children of these groups, and others similarly bearing scars of service or suffering. These distinctions are not, of course, allowed to determine the allocation of crucial goods, and certainly not tragic ones.

Reflecting, among other things, this allegiance to a sentimental egalitarianism Italian society bears a substantial distrust of uncontrolled money markets. It also has no tradition of the jury. Far from being objects of cultural faith, the jury, and by extension the parajury, are seen as obviously corruptible as well as, or perhaps because they are, unprincipled. This view reflects a general rejection of modes which fail to swear to an ideal. By its very nature, the jury supposes the need for decisions which are *ad hoc* and unprincipled in the sense that they do not even profess to be governed by general principles.

In Italy there is even a wary antagonism toward discretion exercised by judges. Nominally, such discretion is absent in reaching verdicts; and in determining sentences, long lists of aggravating and mitigating circumstances are supposed to add or detract periods from a basic term, thereby supplying a calculus for every crime. [87] If much of this is a charade, the important point for us is that a charade is deemed necessary, that is, some accommodation is required because no ideal of sufficient generality to claim the name can dictate appropriate action in specific cases. A jury epitomizes the rejection of such an ideal; moreover, it depends on a general belief in the incorruptibility of procedures since the introduction of discretion and aresponsibility leaves only the procedures bare for scrutiny. Few Italians would count themselves so credulous as to assume mere procedures warrant a presumption of correctness or of good faith.

The Italian distrust of uncontrolled money markets reflects two complementary features of that elegant, yet historically commercial, society's attitude toward wealth and allocations: The profession of simple egalitarianism and the commitment to the assumption that status, if it can be introduced *sub silentio*, ought to count as much as money in determining eventual outcomes. This distrust has brought forth the flowering jungle of price, rent, and other controls which insinuate the state, though not necessarily decisively, in so many market decisions. A society that was willing to create the complex system of subterfuges by which the results of simple egalitarianism are avoided would scarcely abstain from modifying the mechanics of a laissex-faire egalitarianism.

KIDNEY ALLOCATIONS IN ITALY[88] / Without pretending that we have surveyed all, or even most, of the principal cultural influences determining the allocation of tragic goods in Italy, or that we have seen anything so fantastic as a national character emerge from the preceding discussion, a review of the Italian approach to a tragic choice ought at least to reflect the cultural features noted above.

The general approach to the allocation of artificial kidneys in Italy has been structured by the statement of guidelines for responsible allocations which would not contravene the general principle of simple egalitarianism. One such guideline is: To the first in need goes the right to the good. This far exceeds even the corrected egalitarianism of the United States, since even nonclass-related efficiency criteria are discarded. In Italy, it has been applied to give artificial kidneys to patients suffering from terminal illnesses which dialysis would not relieve.[89] Why, after all, should their shorter lives be measured against lives that would have been longer from no merit of their own? Measurements of this kind are regarded as mere utilitarianism. If people are to be treated as if they were the same, the patient for whom dialysis offers little likelihood of success should have no less a chance to receive an artificial kidney than the patient whose condition makes dialysis a promising imperative.[90]

The hospital committee, a parajury, is rejected out of hand as a method of selecting recipients.[91] The money market is similarly rejected, though emigration is not prohibited.

Nonmoney or mixed markets—such as a market in time, through which the patient or his hired representatives can continue to press his case, or a market in influence—play roles analogous to that of a money market. To some degree they have been exchanged for a pure money market. Of course, ultimate allocation will depend on the decisions of bureaucrats or physicians who, though allegedly applying austere guidelines which must appear compatible with simple equality, do so through a system that is aresponsible and nonrepresentative.[92]

The first-order determination is obscured and not confronted. But it may be that a country that had long been poor would find it less damaging to humanistic values to face such a determination. Poverty and hunger and illness had not been incompatible with human dignity in the old, poorer society. Maybe the notion that a society cannot save everyone can still be more easily accepted.

Certainly the fact that the first-order determination in Italy initially limited the number of kidney treatment recipients to a very few acted to ease the stress imposed upon the complex second-order decision. Indeed, as more artificial kidneys were produced, Italy's system of allocation began to truly threaten fundamental values. This system depended on uncontrolled decisions by doctors operating under unenforced guidelines. The guideline by which preference was to be accorded to recipients by virtue of their priority in time allowed great malleability in its aresponsible application. Like simple equality in education it may well have been a charade, and with the availability of more kidneys came more skepticism that the system was corrupt. The result was a shift to an allocation principle based on sufficient abundance: Artificial kidneys were to be made available to "all who needed them."

This level of distribution was not prohibitively expensive since it entailed only that expenditure which would make plausible the claim of "kidneys for all who need them"; a claim whose requirements are elastic.[93] But had this alternative not been relatively accessible, the likely result would have been attempts to enforce first-in-time strictly. This would have served merely to replace doctors with bureaucrats and one may speculate that practices would have continued to be influenced by money and nonmoney markets. We doubt whether this would have surprised anyone.

Italians agreeably admit that the allocations entailed by simple egalitarianism or the various distributional guidelines promulgated in conformity with it, are unrealistic as a practical matter, and that the actual results produced by a complex system of modifications of these guidelines in operation are unsatisfactory. "But," they ask, "what other results, given a

situation of scarcity, are more satisfactory?" At least the ideal is
a proper and humane one, and this is more than can be said of
many societies whose allocations reach no better results. [94] One
is struck by the similarity between this point of view and the
justifications in our own society of inefficient but conceivably
perfectible criteria for decision (definitions of death or guilt or
negligence) in the face of proposals which depend on more
precise but clearly imperfectible alternatives.

KIDNEY ALLOCATION AND EGALITARIANISM IN ENGLAND/ England's initial approach to the allocation of artificial kidneys
can be described as quite distinct from that tried either by Italy
or the United States. Since the operative mechanism usually
was individual decisions by doctors and hospitals, it is hard to
be sure how allocations were in fact made. Nevertheless, the
impressions one gets from articles written and from informal
descriptions of the process suggest a very different pattern.
While Italy sought to avoid a tragic conflict by simply not
applying, without ceasing to proclaim, principles of absolute
equality, America, as we shall see, generally permitted allocations based on therapeutic and other efficiency considerations
so long as the results did not coincide with well-recognized
patterns of race or class discrimination. England, by contrast,
seems to have opted for a third alternative: clinical judgment,
which could readily reduce itself to a sort of mechanistic, New-
tonian efficiency-determined egalitarianism. [95]

This approach would treat equally those recipients who are
equal with respect to exterior, observable therapy-related
criteria. The criteria are applied unswervingly and damn the
implications for general equality. Thus hemodialysis is allocated so as to achieve the highest rate of success, given a limited
number of kidneys available. [96]

In England the aged and the young seem to have been
excluded from the pool of possible recipients, because the aged
are less good medical risks (since they are prey to all kinds of

other diseases, stand stress less well, and so forth), and because the young were less likely to adhere to the strict regimen then believed necessary to successful hemodialysis.[97] Many other categories of candidates were excluded on the grounds that they were poor medical risks for recovery. Thus far the English program is not much different from the American use of various therapeutic efficiency standards.[98]

But the English system may have gone on to make exclusions of other classes of poor risks that would doubtless have been unacceptable in an American system. Some have stated that laborers were excepted from the pool because physical strain made treatments less likely to work in them than in, for example, academics. Those who would not closely follow the Giovanetti diet—a strict and unpleasant menu helpful in carrying recipients over periods in which the artificial kidney was not working well—were also excluded at least in one hospital.[99] Adherence to the diet, as Professor Giovanetti himself noted, tended to be linked to socioeconomic class though it, to some extent, also might reflect an individual's desire to live. (Giovanetti, at Pisa, rejected the diet as a way of selecting recipients because "it would violate all humane principles."[100]) Psychological health was also suggested as a criterion, seemingly without regard to whether it might in fact tend to favor the higher classes.[101]

This mechanistic efficiency carries with it a certain kind of egalitarianism, by virtue of what it excludes.[102] That is, individual desires to live are, in the main, ignored;[103] no weighing of the relative value to society of one life or another is done either. Efficiency in this manner reduces itself to getting the most life-years out of the limited number of machines. Everyone's desire to survive and live in treatment is assumed to be equal. So is society's desire to have each one live.

We cannot say for sure how fully this approach was applied in England. And, of course, the increasing availability of kidney machines made the question largely academic. But to the extent it operated, it put into effect a remarkable, troubling analogue of an educational system in which examination scores determined advancement.[104]

ALLOCATION OF ARTIFICIAL KIDNEYS IN AMERICA / The procedures by which artificial kidneys and transplants have been allotted in the United States present an interestingly different pattern. As befits a land of plenty and a society convinced that an orgastic future awaits it if only the proper plans are made, the principal object of the tragic allocation in America has been to avoid owning up to having made a first-order determination. From this as much as from our democratic ideology follows the consistent reliance on limiting second-order criteria to those which seem unchosen, and correcting second-order results before they reveal discriminations which offend a qualified egalitarianism, that is, that persons ought to be treated as equals if they are similar according to generalized efficiency criteria, but also if not treating them as equals displays a disfavored group in some prominent way.[105] Here then, as in America's approach to military conscription and to education, efficiency plays a significant role, but becomes suspect when it results in an obvious discrimination against a well-defined socioeconomic group.

Our first approach was a purely technical one: Kidneys went to those people in whom the kidneys were likeliest to work, or to those in whom there was a substantial experimental interest. These decisions were left up to doctors and hospitals which faced a scarcity not of their own making. If it appeared that every patient who was really likely to benefit would get a kidney, then attention was never focused on the first-order determination and no decisions threatening egalitarian or humanistic values needed to be made.

This approach broke down because it did not fit the facts of the matter. On the one hand, the use of a customary approach to the first-order determination quickly drove the number of artificial kidneys available up to levels sufficient to provide more than enough to that group for whom successful dialysis was almost a sure bet, as well as for justifiable experimentation.[106] The existence of a perimeter enclosing a group of sure bets became rather unconvincing as the line was advanced and the enclosure expanded; suspicion was voiced that some medical bets were surer than others because of previous or present wealth advantages. On the other hand, it became apparent that the remaining scarcity was very much the product of a societal decision.[107]

The first difficulty was met by a variety of measures—none of them completely successful. A first-come-first-served basis was tried. But some of the patients first to come asking were poor recipients.[108] A modification by which a first-come-first-served approach was limited to equally good recipients ran into the problem that there was a continuum between better and worse recipients. It was not easy simply to draw a line and treat all those above the line as equally good and those below the line as unacceptable (though this too was suggested).[109] Trade-offs between relatively good recipients and relatively first in time were almost impossible to administer and accordingly raised doubts about the nature of what had become aresponsible, unrepresentative, and technically uncontrollable decisions. Were the doctors favoring friends? Or those who could pay? Or those they deemed worthiest? Doctors themselves tended to refuse to be put in so vulnerable a role.[110]

Of course many doctors and hospital groups recognized that a first-come-first-served approach made choices, and made them mindlessly. Some of these physicians and administrators attempted to confront the problem of second-order determinations directly. The Seattle God Committee was a courageous attempt to do this, and its experience illustrated both the advantages and dangers of thinking too clearly in this area. A parajury was set up (with "selected representatives of various groups" and with medical experts as well, at least on the sidelines). The Committee chose those who, considering also relative chance of success, were most deserving to live. The

Committee was aresponsible and neither the guidelines applied nor their outcomes were framed in terms of societal utility or of individual desire, though both may well have been implicitly used.[111] Had it worked it would have been able to give weight to efficiency (both in the narrow sense of clinical judgment and in a broader sense involving individual or social desires) and to correct that efficiency so that no group would be too obviously disfavored. Corrected egalitarianism would have had its due, through a peculiarly American device, the aresponsible agency.

The Seattle God Committee could not, however, avoid the inherent defects of aresponsible allocations in tragic contexts. An avalanche of criticisms of the approach followed. These ranged from attacks on the standards used, or not used, to the simpler criticism that the approach dramatized the second-order choice and spotlighted thereby the fact that a first-order determination against a fundamental humanistic value—the perpetuation of life—had been made.[112]

Some commentators suggested a return to relying purely on medical judgments, now described in terms resembling the criteria of absolute worthiness (improperly, of course, since, in the absence of scarcity, less good medical risks would certainly be given kidneys).[113] Other, wiser writers, instead, doubted the desirability of giving such broad powers to physician-investigators and noted the relationship between decisions made in this way and socioeconomic discriminations. They argued, however, that such discriminations could be limited if basic medical criteria were openly promulgated. Lotteries and like approaches reflecting a simple egalitarianism were recommended if too many good potential recipients still remained. Among the most intriguing proposals was the suggestion that if all who are worthy could not receive a kidney, none should![114] None of these approaches gained general acceptance. Lotteries, as might have been expected, were of little use: The premises on which they depend—that patients are viewed as equals, and that they view themselves as equal in desire to live

—were not present. Furthermore, lotteries tend to attract attention; thus use here emphasized the impersonal and certain first-order determination.[115] The all-or-none proposal, while fervently and ably argued, attracted few adherents because it, too, would have emphasized a first-order decision society does not wish emphasized, and perhaps because it accords absolute equality a primacy over all other values, including life, which does not, for better or worse, reflect the value structure of our society.[116]

The result of all this, and of the ready rejection of both responsible collective and market allocation approaches,[117] was the redetermination of the first-order decision. The advantages of a customary approach had been lost because the first-order determination imposed too many difficult second-order decisions, and the breakdown of the attempt to use long-lived aresponsible agencies destroyed the possibility of achieving an acceptable result consistent with qualified egalitarianism. At about the same time, the cost of kidney machines diminished sufficiently to permit a fresh, admittedly chosen first-order decision which could provide hemodialysis for all who might benefit. Only those who saw as clearly as the much-maligned Seattle doctors realized that this was a new subterfuge. A system which offers "kidneys for everyone" distinguishes those dying from renal failure—and prices their lives exceedingly high—from those dying from other diseases, who for similar expenditures could also have been saved.[118]

COMPARISONS: SUMMARY / In the allocation of kidneys, many accountable decisions are possible. Wide scope is allowed to sheer efficiency concerns, responsibly defined and decentrally applied. Decentralization works so long as the decision is a technical one because societies can count on a general perception of the professionalism of doctors and because an informal system of peer control does on the whole function successfully.

It is unlikely that, presented with these possibilities and the insistent tragedy of the kidney problem, the three societies we have been discussing came by chance to their separate approaches. From all that has gone before, and from his likely background in this culture, the reader should probably have expected that, for example, since privacy costs are not too great and since aresponsible and pararesponsible agencies provide flexible structures within which social and individual efficiency grounds can be measured against socioeconomic status, such agencies would be likely to have been employed in a society like the United States that has traditionally regarded them highly. And much the same sort of thing might be said with respect to the Italian choice of a first-need-in-time approach.

The fact of similarities, however, is just as significant as that of differences. Consider, for instance, the unwillingness of any of these countries to let the market operate here, except at the very fringes, for instance, by permitting emigration (which they all did). Nor have any been willing to seriously consider removing a patient from dialysis simply because a somewhat worthier—on any criterion—candidate is in need.

The most important similarity is found in the way each of the three societies ultimately seems to have dealt with the allocation dilemma. After trying different second-order approaches, each of these countries gave up, and modified the first-order decision so that it could be said that they were attempting to accommodate every reasonable candidate. The first-order determination had been too stark, and the weaknesses in second-order approaches too demoralizing, to permit a continuation of what at first appeared to be acceptable methods. These were culturally and economically cognate societies, it must be remembered. Perhaps underneath the slogan "kidneys for all who need them," different approaches still operate, but in the end the slogan had to be the same.

With this we conclude our consideration of those elements in the pathology of tragic choices, as it were, which originate with the culture to whom the choice has been committed. We have observed various conceptions of equality at work. Other illustrations of these conceptions come to mind: the egalitarianism of the playing field, for example, in which only some play because someone has chosen them, and not on account of who they are or whether even they wish to play, but simply because they play well; the egalitarianism of the fishing village, in which everyone has a significant task and everyone shares in the catch according to his needs; and finally the egalitarianism of the barn-raising, in which those who are newcomers to the town are assimilated into a general minimum of prosperity, precisely because they are newcomers. We have not, and do not wish to claim much for these impressionistic sketches of complex and subtle societies. Rather we have been looking for traces of patterns, "figure[s] in the carpet," which are indispensable elements whenever different societies confront similar tragic choices.

7

THE TRAGIC DILEMMA
AND CYCLES

I<small>T HAS BEEN</small> the business of this book not to resolve tragic choices by means of discoveries of new methods, but to make it possible for us to get a clearer view of the state of affairs that troubles us. By complex mixtures of approaches, various societies attempt to avert tragic results, that is, results which imply the rejection of values which are proclaimed to be fundamental. These may succeed for a time. But it will become apparent that some sacrifice of values has taken place; fresh mixtures of methods will be tried, structured, as we have seen, by the shortcomings of the approaches they replace. It may not be so obvious that this will happen with the tragic situation in which the focus of attention has narrowed to the precise technological good at stake—iron lungs, say—and has ignored the rest of the family of such goods—cardiac shunts, marrow transplants, and the like—whose availability waxes and wanes as such attention changes its focus. This focus will not last, and even if it could, it could not withstand the stresses and assaults generated by the underlying, temporarily obscured, conflict of values. An awareness of the tragic facts will recur just as certainly as do the dilemmas of the draft or birth limitation. When we have observed this recurrence and continuity of tragedy, it becomes apparent that a special type of mixture is being used by societies over time, namely, the mixture or alternation of mixtures. Such a strategy of successive moves comprises an intricate game which better than any other method or set of methods reflects appreciation of the tragic choice.

It is the most subtle of methods because it depends on methodology being constantly replaced; yet alone among mixtures and methods, cycle strategy does not depend, for its success, on subterfuge. It may represent a forthright way of facing tragic choices since it accepts the fact that society faces the paradox of being forced to choose among competing values in a general context in which none can, for long, be abandoned. The mode of change may, of course, be customary; it may involve subterfuges; and the very existence of cycles may not be recognized. But the admission that cycle strategy occurs is an admission that society is attempting to preserve essential yet conflicting values. This admission has the virtue of affirming honesty, a not insubstantial value in a society which must cope with change.

Why do approaches to tragic allocations change? Such changes are not mindlessly made; they have, in fact, represented quite rational responses preceded by discussions as rational as discussions termed rational usually are. The criticisms of the pre-existing system have described in generally accurate detail its fundamental flaws and have invoked the basic values which that system degrades. But the defenders of the pre-existing system are just as rational. They usually are penetrating in their recognition of the flaws inherent in the proposed reform. And when the reform is accepted and has become the vested method, it is eventually seen to display the very shortcomings which its critics had predicted (and to degrade those values they had sought to protect). Are these *mistakes?* If they are not, why do we move restlessly from one system which proves inadequate to another?

The answer is, we have come to think, that a society may limit the destructive impact of tragic choices by choosing to mix approaches over time. Endangered values are reaffirmed. The ultimate cost to other values is not immediately borne. Change itself brings two dividends, though all too often of an illusory kind we have associated with subterfuges. First, a reconceptualization of the problem arouses hope that its final price will not be exacted; the certainties of the discarded method are replaced. Second, the society is acting, and action has some palliative benefit since it too implies that necessity can somehow be evaded if only we try harder, plan better than those we followed, avoid their mistakes, and so forth. More important, because more honest, the deep knowledge that change will come again carries with it the hope that values currently degraded will not for all that be abandoned.

That this notion of flux is intimately tied to the tragic circumstance can be seen from the contrasting relative stability of methods at the fringes of tragic choices. For instance, the first-order determination of the total number of soldiers needed or the market inducement of some volunteers or the responsible rejection of those below or above certain ages have all remained stable components of the conscription system. But, as we discussed above, virtually all the classical approaches to allocation have, in various mixtures, been tried as devices for resolving the tragic choice of forcing some men to fight while others are left safe at home. None of these mixtures has long survived the war for which it was to be a reform measure.

Moreover, what is stable and what is irreducibly tragic is also changeable. For example, conscientious objection to conscription was at one time not accepted but now seems a stable element in that system. Values, even fundamental values, evolve and change. What becomes stable, what remains stable, depends on the evolution of values in society.

We do not, of course, mean to suggest that any particular order of succession will occur. Nor are we saying anything much about the mechanism through which the changes come about. Indeed, a challenging empirical study worth a book of its own could be made of these matters. Perhaps changes come about because disfavored groups spurred by an awareness of their disfavor seek political power. Perhaps such changes occur because critics explicitly concerned with the values undermined by the previous system challenge that system and call on those disfavored by it to ally in overthrowing it. Many permutations are possible, and all are worth study. Similarly, one cannot say much about the lifespan of any given approach. Too much depends on the relative strengths and needs for reaffirm-ance of particular values at particular times in a particular society.

Our story, of course, can have no happy ending, and so it is especially agreeable at this point to have drawn attention to the noble uses societies have made of classical allocation methods by rejecting each of them across time. Since the values en-dangered by any given approach vary, a society which wishes to reject none of them can, by moving, with desperate grace, from one approach to another, reaffirm the most threatened basic value and thereby seek to assure that its function as an under-pinning of the society is not permanently lost.

We doubt whether there could be an open society whose values were sufficiently consistent to obviate the possibility that scarcity would bring about tragic choices. Morality—since the terms in which it is stated and by which it is understood must be grounded in culture and tradition—is not simply the aggregate demand of individuals atomistically wishing to do right. And therefore a moral society must depend on moral conflict as the basis for determining morality unless, of course, a lawgiver decrees inflexible rules, the obedience to which constitutes right and wrong. Then morality would not have to make sense. In such a totalitarian society there could be conflict, but no conflict of values. There could be pathos, but no tragedy.

But this is not the culture in which we live. Indeed, a culture such as ours which implicitly recognizes contradictions in its moral scheme by the use of a strategy of cycles has opted to remain sensitive to values it continues to cherish at the moment they are most frail, while being amenable to change, including moral change. The alternative, as we have seen, would be the final rejection of some fundamental values. We could simply discard those basic values which, with others, evoke the tragic dilemma. We could, at a cost, keep a slave army, forbid certain groups from procreating, or try, by the use of absolute worthi-ness language, permanently to hide the choices made, and so on. Perhaps we have even done so. It is doubtful, however, that even if we did accept this sort of solution to some tragic choices we could do so as to many.

If we did, we would be a different society. Surely it is a fact that our society will be different from what it is presently. Yet we can hope that it will retain that diversity which entails tragedy. We do not live in the timeless days of a dog or sparrows. As we become aware of what we, as a society, are doing, we bear responsibility for those allocations that will be made as well as for what has been done in our names. If one understands more than before for having read this essay, one can still appreciate that tragic decisions need be made and are not the easier for the understanding.

NOTES

Chapter 1

EPIGRAPH. Euripides, *Hippolytus,* ll. 189–97, *The Complete Greek Tragedies, Euripides I,* ed. D. Grene and R. Lattimore (Chicago and London: University of Chicago Press, 1955).

1. "Tragedy, then, is the imitation of a good action, which is complete and of a certain length, by means of language made pleasing for each part separately; it relies in its various elements not on narrative but on acting; through pity and fear it achieves the purgation of such emotions" (Aristotle, *On Poetry and Style,* trans. G. M. A. Grube [Indianapolis: Bobbs-Merrill, 1958], chap. 6, p. 49b). Cf. W. Kaufmann, *Tragedy and Philosophy* (Garden City, N.Y.: Doubleday, 1968), pp. 46–47.

2. William Arrowsmith, "The Criticism of Greek Tragedy," in *Tragedy: Vision and Form,* ed. W. Corrigan (San Francisco: Chandler Publishing, 1965), p. 332.

3. See Aeschylus, *Agamemnon,* l. 211, as phrased by Arrowsmith, in *Tragedy,* p. 333.

4. R. B. Sewall, "The Tragic Form," in *Tragedy: Modern Essays in Criticism,* ed. L. Michel and R. B. Sewall (Englewood Cliffs, N.J.: Prentice-Hall, 1963), p. 120.

5. C. Brooks, "Introduction," in *Tragic Themes in Western Literature,* ed. C. Brooks (New Haven, Conn.: Yale University Press, 1955), p. 5.

6. Euripides, *Bacchae,* l. 204, spoken by Teiresias, in *The Complete Greek Tragedies, Euripides V,* ed. D. Grene and R. Lattimore (Chicago and London: University of Chicago Press, 1955).

7. Of course *efficiency* can be defined so that it includes all of this; for our purposes here, however, such a definition would only be misleading.

8. The influence of corrected egalitarianism in the American concept of equality is illustrated in Chapter 4. On simple or naïve egalitarianism, see Chapter 2, note 9.

9. [This] acceptance springs from a desire for knowledge, for the deepest kind of self-knowledge, knowledge of the full meaning of one's ultimate commitments. It is the glory of Oedipus that he insists upon knowing *who* he is. But so does Rosmer and so does Hamlet and so do all the rest. Even Becket needs to know whether he is acting out of human pride or out of submission to God's will, and will not really know until he has tested his conviction to the final limit, which is death. . . . With this in mind, it is all the more strange, and glorious, that man should so yearn for such knowledge (Brooks, in *Tragic Themes,* pp. 5–6).

10. Arrowsmith, in *Tragedy*, p. 342.

11. A particularly striking example of society's demand for a victim appears to have been the execution of Private Eddie Slovik in World War II. Recent testimony indicates that when it was decided that "a cautionary execution was . . . necessary . . . they combed the military prisons" and made up "a pool of six deserters . . . considered for execution." Originally, "a Jewish soldier had been chosen to die, but . . . after psychological examinations [of the six] the general staff ordered that Private Slovik be executed instead" (*New York Times*, June 30, 1977, section A, p. 14).

12. In the pages that follow, we will describe the ways in which choices have been made in the allocation of hemodialysis and kidney transplants, the bearing of children, and wartime military service. As we noted earlier, the use of such examples entails a substantial risk that analysis may be confused with prescription. Our object, however, is not to prescribe the best way to make these particular tragic choices. Rather it is, by examining the strengths and weaknesses of institutions and approaches used to make allocations in particular situations, to chart the general outlines of all such choices.

13. J. L. Austin, "A Plea for Excuses," in J. L. Austin, *Philosphical Papers*, ed. J. O. Urmson and G. Warnock (London: Oxford University Press, 1961), p. 126.

14. See L. Wittgenstein, *Tractatus Logico-Philosophicus* ¶6.371, trans. D. F. Pears and B. F. McGuinness (New York: Humanities Press, 1961), p. 143.

Chapter 2

1. Kenneth Boulding has proposed, for example, that every woman be alloted two "child rights," which could then be bought and sold freely (K. Boulding, *The Meaning of the Twentieth Century* [New York: Harper & Row, 1964], pp. 135–36). Under this plan, the market determines the cost and distribution of available child rights, but does not determine the total number of child rights available; the latter decision is made collectively in determining the initial entitlement, that is, exactly how many child rights will be allotted to each woman prior to trading.

2. A Pareto superior move is one in which everyone is left at least as well off as before and some are made better off. For a further discussion of this and other, related, Pareto concepts, see Chapter 4.

In his discussion of the use of psychosurgery on "consenting" prisoners, for example, Robert Burt examines the costs of such surgery not only to the prisoners/patients but also to society at large. He characterizes the latter costs as derogations of "ill-defined but powerful notions of human dignity and inviolability," and concludes that by "withholding the possibility of legally consented psychosurgery [from a prisoner], we are . . . protecting ourselves more than him" (R. Burt, "Why We Should Keep Prisoners from the Doctors," *Hastings Center Report 5* [1975]: 25, 27, 34).

3. We will use the term *merit wants* to identify the desire for those goods (or for freedom from those bads) whose allocation on the basis of the existing wealth distribution engenders external costs which would not occur were the allocation based on a different distribution. In our terminology the sale of kidneys for transplant by live donors would involve a merit good if a society objected to such a market on the ground that the bulk of the donors would be the very poor. See Chapter 4.

4. The design of wealth-neutral markets is discussed in Chapter 4.

5. This is true whether the process of political decision making takes the form of a representative democracy, as in the United States, or some other form. It is the ultimate scarcity of the resource to be allocated, not the form of the political system through which it may be allocated, which makes an allocation decision tragic.

6. See Chapter 6.

7. The use of the various allocation methods to allot wartime military service in the armies of the United States is described in Chapter 6.

8. Even if any single allocative decision were best made collectively, from the viewpoint of social desirability and efficiency, it would not follow that all allocative decisions would be better made collectively than through a market system. A single decision can be brought to the attention of many individuals, receiving careful study and consideration of all implications of alternatives, before a decision is made. But as the number of decisions to be made increases, legislative or administrative bodies will be able to devote fewer and fewer resources to each decision.

Analogous problems arise if a market is overburdened. Perfect markets do not exist; to make markets relatively good allocation devices requires the enforcement of laws to insure competition, such as the antitrust statutes attempt to do, and positive steps to equalize knowledge, as may be accomplished through the securities laws. The more decisions there are to be made through the market, the more expensive these perfecting devices become; if too many decisions are left to the market, it may be too costly to insure the kind of market which will make the decisions well. Further, the market may be overburdened not only by increasing the numbers of decisions to be made but also by changing perceptions of the measures required to create a sufficiently perfect market. If, for example, only wealth-neutral markets are acceptable as allocation devices, then the cost of making the market wealth neutral, for each decision, must be added to the costs of making it competitive and open. See the discussion of wealth-neutral markets in Chapter 4.

Because market decisions and collective decisions do not become overburdened cumulatively or in the same way, there is good reason to think that a system which employs both is less likely to be overburdened than a system with only one or the other. In structuring the decision method for any particular set of choices, then, the important consideration is not simply whether the decisions in question are likely to be made better through the market system or through the collective (political) system but is, rather, a question of the comparative advantage of using each approach.

9. We shall use the term *simple egalitarianism* to identify the sweeping conception of equality which insists upon treating everyone within the eligible group as equal—either all have an equal chance at the pay-off, or pay-offs are distributed in an equal amount to all group members. On merit wants, see note 3, this chapter.

10. The hierarchic conception of society pervasive in France and the Low Countries at the close of the Middle Ages led to the conclusion that the common people were created to till the soil, while nobles were meant to cultivate justice and virtue. But as incidents of their high estate and many privileges, the nobility had the tasks of defending the people from oppression, combating violence and tyranny, and maintaining peace. So far as there was any shared conception of equality of all men, it was a religious or spiritual equality based on the idea of *momento mori*, and had nothing to do with the hierarchic structure of

temporal society (J. Huizinga, *The Waning of the Middle Ages* [London: E. Arnold, 1924], pp. 46–54).

11. A society which embraced the value of human equality might seek to overcome such dissonance by choosing or inducing the most worthy members to make the required sacrifices. See Chapter 3.

12. Of course, the higher value as well might become dominant, if it were argued that all lives are equally precious and that, for example, the expenditures to save the convict should therefore be matched by expenditures to provide the aged with hemodialysis. But society can no more afford the cost in resources of these general expenditures than it can afford the cost to its values incurred by refusing to make any dramatic affirmations of the value of life. See Chapter 5.

13. New York Times Co. v. United States, 403 U.S. 713 (1971). In the course of the argument of this case, Justice Stewart asked the counsel for the *New York Times* whether, if publication of the papers at issue in the case would necessarily lead to the death of one hundred people, a ban on publication would then be justified. In reply, counsel for the *Times* simply pointed out that the case at bar did not involve the situation described in the question. In his concurring opinion, Justice Stewart made clear that he agreed with counsel for the *Times:* "I cannot say that disclosure of any of [the papers] will surely result in direct, immediate, and irreparable damage to our Nation or its people" (403 U.S. 730).

14. Justice Hugo Black no doubt would have agreed. We imagine that he would have pointed out that we consistently waste many more than a hundred lives for things we value much less dearly than freedom of speech, and that the most important point is not that lives are lost but that we should have absolute rules (such as the rule against prior censorship) so that courts do not make the decision to sacrifice lives in order to preserve other values.

15. Attempts to weigh precisely the social costs and benefits associated with different responses to a tragic choice result more often in the valuation of only what we can measure than in the measurement of all that we value. Costs which are difficult to measure, such as the affront to the value of human life entailed by a decision to authorize medical experimentation with the terminally ill, will often be left out of the accounting altogether, though the resulting narrowness of the premises will poison the conclusion. L. Tribe, "Trial by Mathematics: Precision and Ritual in the Legal Process, *Harvard Law Review,* 84[1971]: 1,329. John Stuart Mill noted this weakness in the method of the first systematic analyzer of the costs and benefits associated with social rules and institutions, Jeremy Bentham (Mill, "Bentham," *The Philosophy of John Stuart Mill,* ed. M. Cohen [New York: Modern Library, 1961], pp. 18–22).

16. To laissez-faire egalitarianism, for example, differences in wealth are not incompatible with the view that people should be treated equally. On this and other ideal types of egalitarianism, see Chapter 1. Some of the consequences of different conceptions of human equality embraced by three different societies are examined in Chapter 6.

17. After the Social Security Amendments of 1972, which provided payment for hemodialysis, the official allocation system in the United States did consist of giving treatment to all who asked as long as treatment facilities remained available. In reviewing the treatment of chronic kidney failure, the Office of the Comptroller General identified as a pressing problem the limitations on access to treatment resulting from varying knowledge among physicians about the availability of treatment (United States General Accounting

Office, *Treatment of Chronic Kidney Failure: Dialysis, Transplant, Costs, and the Need for More Vigorous Effort. Report to the Congress by the Comptroller General of the United States* [1975], p. 13).

18. In addition to destroying the illusion of first-order sufficiency fostered by a first-come-first-served system and necessitating difficult second-order decisions, such treatments of the second-rate recipient also entail onerous process costs. Whether the second-rate recipient is denied any treatment, or is offered treatment only until a first-rate recipient comes along, utter demoralization is the result. (On process costs, see Chapter 3.) The first-come-first-served system can seek to eliminate these costs by refusing to recognize any distinction between first- and second-rate recipients. But a system so dominated by simple egalitarianism obviously plays havoc with other values, such as the desire to see medical resources used to best effect (what Professor Al Katz terms "the goal of therapeutic success," in "Process Design for Selection of Hemodialysis and Organ Transplant Recipients," *Buffalo Law Review* 22 [1973]: 375), and some accommodation of values becomes essential. Even in the Italian system, which is strongly committed to the pure first-come-first-served method of allocation, a few machines are nonetheless held in reserve for the treatment of acute kidney failures. See Chapter 6, note 90.

19. See the discussion of the allocation of artificial kidneys in Italy, in Chapter 6.

20. Professor Al Katz's proposal for the selection of patients for hemodialysis and kidney transplants incorporates random selection at several points in the model process (A. Katz, "Process Design," pp. 373, 393, 395, 416–17). Katz writes that "[w]here it is suggested that random selection may be the only fair process three circumstances seem to coexist: (1) the consequence of the decision to be made is literally critical; (2) there is a real temptation to value one human life more than another; and (3) there is no morally acceptable basis for making judgments of relative desert" (p. 402).

21. For a discussion of various incentives and their probable effects, see J. Noonan, "Unintended Consequences: Laws Indirectly Affecting Population in the United States," in R. Parke, ed., for the United States Commission on Population Growth and the American Future, *Aspects of Population Growth Policy* 6 (1972): 115, 122–38.

22. The *Ad Hoc* Committee at Harvard Medical School to Examine the Definition of Brain Death suggested that death be defined as the absence of any *"discernable central nervous system activity"* (H. Beecher, "Scarce Resources and Medical Advancement," *Daedalus*, Spring 1969, pp. 275, 292). As Beecher acknowledges, the new definition is a sharp break from the traditional focus on the cessation of respiratory and cardiac activity (p. 294). The standard suggested is often referred to as the "flat EEG" definition of death, but the Harvard committee regarded the isoelectric electroencephalogram as having "confirmatory value" of cessation of central nervous system activity only after the physician has examined for at least fourteen different physiological indicators for at least twenty-four hours (pp. 292–93).

The emphasis on the involvement and judgment of the physician in the death decision may allay fears that a technical definition is being applied mechanically at the cost of some lives which might be saved. Even though it is unclear that the judgment of the physician will avoid that cost, it is at least possible that it will. On the importance of such perfectability in a decision-making procedure, see this chapter, below, and Chapter 3.

23. Edmund Burke was a forceful apologist for this position.

> Instead of casting away all our old prejudices, we cherish them to a very considerable degree, and . . . we cherish them because they are prejudices: and the longer they have lasted and the more generally they have prevailed, the more we cherish them. We are afraid to put men to live and trade each on his own private stock of reason; because we suspect that the stock in each man is small, and that the individuals would do better to avail themselves of the general bank and capital of nations and ages. Many of our men of speculation, instead of exploding general prejudices, employ their sagacity to discover the latent wisdom which prevails in them. If they find what they seek, and they seldom fail, they think it more wise to continue the prejudice, with the reason involved, than to cast away the coat of prejudice, and to leave nothing but the naked reason (*Reflections on the Revolution in France* [Oxford, 1907] p. 95).

Cautioning against the notion that a legislative assembly could tear down a social order and build it up again in three days, Burke termed the raising of fit social institutions to be "the work of ages," for "mind must conspire with mind. Time is required to produce that union of minds which alone can produce all the good we aim at" (pp. 186–87).

Chapter 3

1. The following section must necessarily be without those details and refinements which a student of political decision-making bodies could provide, for we are not political scientists and can make no claim to familiarity with much that political scientists have written on the subject. For that reason, along with limitations of space, we move rather quickly in our discussion to those political-collective allocation devices which employ legal institutions (e.g., juries) in the allocation of tragic goods. These after all are the mechanisms (along with economic approaches, like markets) with which we are most familiar and to whose analysis we can make the most useful contributions.

2. In applying the due-process requirement of the Fourteenth Amendment, the Supreme Court has abandoned, in one area of the law after another, the approach of testing state laws and procedures to determine "whether they offend those canons of decency and fairness which express the notions of justice of English-speaking peoples" (Adamson v. California, 332 U.S. 46, 67 [1947] Frankfurter, J., conc.). That principle, which allowed considerable diversity among the states' laws, has been displaced by a process of incorporation through which the specific constitutional guarantees of the Bill of Rights have been made applicable to residents of every state, creating uniform national standards. See Duncan v. Louisiana, 391 U.S. 145, 146–47, and nn. 1–9 (1968). But cf. Moore v. City of East Cleveland, 431 U.S. 494, 97 S.Ct. 1,932 (1977).

3. See Chapter 3.

4. The data relevant to decisions about experimentation with humans, for example, may already be semipublic before the decision maker uses the information to justify his decision. See this chapter, below, and Chapter 6.

5. The classic Holmes-Knowlton debate on the role of courts and juries in setting standards for negligence in torts illustrates the traditional focus of inquiry. Holmes argued in favor of judge-made rules, of precedents which would automatically govern, providing certainty after the fact and predictability before it. We would know, for example, that holes of less than a certain depth in

a public street were not deemed negligence, while those of more than that depth were. Knowlton, who with many other judges held the contrary and ultimately prevailing view, argued that too many differences were ignored by Holmes's approach, and substantive unfairness would result. In one such case described by Holmes as "simple," for example, Knowlton listed a series of relevant facts and concluded that in such "complex" situations rules and precedents have little role (Lorenzo v. Wirth, 170 Mass. 596, 49 N.E. 1,010[1897]).

6. In criticizing proposals for replacing the rule of contributory negligence with one of comparative negligence, now Justice Lewis Powell stressed the "privileged" status of plaintiffs in damage suits, which he attributed to the popular image of poor, injured plaintiffs facing rich and powerful corporations (L. Powell, "Contributory Negligence: Necessary Check on the American Jury," *American Bar Association Journal* 43 [1957]: 1,005, 1,006–7). See also G. Calabresi, "Access to Justice and Substantive Law Reform: Legal Aid for the Lower Middle Class," in *Emerging Perspectives and Issues in the "Access-to-Justice" Movement*, ed. M. Cappelletti, vol. 3, Florence Access-to-Justice Project Series (Dobbs Ferry, N.Y.: Oceana, 1978). But see Harry Kalven's review of empirical studies which suggests the absence of any systematic proplaintiff bias in juries ("Comment on Maki v. Frelk," *Vanderbilt Law Review* 21 [1968]: 897, 902–4).

7. There are, for example, symbolic and rhetorical purposes prompting the demand for laws allowing abortion-on-demand. But few people would be willing to support the absolute rule were it not that such a rule minimizes the cost of equal access to abortions. Any rule which discriminates between some situations in which abortion will be allowed and some in which it may not gives greater access to the articulate and the well represented; in this way, new inequities are introduced by a rule intended to avoid (other) unjust results. If inequalities of access based on differences in wealth and articulateness are perceived as serious enough, some, even many, become willing to endorse an absolute rule which eliminates those costs, even though it means that in some specific cases they must live with results which they regard as objectionable in terms of other values.

8. Professor Frank Michelman has discussed the costs in terms of human dignity which a system of litigation may exact by excluding some people from access to the system: "[Dignity values] seem most clearly offended when a person confronts a formal, state-sponsored, public proceeding charging wrongdoing, failure, or defect, and the person is either prevented from responding or forced to respond without the assistance and resources that a self-respecting response necessitates" (F. Michelman, "The Supreme Court and Litigation Access Fees: The Right to Protect One's Rights—Part I," *Duke Law Journal*, vol. 1973, pp. 1,153, 1,173). Similar costs are also incurred, along with others, when decisions are made in ways other than through litigation.

9. See Chapter 5.

10. And, incidentally, whether they are worth paying may depend in part upon the distribution of costs. One is likely to view responsible decentralized decision-making differently depending on whether or not the cost of equal access can be allocated in a way consistent with the society's proclaimed notions of distributional equity.

11. For example, it is very different for a nation or some subdivision of it, such as a state, to say that graduate students will be exempted from the draft but carpenters' apprentices will not than it is for juries in two specific cases, with specific and therefore dissimilar facts before them, to decide that one young

man may continue his education and another young man must serve his country. Because no reasons for the decisions are given, the preference is viewed, at least at first, as highly particularized, reflecting an unanalyzable bundle of differences between the two men.

12. In conversation with one of us, Justice Hugo Black once suggested that the jury system was accorded its prominence and protection in the Constitution because its aresponsibility allowed it to disregard legal rules when the rules produced results contrary to community standards, and its representativeness insured that it would do just that.

13. There are other reasons, of course, for using juries, such as their ability to sift evidence, assess the credibility of witnesses, and find facts. The value of such other, readily acceptable, functions in legitimating the institution of the jury is discussed in Chapter 4.

14. See this chapter, below.

15. For a description of the Seattle God Committee, see Chapter 6. For an account of the systems of conscription used in the United States, see Chapter 6.

16. This assumes, plausibly, that the information necessary for the experimentation decision is recognized to be the same as the information required for intelligent treatment, and so has already been revealed to the patient's doctors before it is required for the experimentation decision.

17. See below, and G. Calabresi, "Access to Justice and Substantive Law Reform." This assumption presents no difficulty if articulateness appears to be a relevant criterion for allocation of a good. Admission to law school, for example, may fairly depend, in part, upon articulateness because the study and practice of law require skill in communication. But the assumption is untenable when we perceive that the good to be allocated—the acquittal of an innocent man in a criminal trial, for example—should not be granted or withheld on the basis of a defendant's articulateness.

18. See e.g., ibid.

19. From 1924 to 1968, for example, Texas executed thirty-eight wife-killers but no husband-killers (R. Koeninger, "Capital Punishment in Texas," *Crime and Delinquency* 15 [1969]: 132, 138).

20. See note 2, this chapter.

21. The particular difficulty of reconciling the desire for representativeness with the tenure of parajuries is discussed in this chapter, below.

22. Furman v. Georgia, 408 U.S. 238 (1972).

23. Ibid., pp. 240, 249–52, 255–57 (Douglas, J., conc.).

24. "These death sentences are cruel and unusual in the same way that being struck by lightning is cruel and unusual. For, of all the people convicted of rapes and murders in 1967 and 1968, . . . the petitioners are among a capriciously selected random handful upon whom the sentence of death has in fact been imposed" (ibid., pp. 309–10 [Stewart, J. conc.]).

25. The tendency of juries to make ever-larger awards in accident cases, with no apparent consideration of the costs which a series of such decisions may impose on the society, illustrates this problem with a discontinuous aresponsible decision maker.

26. See Chapter 1.

27. Stated most strongly, the absolute worthiness approach claims that the standard of worthiness should control allocation even if there is no scarcity. After studying the allocation methods used by various hemodialysis treatment centers in this country, one commentator concluded that standards applied to exclude applicants were not fixed, but varied according to the availability of

treatment facilities (Note, "Scarce Medical Resources," *Columbia Law Review* 69 [1969]: 620, 654). On the premise that "[t]he most obvious use of a rule of exclusion is to eliminate those who would not be considered even if the resource were available to unlimited supply," this observer suggested refinements in the exclusionary rules which would improve their usefulness (pp. 655–56). But it is clear that the suggestions are made with the object of selecting a number of recipients compatible with existing facilities and are not aimed at identifying for exclusion all of those who should be denied treatment even absent scarcity of medical resources.

There is greater justification for using exclusion based on medical criteria to limit the size of the applicant group to the number that can be treated. It is an almost universally accepted standard for selections that the patient whose chances of survival will be most greatly increased by the use of a resource will be preferred over others. Effect can be given to this principle by setting a minimum increase in survival probability which will allow all who fall above the minimum to be treated (Ibid., pp. 655–56).

28. The economist would view the move to increased continuity as a way of internalizing, to the agency, some of the costs (of all kinds) of a future shortfall of resources which must necessarily follow from profligate present allocations.

29. The Seattle God Committee, for example, was a lay committee which selected, from among eligible candidates, those who would receive treatment at the Seattle Artificial Kidney Center. Its membership consisted of a lawyer, a minister, a housewife, a banker, a state government official, a labor leader, and a surgeon. The committee was assisted in its deliberations by a medical advisory panel made up of personnel associated with the kidney treatment program. The membership, mission, and activities of the committee were reported widely in the popular press; see, for example, S. Alexander, "They Decide Who Lives, Who Dies," *Life,* November 9, 1962, p. 102; *Newsweek,* June 11, 1962, p. 92; and *Redbook,* November 1967, pp. 80, 133. For further discussion, see Chapter 6 and note 111 in that chapter.

30. In considering the representativeness of juries in the judicial setting, the Supreme Court has made it clear that there is no requirement that any particular jury be representative of the community's population. Most recently, in considering a claim that a petit jury venire without women denied a defendant's constitutional right to a fair trial, the Court reaffirmed that "the American concept of the jury trial contemplates a jury drawn from a fair cross-section of the community" (Taylor v. Louisiana, 419 U.S. 522, 527, 95 S. Ct. 692, 696 [1975]). "It should also be emphasized that in holding that petit juries must be drawn from a source fairly representative of the community we impose no requirement that petit juries actually chosen must mirror the community and reflect the various distinctive groups in the population. Defendants are not entitled to a jury of any particular composition" (p. 538).

31. An occasional bad decision, unlikely to be repeated, raises less alarm about the functioning of a decision-making system than does an existing or likely pattern of error. The Supreme Court, for example, uses its writ of certiorari to bring before itself legal questions of general significance for the legal system, questions which present themselves repeatedly for decision in the lower courts (see Supreme Court Rule 19). But only on extraordinary occasions does the Court intervene to correct mistakes by the discontinuous decision makers—juries—within the legal system.

32. We might also use a committee because, at the outset, we lack the knowledge required to make centralized, responsible decisions. In such cases,

we identify the problem, then use the committee to gather information and develop, through case-by-case decision making, the standard to be applied. Agencies such as medical experimentation committees are sometimes employed for these purposes. When a committee is proposed in this kind of situation, the issue is not whether it is the best form of decision maker to handle a tragic choice, but whether use of the agency is a suitable way to develop responsible standards. To the extent that we use decentralized decision-making agencies for this purpose, the requirement that they explain their results is essential and not a bit paradoxical. See G. Calabresi, "Reflections on Medical Experimentation in Humans," *Daedalus*, Spring 1969, pp. 387, 400–403.

That we do not require juries to give reasons for their decisions suggests that they are employed for some other purpose than that of information gathering and rule development.

33. See C. Fried, *An Anatomy of Values* (Cambridge, Mass.: Harvard University Press, 1970), pp. 207–36, commenting on G. Calabresi, "The Decision for Accidents: An Approach to Nonfault Allocation of Costs, *Harvard Law Review* 78 (1965): 713, 714.

34. Appellate decisions often transform the question to be decided from one involving human actors whose behavior has created the necessity to decide to an abstract proposition. The case of Gideon v. Wainwright (372 U.S. 335 [1963]), for example, is recalled as a decision about whether defendants in state courts have a constitutional right to the assistance of counsel, not a decision about the continued imprisonment of "a fifty-one-year-old . . . man who had been in and out of prisons much of his life. He had served time for four previous felonies. . . . He had never been a professional criminal or a man of violence; he just could not seem to settle down to work, and so he had made his way by gambling and occasional thefts" (A. Lewis, *Gideon's Trumpet* [New York: Random House, 1964], p. 5).

35. The affront to the community's sense of justice, fairness, or sanctity of life will result as surely from actions which are widely perceived as unjust, unfair, or against life, even if, upon analysis, the actions actually support those values, as from actions which are in fact contrary to such values. See G. Calabresi, *The Costs of Accidents* (New Haven, Conn.: Yale University Press, 1970), p. 294. See Chapter 2.

36. It is not surprising, for example, that the British Broadcasting Corporation, subject to institutionalized elite criticism, devotes more of its resources to the Third Program than would be justified by the number of people who listen to that program. An analogous situation occurs in programming for RAI-TV in Italy. In both cases, the elite critics are drawn from those very groups who form a disproportionately large part of the audience for the favored programs. Thus the likelihood that elite criticism will be unrepresentative carries with it the danger that it will be consciously used to benefit the elite. Consciously or unconsciously, the criticism by an elite will serve to restrict the decisions of the pararesponsible agency to those which serve either the purposes or the ideals of the elite. Attacks on the traditional system of elite criticism of legal decisions by courts, lawyers, and academics should put us on our guard against a too easy assumption that criticism by an elite will solve our problems. See, e.g., F. Rodell, *Woe Unto You, Lawyers* (New York: Reynal & Hitchcock, 1939), and F. Rodell, "Goodbye to Law Reviews," *Virginia Law Review* 23 (1937): 38.

37. See Chapter 2.

38. See, e.g., G. Gunther, "The Subtle Vices of the 'Passive Virtues': A Comment on Principle and Expediency in Judicial Review," *Columbia Law*

Review 64 (1964): 1; compare A. Bickel, *The Least Dangerous Branch: The Supreme Court at the Bar of Politics* (Indianapolis: Bobbs-Merrill, 1962), and J. Deutsch, "Neutrality, Legitimacy, and the Supreme Court: Some Intersections between Law and Political Science," *Stanford Law Review* 20 (1968): 169.

39. Bickel, in his Holmes Lectures, described as unprincipled only those judicial decisions which are so muddled or so self-contradictory that they could not be said to stand for anything. Such decisions were, in his view, pernicious because they could not be criticized on any of the grounds that the principle they expounded was incorrect, undesirable, or improper for a court to employ. Neither could they be criticized as being wrong in the specific case because facts are ephemeral and the critic could never be sure of the precise facts which faced the court when it made its unprincipled decision. Since such opinions are immune to standard forms of legal criticism, Bickel reasoned, they are dangerous and must be avoided. We are inclined to agree with him but only until the last step. Such opinions, since they cannot be criticized on other grounds, must at least be criticizable on the ground that they are unprincipled. This fact does not, however, mean that their use in some situations is unjustified. Indeed, precisely because they are so readily attacked as unprincipled, such decisions may represent a technique as passive as any of the "passive virtues" extolled by Bickel. When a court is working its way toward a new doctrine but does not yet know which of various competing principles will be appropriate, the opinion which does not stand for anything, if used sparingly, may be the least willful step the court can take. It may permit the court to test the water without imposing its will on later courts. In time, however, that, or some subsequent, court must either move on to an opinion which stands for something, and hence can be attacked and defended, or properly be made to retreat on the ground that the intermediate position was self-contradictory and unprincipled. See A. Bickel, *The Supreme Court and the Idea of Progress* (New York: Harper & Row, 1970), and A. Bickel, *The Least Dangerous Branch*.

40. Of course, some administrative agencies do make tragic choices. Some types of draft boards, during some periods of our history, have made just such decisions; see Chapter 6.

41. For example, we use fault language to evaluate claims for damages in automobile accidents, even though the structure of insurance rates indicates that the incidence of involvement in accidents is highly correlated with age, socioeconomic status, and, to a lesser extent, with race. Similar patterns in the characteristics of those convicted in the criminal law system raise like questions about our use of language of absolute worthiness to describe criminal guilt.

42. Before the Supreme Court's July 1976 decisions regarding the death penalty, we would have noted Furman v. Georgia, 408 U.S. 238 (1972), as an instance in which an absolute worthiness system was rejected because it was perceived that worthiness had little or nothing to do with the selection made. See earlier in this chapter. But *Furman's* condemnation of the death penalty system has not resulted in complete rejection of the system, even though in the 1976 cases the Court did invalidate for the first time a system of mandatory death penalties for certain crimes, apparently at least in part because the law did nothing to curb the unbridled discretion of the jury which the Court condemned in *Furman*. See Woodson v. North Carolina, 428 U.S. 280, 96 S.Ct. 2,978 (1976), and two companion cases, in which the Court refused to invalidate a new set of state death penalty laws which it described as more attentive than their pre-*Furman* predecessors to the assumptions of the worthiness system. (On the actual methods by which these statutes seek to guide and

control jury and court discretion, however, one should compare the Court's approving description of the Georgia statute in Gregg v. Georgia, 428 U.S. 153, 196–98, 96 S.Ct. 2,909, 2,936–37 (1976), with Professor Charles Black's account of the "grimly silly statute" approved in Jurek v. Texas, 428 U.S. 262, 96 S.Ct. 2,950 (1976) (C. Black, "Due Process for Death: Jurek v. Texas and Companion Cases," *Catholic University Law Review* 26 [1976]: 1).

Recognizing the stability of the death penalty system in our society (see Justice Potter Stewart's comment on new federal and state death penalty laws following *Furman*, 428 U.S. 153, 179–80, 96 S. Ct. 2,909, 2,928), the Court has given the states, through its decision in *Gregg* another opportunity to administer the death penalty without the randomness and invidious discrimination condemned in *Furman* and again in *Woodson*. Only experience with the operation of these new statutes will show whether guidelines for judges and juries such as those approved in *Jurek* can remove the unconstitutional elements of caprice and prejudice from the system. For our part, we expect that the problems of mistake and arbitrariness will be found to be, as Professor Black has argued, incurable characteristics of any death penalty system (C. Black, *Capital Punishment* [New York: Norton, 1974]; P. Bobbitt, book review, "Strategies of Abolition," *Yale Law Journal* 84 [1975]: 1,769; C. Black, "Due Process for Death").

43. See, e.g., Nixon, "Changing Rules of Liability in Automobile Accident Litigation," *Law and Contemporary Problems* 3 (1936): 476. See earlier this chapter and notes 5 and 6.

44. Indeed such questions arise even in some relatively nontragic areas, involving no allocation decisions, which have been traditionally assigned to aresponsible, representative agencies. The moves toward no-fault divorce and strict liability in automobile accidents, for example, are due in part to the questioning of whether the privacy and equal access costs are sufficiently great and the perfectibility premise sufficiently dubious to justify a move away from a perfectible, aresponsible agency to a simpler, if clearly imperfectible alternative. See Calabresi, "Access to Justice and Substantive Law Reform."

45. F. Duerenmatt, *The Visit* (New York: Grove Press, 1962).

46. Margaret Mead, "Research with Human Beings: A Model Derived from Anthropological Field Practice," *Daedalus*, Spring 1969, pp. 361, 371–74.

47. Rupert Brooke gave poetic expression to that when he wrote "The Soldier" (*The Collected Poems of Rupert Brooke* [New York: Dodd, Mead, 1915], p. 115).

Chapter 4

1. See G. Calabresi and D. Melamed, "Property Rules, Liability Rules, and Inalienability: One View of the Cathedral," *Harvard Law Review* 85 (1972): 1,089, for a discussion of entitlements.

Any change in which, after the change, no one is worse off than before and some are better off than before is called a move to a Pareto superior position. A position from which no moves to Pareto superior positions are possible, because after any move there will either be some who have lost, as a result of the change, or none who have gained, is called a Pareto optimal position. It is optimal in the sense that any change cannot be shown to be better with unanimous agreement. In traditional economic thought, compensation of losers by winners serves to establish Pareto superiority if the amount of compensation is accepted, voluntarily, as sufficient by the losers. Only then can the change be described as, in the end, involving no losers.

For a concise description of welfare maximization through the market, see F. Bator, "The Simple Analytics of Welfare Maximization," *American Economic Review* 47 (1957): 22, 33–36. The deficiencies which require modifications of the market structure are analyzed in F. Bator, "The Anatomy of Market Failure," *Quarterly Journal of Economics* 72 (1958): 351, 356–77.

2. See R. Coase, "The Problem of Social Cost," *Journal of Law and Economics* 3 (1960): 1, and G. Calabresi, "Transaction Costs, Resource Allocation and Liability Rules: A Comment," *Journal of Law and Economics* 11 (1968): 67. See also W. Nutter, "The Coase Theorem on Social Cost: A Footnote," *Journal of Law and Economics* 11 (1968): 503.

3. Liability rules may be defined as rules which establish initial entitlements and set objectively determined prices at which the entitlements may be purchased without the consent of the owner. The entitlement to be free of bodily injury unintentionally caused by another is an example of a liability rule, if the entitlement may be destroyed at a cost objectively determined by the state (G. Calabresi and D. Melamed, "Property Rules, Liability Rules, and Inalienability," pp. 1,089, 1,120).

Though he notes that transaction costs may occasionally require state intervention, George Stigler describes the Coase theorem as generally suggesting that the "manner in which the law assigns liability will not affect the relative private marginal costs of production," so that, in his example, it does not matter whether the liability rules make the rancher pay the farmer for crops destroyed by his cattle, or leave the farmer to pay the rancher to keep the cattle out of his crops (G. Stigler, *The Theory of Price*, 3d ed. [New York: Macmillan, 1966], pp. 110–14).

4. If one can assume costless markets in one's theories, one can assume as well costless, perfect nonmarket approaches. Under such a set of assumptions, either the market or the nonmarket approach would be as good as the other. In practice, then, the engaging question must be which in fact costs more to establish in a particular situation and who bears the cost under each of the two approaches.

5. But government intervention to achieve such an arrangement can only be justified according to the standard of potential Pareto superiority with tolerable distributional effects. Government intervention may establish the nonmarket allocation by direct coercion or by coercing some people to give up some of their wealth (through taxes) to pay for the government action in establishing the arrangement. In either case, the coerced move is not Pareto superior to inaction because those who are coerced are left worse off than they formerly were. Where we nonetheless regard such efficiency motivated intervention as a good thing, it is because we think that the gainers have gained more than the losers have lost, and that the redistribution from losers to gainers, if not desirable, is at least acceptable. For a theoretically interesting but practically unimportant exception involving voluntary contributions to government, see K. Wicksell, "A New Theory of Taxation," translated and reprinted in R. Musgrave and A. Peacock, *Classics in the Theory of Public Finance* (London and New York: Macmillan, 1958), pp. 87–97.

6. Under this arrangement, fertile couples determine for themselves the price at which they will surrender their entitlement to have children. In G. Calabresi and D. Melamed, "Property Rules, Liability Rules, and Inalienability" (pp. 1,089, 1,092), this is called a "property-rule" approach.

7. One of us has elsewhere termed this the "liability-rule" approach; see note 3, this chapter.

8. See G. Calabresi, "Transaction Costs, Resource Allocation, and Liability Rules," pp. 69–70.

9. We could attempt the costly process of estimation and internalization of the costs of the destruction of these basic social goals. But the very nature of the goals makes it most likely that the costs would be too great to be worth paying, even after we had borne the burden of identifying and estimating them.

10. There may be other reasons for preferring a collective first-order determination to an attempt to assign costs to various activities and then to allow market forces to determine first-order levels. One reason for such a preference is the tendency of cost-assignment techniques to slight those values and costs which are less easily monetizable than others; see L. Tribe, "Trial by Mathematics: Precision and Ritual in the Legal Process," *Harvard Law Review* 84 (1971): 1,329. This possibility leads us to expect that political decisions as to nonmonetizable costs and benefits are more likely to reflect our desires than market decisions. A second reason for choosing the political approach instead of market decisions is that the cost of evaluating the nonmonetizable costs and benefits and introducing them into the market may not be worth the benefits that market judgments would bring; see G. Calabresi, *The Costs of Accidents* (New Haven, Conn.: Yale University Press, 1970), pp. 98–99.

11. In the terminology of *The Costs of Accidents*, method (a) is that form of specific deterrence which most closely approaches general deterrence, and method (b) is that form of general deterrence which most closely approaches specific deterrence (pp. 68–69). In method (a), the collective decision as to how much of the activity—bearing of children—will be allowed may be coupled with a market system or some other allocation method which takes individual desires into account in allocating the available supply. Method (b) in contrast, allows individual desires to determine the quantity of the activity after costs have been assigned—a general deterrence approach—but the assignment of costs to the activity will reflect collective judgments about the acceptable range of the resulting first-order determination; see Chapter 2.

12. Such problems arise when the actual distribution of the collectively determined quantity becomes apparent, and some people realize that the collective first-order decision has so limited the scarce good that they will receive none of it. For example, Justice Potter Stewart understood that a collectively determined rule against prior censorship could become, in a specific case, a "judicial sentencing to death" of a certain and known number of people, even though those lives were not assigned a cost when the rule was adopted; see Chapter 2.

13. E.g., R. Musgrave, *The Theory of Public Finance* (New York: McGraw-Hill, 1959), pp. 13–14; and J. Tobin, "On Limiting the Domain of Inequality," *Journal of Law and Economics* 13 (1970): 263.

14. For a good to be a merit good it is not necessary that all unequal distributions of the good be regarded as objectionable. Rather, it is enough that it be objectionable—i.e., that sufficient external costs be created—if that good is allocated according to the prevailing distribution of wealth.

15. See Chapter 6.

16. If merit goods are distributed on some nonmarket basis (or through a wealth-neutral market) because of precautionary concerns about choices made under conditions of poverty, it means that even those who would be able to choose well in the face of poverty will be deprived of the choice. A compulsory

retirement pension plan, for example, will penalize those who would choose well for themselves regarding provision for retirement. But the variety of capacities to choose well under adverse conditions means that any system of allocation which allows some people to maximize with respect to their choosing capacity will deny others the opportunity to do so. A fully laissez-faire market arrangement allows only those who truly know best for themselves under all conditions to maximize. Again, the test being applied is a potential Pareto standard, not a pure Pareto standard.

17. The future cost is uncertain because of the uncertainty about everyone else's future wealth.

18. If the futures market in child rights were too expensive, a distribution in kind (e.g., through a voucher system) might be made independently of the wealth distribution. This would assure that, whatever the wealth distribution, child rights (or other merit goods) would be possessed by all people. The costliness of the futures market, however, is not a justification for prohibiting the sale of the vouchers once they are distributed; such a prohibition can only be justified on the precautionary- and externality-based grounds already discussed.

19. See, e.g., "Muskie Calls for Changes in Unfair Draft System," *New York Times*, February 18, 1969, p. 4; M. R. Killingsworth, "Topics: Civilian Service Instead of the Draft," *New York Times*, February 15, 1969, p. 28; and "James Donovan Urges That Women Be Drafted," *New York Times*, February 23, 1969, p. 41.

The use of markets in time to allocate merit goods is examined in D. Nichols, E. Smolensky, and T. N. Tideman, "Discrimination by Waiting Time in Merit Goods," *American Economic Review* 61 (1971): 312. The authors note that goods allocated by charging time (in the form of waiting in queues) rather than money will generally end up distributed quite differently than would the same goods if distributed in an ordinary money market. They suggest that public subsidy objectives can be accomplished efficiently by selling merit goods as a variety of time-money pairings, allowing those with a relatively high marginal value of their time to purchase the good quickly, for money, while others spend more time and less money to secure the good. Of course, if only a market in time exists, those with a high marginal value of time will be able to hire others to stand in line for them. But where, as in the compulsory military service context, such substitution is prohibited because it is objectionable on noneconomic grounds (see Chapter 6), formal provision of a variety of time-money pairings is important. In the example in the text, the various public service options would reflect a range of time-risk pairings, rather than time-money pairings, but the effect is analogous. Those with a relatively high marginal value of time would pay more, in terms of risk incurred during public service, in order to secure the good being allocated, completion of the obligation of service.

20. The opportunity costs of time vary widely among persons. If higher opportunity costs of time are correlated with higher wealth levels, then the market in time charges higher prices to those in higher wealth categories—a form of wealth-neutral market. But it is a rough form of wealth neutrality. To some people, time is precious not because it is readily convertible into money or wealth, but because of other aims and activities. To someone suffering from a terminal illness, for example, a high subjective value on time (hence relatively higher prices in the time market) is unrelated to wealth.

21. In the union territory of Delhi, the Indian administration gave priority

in allotment of subsidized housing to bachelors, newly marrieds, and persons with fewer than three children, another example of a nonmoney market (The Population Council, "India," in *Country Profiles* [May 1976], p. 43). In the vote-denial proposal in the text, however, the penalty for "excess" procreation falls directly on parents, and not on the children, while exclusion from public housing penalizes children as well as parents. A plan something like the no-vote plan in the text was put forward by the Indian government in April 1976 when it proposed that representation in the lower house of Parliament and in the state legislatures be frozen as determined by the 1971 census (ibid, p. 45). Of course deprivation or reduction of political power may reduce publicly allocated resources available to children in large families (or, in the Indian proposal, to children in regions or states with above average population growth rates). This indirect effect only points up the difficulty of finding any market-type incentive system which affects parents but not their children.

22. But see note 21, this chapter.

23. With nonmoney markets, and what serves to legitimate them, compare jury systems which draw their legitimacy less from their defensive posture— the capacity to avoid conflict between the wish to recognize differences and the desire to affirm egalitarianism (which cannot be stated without undermining the capacity)—than from their affirmative and openly acknowledged advantages in finding facts and evaluating witnesses; see Chapter 3.

24. The effect of using the mixed time-money market might be to allow children to an ascetic who loves to waste time and doesn't really care much for children, and to deny them to a time-conscious hedonist who adores having lots of goods, including children. This inability of even modified markets to test relative desire presents a problem for wealth-neutral markets as well as mixed time-money markets; see below, this chapter.

25. These responsibly determined social preferences might even be embodied in laws enforced by courts.

26. See the discussion in Chapter 6 of the approach to the allocation of hemodialysis followed in Italy.

27. The Boulding Plan is described in Chapter 2, note 1. Boulding apparently realized that one of the problems with his proposal was its wealth dependence. He wrote, "Perhaps the ideal situation would be found when the price was naturally zero, in which case those who wanted children would have them without extra cost. If the price were very high the system would probably have to be supplemented by some sort of grants to enable the deserving but impecunious to have children, while cutting off the desires of the less deserving through taxation (K. Boulding, *The Meaning of the Twentietn Century* [New York: Harper & Row, 1964], p. 136). Boulding's ideal situation will occur only waen individual decisions about childbearing produce a total number of children just equal to the number determined collectively to be desirable. In such a situation, however, there would be no need for Boulding's plan.

28. Insurance rate categories present a similar pattern: rate categories can be broad enough to spread risks over a suitably large group of people, because of our limited statistical knowledge of future risks, but narrow enough to allow charges which reflect major differences in each individual riskiness. If we knew enough about future risks (which probably amounts to saying, if we knew exactly what would happen in the future), each category would include only one person, and insurance would only be a form of saving. In the wealth-neutral market in child rights, there must be categories broad enough to create an

effective market, but narrow enough to satisfy the egalitarian aspirations which motivated the design of the market in the first place.

29. In the wealth-neutral market for child rights (see above), for example, we assumed that absent wealth differences, every category (though not every individual in each category) would place the same value on having children.

30. Under the Yale plan, a student may defer payment of part of his or her educational expenses; payments on the amount deferred are then made semiannually over a period of up to thirty-five years beginning with the year after the student's education at Yale is completed. The amount to be paid each year is computed by applying a percentage, determined by the amount of tuition deferred, to a repayment base calculated by reference to gross income. The participant's obligation to pay continues until payments by all members of the group to which the participant is assigned equal the total amount deferred by the group, plus compound interest, or until the participant has repaid 150 percent of his or her original deferred amount plus compound interest. If any participant defaults, other members of the participant's group must pay more than otherwise would be necessary to discharge the group's obligation.

31. See Chapter 1.

32. Of course, there will be instances in which the first-order determination is inflexible, whatever the costs of the resulting second-order solutions. While complete inflexibility is unlikely, it is likely that resistance to first-order alterations on account of second-order considerations will increase as the deviations from the optimal first-order level increase. The costs of not inducting enough men into the army during wartime, for example, means that the range of flexibility below the optimum number of men under arms is limited.

33. These problems can be subsumed under the economist's familiar term *external costs,* for they arise because some benefits and costs cannot readily be made to influence the decisions taking place within the market. But we will avoid the term in discussing some of the problems of wealth-neutral markets, for the term is associated with too many, too different kinds of problems to be of much use to us here.

34. See Chapters 2 and 4.

35. To pose another example, are we prepared to say that we are indifferent among the family with two children, the family with any number of children, and the intentionally childless family, so long as a wealth-neutral price is paid for each child? Many of our students seem offended by a family of fifteen, even if the average number of children in society satisfies population aims; other people hold to the view that a childless marriage is somehow immoral, again regardless of general population levels and growth. It may well be that these attitudes became part of socially taught values because they were at first closely linked to control of population growth, but now either have been divorced from their original aim and taken on a life of their own or have not yet been undermined by changing conditions.

36. We will have more to say about this problem when we discuss markets in risks later in this chapter.

37. Even if the society can agree on an initial use of the market either in money or in wealth-neutral exchange, to effect an allocation, these problems may still arise. It is one thing to say, "Society can afford only so many children, and a wealth-neutral market is the best way to measure desire for the children." But it is quite another to incorporate still more discriminating social preferences into the scheme in money terms, e.g., even if we can recognize a societal

preference for childbearing between ages twenty-two and thirty-five, could we make the price of any child gotten after age thirty-five higher by exactly 20 percent?

38. See, e.g., L. Tribe, "Trial by Mathematics: Precision and Ritual in the Legal Process," pp. 1,329, 1,360, 1,361–65, and G. Calabresi, *The Costs of Accidents*, pp. 97–100, 216.

39. For example, present childbearing incentives arguably place the greatest disincentives to childbearing on the middle classes. If this is so, and if one believed in a eugenic policy with favored procreation by the rich (on the theory that those who are wealthy—successful—are likely to have a good gene pool) and the poor (on the theory that their oppression by the conditions of poverty makes it impossible to know the quality of their gene pool), then one could support the present system of childbearing incentives. Beyond our general lack of affection for eugenic policies, we find this one to be particularly fanciful.

40. Professor Richard Posner made this point in his review of *The Costs of Accidents*, where he wrote that

> [T]he unwillingness of contemporary economists to ascribe an automatic increase in total welfare to any redistribution of income from a wealthier to a poorer person stems not from rejection of the assumption of diminishing marginal utility of income, but from recognition that the interpersonal comparison of utility is arbitrary. If a wealthier person's marginal utility curve happens to be higher than the poorer person's . . . a redistribution of income from the wealthier to the poorer may actually diminish total utility (R. Posner, "Review of *The Costs of Accidents*," *University of Chicago Law Review* 37 [1970]: 636, 643).

41. This is not a Pareto but a potential Pareto optimality approach (see this chapter, above) and assumes that interpersonal comparisons of gains and losses are possible. Interpersonal comparisons would be unnecessary only if everyone were better off choosing for themselves, or if the losers actually were compensated—both conditions clearly impossible in the general case.

42. We do not include as a problem the fact that a wealth-neutral market is Pareto inferior, because it is not clear that it is inferior. Obviously, the rich person who would have to pay heavily for the tragic resource may try to induce a poor man to buy it cheaply and then resell it to the rich man at a profit, leaving both of them better off than they would have been under the wealth-neutral scheme. While this suggests that the wealth-neutral approach, like all nonpure market approaches, involves enforcement costs to protect the system from the pure market, it does not mean that the approach fails the Pareto test, even if the test were the relevant one; see above in this chapter. If the pure market creates external costs, in terms of moralisms, and if the wealth-neutral market is adopted to avoid those costs, it is impossible to say whether the wealth-neutral market which avoids such costs is Pareto superior or inferior to the pure market. And this is true even if the wealth-neutral market has externalities, such as enforcement costs, of its own.

43. See above in this chapter.

44. Markets which have emerged without self-conscious design do not call attention so directly to the pricing of scarce resources which is taking place. An example is the market in childbearing in America; see Chapters 2 and 6. Because the wealth-neutral market is necessarily self-conscious, the choice

between the tragic resource and the goods which must be given up to purchase it is likely to be obvious and destructive.

45. One of us has elsewhere had occasion to discuss this costing problem which makes any value for certain goods impossible to state; see G. Calabresi, *The Costs of Accidents,* pp. 55–58.

46. Indeed, even our choices about the places in which we will live and work entail predictably greater or smaller risks of death. In 1975, the murder rate in the United States was 9.6 murders per 100,000 population. In metropolitan areas, the rate was 11 per 100,000, while in cities outside of metropolitan regions the rate was only 6 per 100,000 (FBI, *Crime in the United States,* [Washington, D.C.: U.S. Government Printing Office, 1975].

47. M. Friedman and L. J. Savage, "The Utility Analysis of Choices Involving Risk," *Journal of Political Economy* 56 (1948): 279, 280, 283–87.

The differences in valuing human life, however, are not simply a function of the erratic workings of individuals' marginal utilities of money; for the variation in the value given to life in different risk contexts is very different from the variation in value given to other goods in similar risk contexts. Nor can one find an adequate explanation for this phenomenon in the notion that the value of life varies with one's wealth (i.e., that the income elasticity of life differs from that of other goods). Both diminishing marginal utility of money and income elasticity of life may well play some role in determining the gambling value we give to life in different risk situations. They do not suffice, however, and we are inclined to conclude that the value humans give to life depends directly on the perceived chance of losing it.

48. The idea of tying oneself to the mast in a period of relative calm, in an attempt to forestall choices which might later appear attractive but which one wishes, on the larger view, to avoid, underlies the usefulness of a written constitution. Merit wants which arise out of precautionary concerns for oneself are another instance in which one may make present arrangements with the aim of foreclosing some future choices which one fears one will make badly; see above in this chapter.

49. Unlike the second-order decisions about childbearing in America, which are rarely perceived as market choices in which choosers respond to various incentives, the decisions in the risk market would be seen as decisions in a consciously created market; see Chapter 2.

50. The demand for intelligibility is often less when one is uncertain as to what is at stake. Policyholders rarely inquire about the exact details of their insurance coverage until their need for indemnity becomes certain. Especially for remote contingencies, knowledge that one is insured for *x* amount against the calamity will generally be satisfactory.

51. Differences in relevant knowledge also present a problem in using a first-come-first-served allocation system; see Chapter 2.

52. If people choose badly about future risks because of their present poverty, then a wealth-neutral market for the risk-resource package will avert bad choices (see above, in this chapter). But to the extent that people choose future risk-resource packages ineptly, that is, in a way they later regret, not because of their present poverty but simply because of the immediacy of the present, the wealth-neutral market is no solution.

53. See G. Calabresi, *The Costs of Accidents,* p. 59, suggesting that one justification for compulsory insurance against injuries can be found in society's inclination to take care of those injured whether or not they are insured.

54. Note that we are talking here about a right to bear children, not a right to adopt a child. A black market in adoption rights is all too possible.

55. See Chapter 6, note 92. The market can affect nominally nonmarket allocations in other, indirect, ways. E.g., under the present system of hemodialysis treatment in the United States, public funds pay the cost of kidney treatment for those who need it. But the uneven dispersal of treatment centers imposes greater costs (transportation, income forgone) on those farther from the center. The Comptroller General found that the farther one lives from chronic dialysis facilities, the less chance one has of being treated (United States General Accounting Office, *Treatment of Chronic Kidney Failure: Dialysis, Transplant, Costs, and the Need for More Vigorous Efforts*. Report to the Congress by the Comptroller General of the United States [1975], pp. ii, 18).

56. See Chapter 6.

57. If we prohibit the re-entry of those who leave the country to secure some tragic good which they cannot acquire in this country (or to avoid some tragic bad), it reflects a collective judgment that those who are more patriotic should be denied the good. Similarly, if we prohibit expatriation of funds to pay for the tragic good abroad, we make a collective decision that only those dishonest enough to sneak the money out of the country will be allowed to have the good. Neither of these approaches was used to control the availability of foreign abortions. But when men left the United States to avoid wartime service during the Vietnam War, we did prohibit re-entry, at least for a time.

58. Except in cases like migration to a neutral land in order to avoid wartime service at home, the emigrant, after all, does not take one of the resources limited by the first-order decision. And he must forgo what, elsewhere, it costs to produce one more of the resource, which necessarily reduces the inegalitarianism perceived in the emigration. Still, if we decide not to make the allocation of the resource through a market, but instead, for example, through a collective first-order decision followed by a lottery, there exists the obvious inequality of having given the wealthy a second chance for the resource since the emigrant can purchase it abroad; this would reflect an inegalitarianism we seem prepared to tolerate around the fringes of allocation systems for tragic goods.

59. The market incentives used to induce volunteers need not be simply monetary. A more complex market arrangement such as special training or duty station options is certainly a practical possibility, and may have the added "advantage" of obscuring the exact nature of the allocation system being used to distribute wartime military service.

60. An allocation system is unlikely to survive for long if it serves no other purposes than giving effect to values we cannot acknowledge openly. The jury, for example, a representative aresponsible decision maker which gives no reasons for its decisions, does give effect to what society views as relevant differences among individuals while avoiding the conflict between the wish to recognize differences and the desire to affirm egalitarianism. But the jury also appears to be a superior fact-finding and credibility judging body, and so serves a value which society can acknowledge openly; see Chapter 3.

61. See, e.g., R. Semple, "Nixon Asks Draft Lottery with 19-Year-Olds First," *New York Times*, May 14, 1969, p. 1; W. Turner, "Criticism and Evasion of Draft Grow with Unpopularity of Vietnam War," *New York Times*, May 14, 1969, p. 20; and "Yale Head Scores Inequities of Draft," *New York Times*, February 29, 1969, p. 27.

62. R. Stevens, *American Medicine and the Public Interest* (New Haven, Conn.: Yale University Press, 1971) pp. 417–26.

63. Rosemary Stevens describes the extent of the private medical system in Great Britain in *Medical Practice in Modern England* (New Haven, Conn.: Yale University Press, 1966), pp. 206–11.

Chapter 5

1. For example, imagine two people, one in need of tragic good *A* and the other in need of tragic good *B*. If the production of *A* for the first person necessarily means that no *B* can be produced, then a decision to concentrate societal resources on producing *A* operates as a second-order allocation between the one in need of *A* and the one in need of *B*. But if no one notices that the latter individual has been denied the *B* he needs, then the decision to produce enough *A* to fill the needs of the former individual will be perceived as life-validating.

2. Though the expense of saving a single, downed balloonist (see Chapter 1) is great, the infrequency of the occasion makes this a relatively economical way of reaffirming our commitment to life. Charles Fried cites the example of a mining enterprise willing to spend vast sums in rescuing a few trapped miners but unwilling to spend proportionately smaller sums to save many lives through better safety precautions (C. Fried, *An Anatomy of Values* [Cambridge, Mass.: Harvard University Press, 1970], p. 207).

3. Charles Fried has examined the effect on resource allocation attributable to "the importance that rational persons would ascribe to the actual circumstances surrounding their death" (C. Fried, "The Value of Life," *Harvard Law Review* 82 [1969]: 1,415, 1,433). Fried argues that allocation of resources to avoid deaths attended by great suffering is a rational response to painful forms of mortal illness, and points out that the alleviation of suffering may be life-affirming (prevention or cure) or life-negating (euthanasia) (ibid, pp. 1,433–34).

4. It has been noted that the certain death which follows end-stage renal disease makes the ordinary disability provisions of the Social Security Amendments (which require 2½ years disability before eligibility for benefits) useless to those with renal failure, and that this fact supports a program for early and direct special assistance to those with kidney diseases (Institute of Medicine, *Disease by Disease toward National Health Insurance? Report of a Panel: Implications of a Categorical Catastrophic Disease Approach to National Health Insurance* [Washington, D.C.: National Academy of Sciences, 1973], p. 3).

5. See Chapter 4.

6. See Chapter 3, note 29; Chapter 6 and note 111 in that chapter.

7. In a pure market, by definition, the first-order decision is determined by second-order decisions; alterations in the latter do not bring about collective intervention. We suggested earlier that the current system of allocating childbearing in the United States, though it gives the appearance of being a market, would not survive a change in second-order decisions which significantly altered the number of children being born. See Chapter 2.

8. See Chapters 3 and 4.

9. A study committee of the Institute of Medicine, for example, has noted that the 1972 extension of the Social Security program to cover expenses of

hemodialysis raises the question of why coverage should not be extended to other catastrophic diseases such as hemophilia and end-stage heart disease. The committee points out that the available health-care resources would be totally absorbed before very many more major categories were added to the health-insurance scheme, and regrets that the first step toward this categorical approach was ever taken in 1972 (*Disease by Disease toward National Health Insurance?*).

10. We do not assert, of course, that the only way in which previously stable second-order criteria become insupportable, so that changes in the allocation of resources occur, is through the ability of disfavored individuals to dramatize their own cases. The ways in which such changes occur merit independent study; see Chapter 7.

Chapter 6

1. One who sets out to fashion public policy to minimize tragedy must realize that his own value system has little to do with which choices and outcomes are tragic to the society and which are not. Instead, the values accepted by society define the constraints within which the policy maker operates. We should distinguish sharply the position of the critic of social values, who objects bitterly to an allocation which his society finds quite acceptable. The task of the critic is to persuade the other members of his society to conform their values to his own, all the time remembering that until they do so, the choice which he finds so objectionable will not pose a tragic dilemma which requires his society to abandon any fundamental values. See also Chapter 1.

2. Though we use the term *good* throughout this discussion, it is worth pointing out that any grant of a scarce good for which there is competition entails a deprivation (a bad) for those who do not receive the good. Each tragic choice allocates both goods and bads; the difference is that some choices focus primarily on the allocation of the good in question, e.g., kidney treatment machines, while others focus on distribution of the bad, e.g., wartime military service.

3. See Chapter 5.

4. For example, to take race openly into account in the criminal process would produce outraged reactions. If we nonetheless think that under some circumstances race must be a consideration in jury selection if defendants of minority races are to receive fair trials, our criminal justice procedures must incorporate such considerations inexplicitly. One proposal for accomplishing this purpose suggested drawing so narrowly the boundaries of the vicinage from which the jury is selected that the segregation of present population distributions produces juries on which members of the race of local defendants are disproportionately high. Because the racial considerations involved are not made explicit and constantly reiterated during the use of the system, the approach would not spawn negative racial attitudes beyond those which made it necessary; moreover, when the latter attitudes fade, the vicinage itself is likely to have changed and no longer to reflect racial segregation. Thus the approach has inherent in it the means of its elimination when it is no longer needed; see Note, "The Case for Black Juries," *Yale Law Journal* 79 (1970): 531.

5. The traditional exclusion of prior criminal records in criminal trials and of prior accident records in torts actions are but two examples.

6. See Chapter 4.

7. Though resort to such approaches represents a failure to identify variables which can be studied to define values and inform decisions, the use of the approaches does affirm certain values. Just as entrail reading affirmed dependence on the gods, the use of a lottery symbolizes utter equality among those eligible for the lottery.

8. See the discussion of process costs at the beginning of Chapter 5.

9. One might object that such a rule would deprive infertile couples of the opportunity to have children, and therefore would not be colorless. But the same technology which makes cloning possible will make bisexual cloning possible as well, so that the problem of the infertile couple would be moot.

10. As of 1970, at least twenty-six states had eugenic sterilization laws, twenty-three of which made sterilization compulsory. "All of the various laws designate[d] feeble-minded or mentally retarded persons as within their ambit, all but two include[d] the mentally ill, some fourteen include[d] epileptics and twelve specifically include[d] criminals—most on eugenic grounds, not on punitive grounds" (D. Meyers, *The Human Body and the Law* [Chicago: Aldine, 1970, p. 28]). The constitutionality of such statutes has been challenged repeatedly, but with success only where the statute failed to provide notice and hearing (Wyatt v. Aderholt, 368 F. Supp. 1,382[M.D. Ala. 1973] or discriminated invidiously in the designation of those to be sterilized (Skinner v. Oklahoma, 316 U.S. 535[1942]); see Meyers, pp. 28–34. Compulsory sterilization laws which avoid these deficiencies have been held constitutional, Buck v. Bell, 274 U.S. 200 (1927); In re Cavitt, 183 Neb. 243 (1968), appeal dismissed *sub nom.* Cavitt v. Nebraska, 396 U.S. 996 (1970).

The scientific basis for compulsory eugenic sterilization has been often and severely criticized. After surveying the state of knowledge about genetics, Harry Kalven, for example, concluded that "there is simply no scientific warrant for a view that criminality is hereditary" and that "the scientific basis for such [sterilization of mentally deficient and epileptic persons] has evaporated" (H. Kalven, "A Special Corner of Civil Liberties: A Legal View I," *New York University Law Review* 31 [1956]: 1,223, 1,232). Evidence contrary to the thesis that epilepsy and mental disorders are inheritable is summarized in E. Z. Ferster, "Eliminating the Unfit—Is Sterilization the Answer?" *Ohio State University Law Journal* 27 (1966): 591, 602–4.

11. E.g., J. Rawls, *A Theory of Justice* (Cambridge, Mass.: Harvard University Press, 1971), and R. Nozick, *Anarchy, State, and Utopia* (New York: Basic Books, 1974).

12. R. P. Friedman, "United States Compulsory Service Systems," in *Compulsory Service Systems*, ed. R. P. Friedman and C. Leistner (Columbia, Mo.: Artcraft Press, 1968), p. 9.

13. G. Walton, *Let's End the Draft Mess* (New York: McKay, 1967), p. 20.

14. R. P. Friedman, p. 9.

15. W. Millis, *Arms and Men: A Study in American Military History* (New York: Putnam, 1956), p. 35, n. 12, pp. 42–46.

16. R. P. Friedman, pp. 10–11.

17. 12 Stat. 597 (July 17, 1862).

18. This account of the Civil War draft in the North is taken from C. Lindsay, "Our National Tradition of Conscription: Experience with the Draft," in *Why the Draft? The Case for the Volunteer Army*, ed. James C. Miller, III (Baltimore: Penguin, 1968), pp. 124–37.

19. R. P. Friedman, p. 12.

20. Ibid., pp. 12–13; E. Murdock, *Patriotism Limited: 1862–65* (Kent, Ohio: Kent State University Press, 1967), pp. 20–21.

21. 12 Stat. 731 (March 3, 1863); E. Murdock, p. 21; R. P. Friedman, p. 13.

By fixing a lower price for exemption than that prevailing in the market for substitutes, the law reduced the seller's surplus which substitutes received. The more recent system of low military wages coupled with conscription of the majority of army personnel decreased, in much the same way, the seller's surplus realized by volunteers.

22. R. P. Friedman, p. 13.

23. 13 Stat. 6 (February 24, 1864).

24. But see L. Hershey, *Outline of Historical Background of Selective Service* (Washington, D.C.: U.S. Government Printing Office, 1952), p. 5.

25. E. Murdock, *One Million Men: The Civil War Draft in the North* (Madison, Wis.: State Historical Society of Wisconsin, 1971), p. 356.

26. G. Walton, p. 19.

27. G. Walton, p. 18, citing D. Lockmiller, *Enoch H. Crowder, Soldier, Lawyer, Statesman*, vol. 27, University of Missouri Studies (Columbia, Mo., 1955).

28. Act of May 18, 1917, 40 Stat. 76 (May 18, 1917).

29. G. Walton, pp. 24–26; L. Hershey, pp. 7–8, 31; R. P. Friedman, p. 17; see 56 *Cong. Rec.* 4,069–70, 4,265–73 (1918).

30. R. P. Friedman, pp. 18–19.

31. Selective Training and Service Act of 1940, 54 Stat. 885 (September 16, 1940).

32. Service Extension Act of 1941, 55 Stat. 626 (August 18, 1941).

33. 55 Stat. 799 (December 13, 1941).

34. A. Blum, *Drafted or Deferred: Practices Past and Present* (Ann Arbor, Mich.: University of Michigan School of Business Administration, 1967), pp. 97–101; R. P. Friedman, p. 20.

35. 62 Stat. 604 (June 24, 1948).

36. R. P. Friedman, p. 21.

37. The following description of the post-1948 system is based on United States National Advisory Commission on Selective Service, *In Pursuit of Equity: Who Serves When Not All Serve* (Washington, D.C.: U.S. Government Printing Office, 1967), pp. 17–29; United States Selective Service System, *Annual Report of the Director to the Congress* (Washington, D.C.: U.S. Government Printing Office, 1967), pp. 3–33. On legal problems raised by appeals within the draft system, see United States Selective Service System, *Legal Aspects of Selective Service* (Washington, D.C.: U.S. Government Printing Office, 1969); and D. Bradford, *Deferment Policy in Selective Service* (Princeton, N.J.: Department of Economics, Princeton University, 1969).

38. M. Laird, *Report to the President: Progress in Ending the Draft and Achieving the All-Volunteer Force* (Washington, D.C.: Government Printing Office, 1972), p. 2.

39. Pub. L. No. 91–124, 83 Stat. 220 (November 26, 1969), repealed the provision of the Military Selective Service Act of 1967 which denied to the President authority to alter the rules governing the order of call-ups. On November 28, 1969, in Proclamation No. 3,945, 34 Fed. Reg. 19,017, President Nixon established a new system of call by lot and one-year eligibility.

40. Exec. Order 11,360 (June 30, 1967), in 32 Fed. Reg. 9,787 (July 4, 1967).

41. Exec. Order 11,527 (April 23, 1970), in 35 Fed. Reg. 6,571 (April 24, 1970).

42. Pub. L. No. 92–129, 85 Stat. 348 (September 28, 1971).

43. M. Laird, p. 11.

44. Ibid., p. 8.

45. Whether or not people with flat feet in fact make bad soldiers is beside the point, for it is societal views which will determine the standards for these second-order decisions. And the exemption of conscientious objectors rests on neither demonstration nor popular perception that conscientious objectors make bad soldiers, but upon the willingness to respect individual choice based on conviction of conscience.

46. It is not clear what grounds supported and justified the exclusion of women from military service, or at least from eligibility for conscription. Several possible grounds have been given: an attitude that held that war was too brutal an enterprise to force women to confront firsthand; a perception that women would make bad soldiers (a view voiced recently in the debate over the admission of women to the United States Military Academy); a belief that women held domestic jobs important to the fabric of society, from which they should not be removed; fear that women soldiers, if captured, would be raped by the enemy; or perhaps a fairness notion that because of their traditional social status, which in practice excluded them from, or restricted their access to, certain desirable occupations, they should be excused from the burden of wartime service (see Chapter 2, note 10). Whatever the explanation, it is clear that the exclusion of women from eligibility for conscription created no conflict in widely held values in the United States during the Vietnam War. Statements such as Donovan's calling for drafting of women (see Chapter 4, note 19) were rare indeed, and for the society as a whole, the exclusion of women was not a tragic choice (see note 1, this chapter).

47. In some instances, the minimal standards for volunteers have been higher than those for draftees. This has usually occurred when volunteers have been allowed to enlist for longer terms than those of conscripts in order to qualify for special training or service rather than being drafted into the general army. In such situations, considerations of social efficiency led to the use of more desirable opportunities to induce longer service than that exacted of conscripts. This contrasts with the more usual situation in which the standards for volunteers are lower than those for draftees, indicating that social efficiency considerations tend to give way in the face of individual desire to serve.

48. Population trends and policies in developed countries are discussed in *Population Policy in Developed Countries*, ed. B. Berelson (New York: McGraw-Hill, 1974). On the United States, see pp. 731–59 (article by C. Westoff).

49. The population density of the Netherlands is approximately 1,000 people per square mile, of Japan approximately 700 per square mile, and of the United States, approximately 58 per square mile (F. Pollara, "Trends in U.S. Population," in *The American Population Debate*, ed. D. Callahan [Garden City, N.Y.: Doubleday, 1971], p. 59). For accounts of population policies and underlying motivations, see P. van Pragg and L. Lohle-Tart, "The Netherlands," and M. Muramatsu and T. Kuroda, "Japan," in Berelson, pp. 294–318, 704–30.

50. The population policies of Israel are discussed in D. Friedlander, "Israel," in Berelson, pp. 52–69.

51. Berelson, p. 771.

52. C. Westoff, "United States," in Berelson, pp. 734–35.

53. *Journals of the American Congress*, vol. 4, Ordinance of May 20, 1785, p. 5,207.

54. On the development of American land policy, see generally, P. Gates, *History of Public Land Law Development* (Washington, D.C.: U.S. Government Printing Office, 1968); and P. Brown and E. Corfman, "Moral-Political Values: An Historical Analysis," in *Population Policy and Ethics: The American Experience*, ed. R. M. Veatch (New York: Irvington, 1977). On the Ordinance of 1785, see Gates, pp. 59–74.

55. 5 Stat. 453 (September 4, 1841). For a description of the policies underlying the provision for prospective pre-emption in the 1841 Act, see P. Gates, pp. 236–40. The history of the earlier, more limited pre-emption acts in 1830 and 1838, as well as an account of the congressional debate surrounding enactment of the 1841 measure, is contained in R. Robbins, *Our Landed Heritage* (Princeton, N.J.: Princeton University Press, 1942), pp. 72–91.

56. 12 Stat. 392 (May 20, 1862).

57. P. Gates, pp. 390–93. R. Robbins recounts the campaign for a land law which would allow settlement of public lands in the West without payment for the land, a movement which began in the 1840s under the inspiration of Horace Greeley and others (pp. 99–116, 178–82, and 206–07).

58. C. Westoff, p. 735.

59. 18 Stat. 477 (March 3, 1875).

60. The statute provided for the exclusion of all immigrant Chinese laborers for a period of ten years (Act of May 6, 1882, 22 Stat. 58). This prohibition was extended for another decade (Act of May 3, 1892, 27 Stat. 24 [1892]), and then another (Act of April 29, 1902, 32 Stat. 176 [1902]). In 1882, the first general United States immigration law was enacted. "It began the policy of collecting a head tax from all immigrants. . . . The law also began the practice of exclusion of undesirables, such as lunatics, idiots, convicts, and those likely to become public charges" (C. Wittke, "Immigration Policy Prior to World War I," in *Immigration and the United States*, ed. P. Tyler [New York: Wilson, 1956], p. 28). See 22 Stat. 214 (1882), described in F. Cavanaugh, *Immigration Restriction* (Washington, D.C.: Catholic University, 1928), pp. 4–5. These qualitative restrictions on immigration were continued in the Immigration Act of 1917 (39 Stat. 874).

61. P. Brown and E. Corfman.

62. This development, beginning with the Quota Law of 1921 (42 Stat. 5 [1921]) and continuing with the Immigration Act of 1924 (43 Stat. 153 [1924]) is described in W. Bernard, *American Immigration Policy: A Reappraisal* (New York: Harper, 1950), pp. 23–34. The 1921 Act used the ethnic composition of the American population in 1910 as the basis for calculating immigration quotas; the 1924 measure, even more "flagrantly discriminatory" (Bernard), used the year 1890 as the base year. In 1927, under the terms of the 1924 Act, the population composition as of 1920 became the basis for quota calculations. The McCarran-Walter Act of 1952 (Pub. L. No. 414, 66 Stat. 163) continued the quota system, augmenting it with alternative criteria for admission of immigrants such as the possession of needed skills or the need for asylum.

63. The Immigration and Nationality Act of 1965 (Pub. L. No. 89–236, 79 Stat. 911) established criteria of admission defined by possession of needed skills, relationship to a citizen, refugee status, and former residence in the Western Hemisphere. The favored qualification, relationship to a present citizen, continues in a more subtle form the system of quotas based on a nationality's past representation in the total population.

64. The roots of these preferences in racism and religious intolerance are analyzed in *Immigration as a Factor in American History*, ed. O. Handlin (Englewood Cliffs, N.J.: Prentice-Hall, 1959), pp. 167–85.

65. H. Gutman, *The Black Family in Slavery and Freedom, 1750–1925* (New York: Pantheon, 1976); D. Moynihan, *The Negro Family: The Case for National Action* (Washington, D.C.: U.S. Government Printing Office, 1965).

66. F. Bancroft, *Slave Trading in the Old South* (New York: Unger, 1959), pp. 2, 4, 8–12; P. Durgnan and C. Clendenen, *The United States and the African Slave Trade, 1619–1862* (Stanford, Calif.: Hoover Institution, 1963), pp. 1,3. According to United States Bureau of the Census, *Historical Statistics of the United States* (Washington, D.C.: U.S. Government Printing Office, 1960), p. 756, the population of Negroes in Virginia was 187,605 in 1770, and 220,582 in 1780. It also reports that the estimated Negro population in South Carolina in 1700 was 2,444; it had grown to 57,334 in 1760, and by 1770, it was 75,178.

67. 2 Stat. 426 (March 2, 1807).

68. The slave population of the United States increased almost sixfold between 1790 and 1860 (United States Bureau of the Census, *Historical Statistics*, p. 9). This source reports a total of 3,953,760 slaves in 1860. F. Bancroft, pp. 67–87.

69. See J. Noonan, "Unintended Consequences: Laws Indirectly Affecting Population Growth in the United States," in *Aspects of Population Growth Policy*, ed. R. Parke, for the United States Commission on Population Growth and the American Future, vol. 6 (Washington, D.C.: U.S. Government Printing Office, 1972), pp. 111–51.

70. See Chapter 2.

71. The demographic statistics in this paragraph are from C. Westoff, p. 733.

72. The statistics in this paragraph are from F. Pollara, pp. 64–65.

73. The first line of criticism is usually grounded on the adverse effects which critics expect that an increasing U.S. population will have on the environment of this country and the world; see, e.g., L. A. Mayer, "U.S. Population Growth: Would Fewer Be Better?" in *The American Population Debate*, ed. D. Callahan, pp. 7–8, 16–17; P. Ehrlich and J. P. Holdren, "Population and Environment," in D. Callahan, pp. 21–30; and W. H. Davis, "Overpopulated America," in D. Callahan, pp. 161–67. The second set of arguments underlies the suggestion that incentives for the poor to procreate should be reduced; see note 74.

74. See R. Elliott et al., "U.S. Population Growth and Family Planning: A Review of the Literature," in D. Callahan, pp. 205–07, 209.

75. A number of proposals are summarized, ibid., p. 206.

76. For example, the Boulding Plan described in Chapter 2, note 1.

77. For example, Joseph J. Spengler suggests rewarding small families financially by increasing their Social Security pensions, but acknowledges that "the arrangements cannot succeed unless the means to control family size are widely available and very cheap in relation to the incomes of the masses" ("Population Problem: In Search of a Solution," *Science* 166 [1969]: 1,234, 1,238, quoted in R. Elliott et al., p. 207). Spengler's plan can claim a rough sort of neutrality, for those who exceed the qualifying limit for pensions can look to their children for support (A. J. Dyck, "Population Policies and Ethical Acceptability," in D. Callahan, p. 356).

78. See Chapter 4.

79. Reports in June 1973 that two young black girls were sterilized through a federally funded family planning program in Montgomery, Alabama, without their consent or the consent of their parents, led to a lawsuit (Relf v. Weinberger, 372 F. Supp. 1,196 [D.D.C. 1973]), and provoked a continuing con-

troversy over the use of welfare programs to prevent procreation by individuals viewed by some as unworthy. Patricia Donovan discusses the debate, and subsequent litigation over the question, in "Sterilizing the Poor and Incompetent," *Hastings Center Report* 6 (1976): 7–8. A recent report of charges that three thousand four hundred American Indians, mostly women, had been indiscriminately sterilized in a three-year period, indicates that such "worthiness" decisions are likely to remain a problem, at least in the near future ("Alleged Sterilization of Indians Denied," *New York Times*, November 24, 1976, p. 12).

80. "India State Is Leader in Forced Sterilization," *New York Times*, August 13, 1976, section A, p. 8, describes the law as enacted. Subsequently, during a national parliamentary election, the central government acted to have such bills set aside; see *New Haven Register*, February 28, 1977, p. 17 (Associated Press article by Paul Chutkow).

81. The statements in this section of the text at times represent first-hand knowledge of the society being described. Authority for most of them could readily be found, but since we feel that such citations would be misleading as to the actual source of the information, they are omitted.

82. See, e.g., Article 3, of the section entitled "Fundamental Principles" in *La Costituzione Italiana* (Florence: Vito Majorica Press, 1971), p. 39. In M. Cappelletti, J. H. Merryman, and J. Perillo, *The Italian Legal System* (Stanford, Calif.: Stanford University Press, 1967), p. 282, this Article is translated as

All citizens have equal social standing and are equal before the law, without distinction of sex, race, language, religion, political opinion, or social and personal conditions.

It shall be the task of the Republic to remove obstacles of an economic or social nature that, by restricting in practice the freedom and equality of citizens, impede the full development of the human personality and the effective participation of all workers in the political, economic, and social organization of the country.

83. See, e.g., M. Cappelletti, J. H. Merryman, and J. Perillo, p. 41. See also J. H. Merryman, *The Civil Law Tradition* (Stanford, Calif.: Stanford University Press, 1969), chap. III.

84. See, e.g., Article 34 of *La Costituzione Italiana* (translated in M. Cappelletti, J. H. Merryman, and J. Perillo, p. 288) and note 14 thereto, indicating its application to higher education and suggesting requirement of state financial assistance to needy students.

85. See, J. H. Merryman, *The Civil Law Tradition*, pp. 71–72.

86. Slightly different social situations call forth very different responses. Thus, in Florence, payment of the fare on buses is almost universal even though there is no ticket taker (tickets are issued by a machine). The fine, of 1,000 Lire, imposed if a person is found without a stamped ticket, is strictly financial and seems to entail no record. Inspectors are so rare that on narrow economic grounds failure to pay the 50 Lire fare would seem the appropriate course. Yet the presence of other passengers, who can see if one has failed to pay and can disapprove, creates exactly the opposite result from the tax situation where cheating can be secret and hence is assumed to occur.

87 See, *I Codici Penali*, ed. G. Lattanzi (Milan: Giuffrè, 1963). Some of the relevant articles of the code are collected (in translation) in J. Michael and H. Wechsler, *Criminal Law and Its Administration* (Chicago: Foundation Press, 1940), pp. 1,298–1,303. See also, e.g., R. Pannain, *Diritto Penale* (Torino: Unione Tipografico, 1962), vol. 1, pp. 421–517.

88. Much of the data in this section was derived from interviews by G. Calabresi with doctors who ran dialysis centers in Italy. The two most detailed interviews were with Professor S. Giovanetti of Pisa, held on June 20, 1973, and Professor Alfredo Costantini of Florence, held on July 4, 1973.

An interesting theoretical discussion of how the problem ought to be approached in Italy is given by F. Mantovani in *I Trapianti e la Sperimentazione Umana* (Padova: Cedam, 1974), pp. 731–51, which relies heavily on American discussions of the issue.

89. This was stated explicitly by Professor Giovanetti, who described people whom he was treating on a first-come-first-served basis even though they were suffering from untreatable cancers. He noted that this had been true even during the early experimental phase, but that perhaps then some attention had been paid to the experimental utility of treating the patient. Professor Costantini suggested that in practice some distinctions were made on the basis of efficiency where the case was clear enough. To admit that such a choice was made, however, would bring down on you the "[Cabinet] Minister, Mayor and [Parliamentary] Deputy."

Mantovani is more ambiguous; he rejects all "social utilitarian" considerations and urges a strict application of a "principle of equality." He does, however, state that purely medical criteria might meet the requirements of the "principle of equality." He quickly becomes troubled by the fact that medical criteria are correlated with socioeconomic status. To correct for these would violate simple, austere egalitarianism, yet not to correct for them would discriminate against disadvantaged groups. Accordingly, he reaches no conclusion; see F. Mantovani, *I Trapianti,* pp. 731–51.

90. Both Costantini and Giovanetti did note, however, that they always had made room for patients suffering from acute renal failure who might be expected to be completely cured after use of the artificial kidney; they both admitted that this was inconsistent with the fundamental no-choice approach. Both expressed their general preference for the "principle of humane nonchoice even if, as a result, lives were lost," and even if the effect of never saying no, but merely sending the patient to another center where there was room but inadequate facilities was, in Giovanetti's words, "somewhat hypocritical." Nevertheless, use of conscious criteria, as they stated occurred in England, would be worse.

91. Constantini said that early on he had tried to set up a committee, "Priests, etc.," but "they wouldn't do it." See also F. Mantovani, *I Trapianti,* pp. 749–50.

92. Remarks like, "I can say 'no room' on the telephone, but not in person," and "What is one to do if a very wealthy family offers to build you several additional dialysis units," suggest the tension between austerely egalitarian guidelines and a responsibility in making the allocations.

93. Giovanetti said that, in 1973, there "probably" were adequate facilities in the North, though not in the South. He added that the demand was less there, originally because of lack of knowledge. He added that television had greatly increased knowledge of the availability of treatment, but that no government funds had been spent on publicizing "dialysis for everyone who needs it." If this was "hypocrisy," it was "clearly unconscious."

The March 1973 issue of ANED, the bulletin of the Association of Dialysis Users, graphically shows the difference between the number of dialysis places in the North and in the South on a population percentage basis. It notes that (as of December 31, 1972) both the general scarcity of places and the worsening of the situation as one moves from North to South is evident; see ANED (Associazione Nazionale Emodializzati), *Foglio Informativo dell' Associazione,* March 1973. It also confirms Giovannetti's statement that many patients moved or traveled great distances in order to obtain dialysis. Mantovani, writing in 1974, asserts that it was clearly the case, as of that date, that the total number of dialysis units in Italy was inadequate; see F. Mantovani, *I Trapianti,* pp. 731–32.

94. Both Costantini and Giovanetti insisted on this point; both also said that, though there was some criticism from the left, the poor received as good treatment as the rich, once they came to the treatment center. Giovanetti noted that lack of knowledge, plus the need to move, did result in some "unconscious" financial bias, but this was bias at the periphery not at the treatment center. He mentioned an unemployed Sicilian laborer, who had moved to Pisa and was being treated, as an example of what was beginning to happen as knowledge became more widespread. Still the role of knowledge, wealth, geographical location, and (for doctors less scrupulous than Giovanetti) personal preferences as informal criteria appeared obvious to the interviewer.

Costantini contrasted the Italian approach with the rigid system, he said, existed in England. He mentioned the case of an English black laborer who was denied dialysis in England "not because he was black, but because he was a laborer," and hence not a proper recipient under the guidelines of the particular English hospital since laborers (as a group) did not do well on dialysis. The laborer's physician (also black) felt bound to exclude him, but had telephoned Costantini in Italy to see if he could fit him in somewhere. Costantini said he had found the man a place at a treatment center elsewhere in Italy and, as far as he knew, the man was still alive.

95. A letter from the Economic Adviser's Office of the Department of Health and Social Security to Guido Calabresi states, "Insofar as the general question of selection of Candidates is concerned I have ascertained within the Department that the method used is that of 'clinical judgement'—which I'm afraid doesn't really tell you very much!" (letter from Gavin Mooney, dated 5 June 1973, on file, Yale University Law Library). See also, e.g., M. A. Wilson's suggestion that the doctors should select hemodialysis patients on the basis of expected therapeutic success (Wilson, "Doctor's Duty to His Patient," *British Medical Journal,* no. 5,540 [March 11, 1967], p. 624; and interview with Costantini cited in note 94).

96. D. N. S. Kerr, "Regular Hemodialysis," *Royal Society of Medicine Proceedings* 60 (1967): 1,195, 1,199.

97. In estimating the costs of a national system of hemodialysis care, Kerr did not include the costs for treating those under the age of fifteen or over the age of fifty-four (ibid., pp. 1,195–96).

Professor Giovannetti asserted that the assumption that children would not be successful hemodialysis recipients is contrary to the experience in Italy. He noted that, though some special facilities were necessary, results were as favorable among children as among adults. Professor Giovannetti also noted that favorable results were obtained in treating the elderly. He specifically denied that these empirical observations of similar effectiveness in people of different ages were the reason for the unwillingness of Italians to draw the eligibility distinctions which he said the English made. Rather, the initial unwillingness to use such distinctions because of a simple egalitarianism described above gave rise to the data supporting the expectation of equal effectiveness in patients of all ages; see interview with Professor Giovannetti, cited in note 88.

98. Rules of exclusion applied to potential hemodialysis recipients at various American kidney treatment centers are described in Note, "Scarce Medical Resources," *Columbia Law Review* 69 (1969): 620, 639–54. The excluding factors include age, treatment requirements, psychological stability, and medical indications of benefit from treatment. See also Note, "Patient Selection for Artificial and Transplanted Organs," *Harvard Law Reivew* 82 (1969): 1,322, 1,324–27.

99. On the use of the Giovannetti diet as a screening device, see D. N. S. Kerr, "Regular Hemodialysis," p. 1,199. See also letter from Gavin Mooney, cited in note 95. It is difficult to substantiate the allegation of exclusion of laborers; Professor Costantini described such exclusions in comparing the Italian and English systems; see note 94.

100. It would not be an exaggeration to say that Professor Giovannetti found the English system, as he perceived it, to be shocking in its (to him) open inegalitarianism (interview with Professor Giovannetti, note 88).

101. E.g., Kerr recounts the treatment history of a "disastrous failure" on dialysis—a patient who "was badly selected, lacking the intelligence or will power to adhere to any strict diet, and without the intellectual resources to benefit from such prolongation of life as she has 'enjoyed' " (D. N. S. Kerr, "Regular Hemodialysis," p. 1,198). Kerr indicates that such candidates have for the most part been screened out of the hemodialysis program, but does not consider the implications of the fact that conventional measures of intelligence and intellectual resources tend to be highly correlated with personal and family wealth, see, e.g., S. Herr, "Civil Rights, Uncivil Asylums, and the Retarded," *University of Cincinnati Law Review* 43 (1974): 679, 701, and sources cited therein.

102. See F. Mantovani, *I Trapianti*, pp. 744 ff., who, in the context of transplants, discusses the possibility that such a mechanistic approach, if applied with enough impartiality, may satisfy what he calls the "principle of equality." In order to achieve such impartiality, he would rely on computers. Leaving aside the fact that computers will give answers determined by the information fed into them, a fact which Mantovani does not discuss, the approach nevertheless troubles him because strictly medical factors correlate with socioeconomic ones (ibid., p. 748).

103. Individual desire to live is recognized as important to treatment success, but it is not taken into account except indirectly by conditioning treatment on adherence to a difficult and unpleasant diet (D. N. S. Kerr, pp. 1,196, 1,199).

104. See letter from Gavin Mooney, cited in note 95. Under the approach which, for a long time, prevailed in England, but which has long since been dismantled, a student's future educational opportunities were determined on the basis of a battery of tests administered at age eleven. The eleven-plus system, with its three-tier school structure, is described and criticisms of the system are discussed in Central Advisory Council for Education (England), *Children and Their Primary Schools*, vol. 1 (London: Her Majesty's Stationery Office, 1967), pp. 153–57.

105. This concern with the treatment of "disfavored groups" is evident in Rawls's formulation of the principle of acceptable distributional inequality (J. Rawls, *A Theory of Justice* [Cambridge, Mass.: Harvard University Press, 1971]). Rawls's principle applies nicely to a society within which can be identified a number of discrete groups, of not too great size, defined by particular socioeconomic, racial, and ethnic criteria as "least favored," whose betterment can justify those inequalities necessary to accomplish it. The fact that concern

focuses on such particular groups, e.g., blacks, poorly educated rural families, makes plausible the notion that the sacrifices demanded of the more favored in order to raise these least favored would be accepted behind Rawls's "veil of ignorance"; but if the least favored were more broadly defined, the sacrifices needed to better their lot would lead to virtual equality among all and, if incentives are important, to a very low total social product. The impact of a principle, for example, which allows only those differences among people which make the poor better off than they would be in a situation in which everyone was treated precisely the same depends upon who is poor and in what terms their poverty is measured. Consider the disfavored group consisting of those who will be killed by collisions with trucks, and cannot be made better off except by returning to that point at which all are equally safe from such "poverty." To take another example, what inequalities are compatible with bettering the lot of the disfavored group consisting of those who will die of cancer? It is arguable that these two groups are the truly least favored in our society. An accurate statement of the distributional principle Rawls actually puts forward should account for these implicit judgments about which disfavored groups will receive special consideration, and how much.

106. For example, a sizable foundation grant allowed Dr. Belding Scribner and his associates to convert the pioneering Seattle dialysis unit from an experimental program with four patients to a treatment clinic with more extensive facilities. During the experimental phase, no special efforts were made to select patients fairly. But the prospect of expanding and regular treatment facilities led the doctors to propose establishment of a lay screening committee to make allocation decisions; see S. Alexander, "They Decide Who Lives, Who Dies," *Life*, November 9, 1962, p. 102.

107. "Anyone who becomes involved in such a [hemodialysis] program soon learns that, aside from the problems of technique, the difficulties are . . . to a large extent social and ethical in nature. How much money should be diverted by society into an expensive procedure that can only deal with a very small fraction of the potentially suitable patients? Which patients should be given the chance and by what criteria should they be chosen?" (Editorial, "Moral Problems in the Use of Borrowed Organs, Artificial and Transplant," *Annals of Internal Medicine* 60 [1964]: 309, 310). The same author comments that while those involved were still lost in the "rosy haze of technological innovation and publicity prone dramas," the first discussions of these social and ethical issues appeared in the popular press. See also F. Mantovani, *I Trapianti*, pp. 731–51.

108. The use of first-come-first-served systems at several kidney treatment centers in the United States is reported in Note, "Scarce Medical Resources," pp. 620, 659–60.

109. One commentator suggested using a rule of eligibility "setting a minimum increase in survival probability which will allow all who fall above the minimum to be treated." But he was forced to admit that experience had shown that it is extremely difficult to predict which patients will be successful recipients of hemodialysis treatment (ibid., pp. 620, 655–56). The same observation is made in D. Sanders and J. Dukeminier, "Medical Advance and Legal Lag: Hemodialysis and Kidney Transplantation," *U.C.L.A. Law Review* 15 (1968): 357, 369.

110. Dr. Belding Scribner of the Seattle kidney treatment center described the need for a decision-making body independent of the medical staff "to represent the community and assure that choices are made objectively and

without outside pressure" (*Newsweek,* June 11, 1962, p. 92). Leach notes that the use of a lay committee spreads the burden of choosing, though he thinks it is a mistake to take the responsibility from the doctors (G. Leach, *The Biocrats* [New York: McGraw-Hill, 1970]).

111. The Admissions and Policies Committee of the Seattle Artificial Kidney Center was created in 1961, as part of the original organization of the Center. Its seven members were chosen to represent all segments of the community in choosing from among those identified by medical experts as suitable candidates for hemodialysis. In selecting those to receive treatment, the Committee established some rules—only residents of Washington state would be eligible, for example—but considered a wide range of factors in an unstructured attempt to choose the best candidates for treatment. These factors included age, sex, marital status, and number of dependents, income, net worth, psychological stability, and past performance and future potential. The Committee worked anonymously; it did not publish any reasons for its choices, though its selections did reveal a pattern of preferences. An account of the Committee's organization and early operation may be found in *Life,* November 9, 1962, p. 102, and in J. W. Haviland, "Experiences in Establishing a Community Artificial Kidney Center," *Transactions of the American Climatological and Clinical Association* 77 (1965): 125, 131–34.

112. Criticism of the selection and application of criteria by the Seattle committee are made in Sanders and Dukeminier, pp. 377–78, which concludes that accounts of committee deliberations "paint a disturbing picture of the bourgeoisie saving the bourgeoisie. . . . This rules out creative nonconformists, who rub the bourgeoisie the wrong way. . . . The Pacific Northwest is no place for a Henry David Thoreau with bad kidneys." Paul Freund also criticizes the Seattle selection procedure, arguing that "in a matter of choosing for life or death, not involving specific wrong doing, no one should assume the responsibility of judging comparative worthiness to live on the basis of unfocused criteria of virtue or social worthiness" (P. Freund, "Introduction, Ethical Aspects of Experimentation with Human Subjects," *Daedalus,* Spring 1969, pp. viii, xiii).

Another critic, Professor Al Katz, arguing for selection of recipients of hemodialysis by lot rather than by a committee applying standards such as those used in Seattle, wrote, "The consequence of the decision is critical to human life, there is . . . a real temptation to value one human life more than another. . . . There is no morally acceptable basis for making judgments of relative desert" (A. Katz, "Process Design for Selection of Hemodialysis and Organ Transplant Recipients," *Buffalo Law Review* 22 [1973]: 373, 402–03).

Internal stress rather than external criticism, however, may have been the direct cause of the demise of the committee. As the technology of kidney treatment improved enough to ease the standards of medical eligibility, more weight in selection was placed on the social and personal factors in selecting patients. Under this increased pressure, the Admissions Committee was unable to function effectively. "The members were slow to take any action and fraught with guilt. In most of the cases they eventually asked the doctors which of the patients they thought would have the best chance of performing well under treatment. In the summer of 1967 the lay panel was discontinued" (Note, "Scarce Medical Resources," pp. 661–62).

113. See J. Katz and A. M. Capron, *Catastrophic Diseases: Who Decides What* (New York: Russell Sage Foundation, 1975), pp. 59–71, 191–96. In their view obvious socioeconomic factors would be eliminated through prior publica-

tion of basic medical criteria. Thus, "socioeconomic considerations would not enter into selection of patients except to the extent (probably inevitable, even if small) that they contaminate the medical criteria in some *disguised* form" (pp. 191–95; emphasis added).

Based on interviews at a number of kidney treatment centers, one observer noted that the medical standards applied to exclude applicants from eligibility for treatment varied in relation to the availability of treatment facilities, and did not appear to reflect any fixed standard of therapeutic eligibility ("Scarce Medical Resources," pp. 649, 654). The author of the study recognized that "the role of exclusion rules does vary with scarcity and this suggests that rules of exclusion are being used for more" than the exclusion of a group clearly unfit for treatment under any conditions. The author nonetheless apparently assumed that there existed some such group of ineligibles, to which treatment would not be extended even were resources unlimited, and recommends ways to improve the use of rules of exclusion to identify that group and that group alone. Primary, though not exclusive, reliance would be placed on the rule of exclusion for medical contraindications, determined by doctors. Those who are not excluded would be equally eligible for treatment; the author recommends a first-come-first-served system (modified by limited exceptions for preferential cases) to select recipients from among this group (pp. 654–56, 662–66).

114. Edmond Cahn made this suggestion in discussing the proper course of action for those in an overloaded lifeboat—the case of United States v. Holmes, 26 Fed. Cas. 360 (C.C.E.D.Pa. 1842), in which the court suggested that those to be cast overboard should have been selected by lot (E. Cahn, *The Moral Decision* [Bloomington, Ind.: Indiana University Press, 1955], p. 71. Paul Ramsey rejects Cahn's conclusion, arguing that the equality of opportunity afforded by the lottery makes it a morally acceptable way of preserving more lives than Cahn's approach promises to save (P. Ramsey, *The Patient as Person: Explorations in Medical Ethics* [New Haven, Conn.: Yale University Press, 1970], pp. 259–66). At least one hospital board adopted the all-or-none approach, not in preference to a lottery but when it appeared that dialysis would have to be allotted on the basis of ability to pay ("Scarce Medical Resources," p. 653).

115. Professor Al Katz suggests the use of a lottery to select hemodialysis recipients from a pool previously limited by the application of all acceptable criteria of selection. These criteria were intended to measure "good therapeutic prognosis" (Katz, pp. 404, 415). But even if it were possible to apply all of these criteria fairly, and even if good therapeutic prognosis were not inextricably linked with socioeconomic status, the problem in the text would remain, for the lottery would signal clearly the inability to provide hemodialysis to all of those whose condition promised to respond well to treatment. J. Katz and A. M. Capron argue that such visibility "may not be a bad result," as it might lead to "'total' treatment for a particular disease" (*Catastrophic Diseases*, p. 195). Their suggestion that unwarranted resources could be kept from such high-visibility diseases through earlier decisions is unconvincing, however, especially if the high visibility is the result of a subsequent need to employ a lottery.

116. Cahn's all-or-none proposal has a decided utilitarian cast, which Cahn apparently did not recognize. In what other terms can one explain the necessity for all to give their lives to uphold values from which we, but not they, will thereafter benefit? Compare Robert Burt's argument that legally consented

psychosurgery should be denied to prisoners because, though the benefit to the individual prisoner might be great, the potential harm to fundamental human values is far greater. He concludes that on balance the prisoner must be required to forgo personal gain through such surgery for the benefit of the rest of us (R. Burt, "Why We Should Keep Prisoners from the Doctors," *Hastings Center Report* 5 [1975]: 25).

117. The pure market approach was, of course, also available and yet its rejection was virtually complete in this area (see J. Katz and A. M. Capron, *Catastrophic Diseases,* pp. 178–96). We had been willing as a society—as we are willing today—to allow those who require extraordinary medical treatment to simply pay for it without our confronting any of the dilemmas that kidney allocations presented. Indeed, in the case of such exotic treatments, we have allowed the market to work not so much because it was thought to test individual desire as because it seemed to free the individual physician and the hospital from having to make difficult second-order decisions and, at the same time, clouded the precise outlines of the first-order determination. The situation of kidney allocations was not, however, amenable to this approach.

It was, in fact, scarcely considered, so obvious were the anticipated criticisms based on existing wealth distribution. Why, however, were there virtually no attempts to introduce a wealth-neutral market? Undoubtedly because there were other shortcomings to a market approach, some even more troublesome in the case of a wealth-neutral market, which the clinching criticism based on wealth distribution made it unnecessary to consider.

First there was substantial doubt whether differences in desire to live were sufficient to make individual desire an important goal for allocations. Second, assuming such differences, it was unclear whether the market, even the wealth-neutral market, could register these distinctions; there was concern that desperation bidding would occur. Third, a market approach would complicate introduction of genuine societal goals like the relative chance that the transplanted kidney would take. Finally, the conscious establishment of a wealth-netural market would emphasize the costing of lives and the first-order decision which brought it about. This can only bring disillusion and invites, in optimistic societies such as our own, a restless despair. The wealth-neutral market is simply too self-conscious to act in successful subterfuge, as does the natural market.

118. A report of a study committee appointed by the Institute of Medicine recommended against a categorical approach to catastrophic diseases, which identifies individual diseases for particular attention and funding, e.g., the extension of Medicare to cover the costs of hemodialysis, effected through the Social Security Amendments of 1972. The study committee recognized that "since resource constraints are operative, equity questions emerge, particularly since the categorical approach for assistance to a small and discrete portion of the patient population may drain resources that could be used to assist larger segments of the population. The justice issue centers on the realization that patients with a certain specific disease condition requiring expensive treatment will be provided access to the health-care system, whereas many patients including those with equally serious conditions will be denied that opportunity" (Institute of Medicine, *Disease by Disease toward National Insurance? Report of a Panel: Implications of a Categorical Catastrophic Disease Approach to National Health Insurance* [Washington, D.C.: National Academy of Sciences, 1973], p. 6).

BIBLIOGRAPHY

Adamson v. California. 332 U.S. 46, (1947).

Alexander, Shana. "They Decide Who Lives, Who Dies." *Life*, November 9, 1962.

ANED (Associazione Nazionale Emodializzati). *Foglio Informativo dell'Associazione*, March 1973.

Aristotle. *On Poetry and Style*. Trans. G. M. A. Grube. Indianapolis: Bobbs-Merrill, 1958.

Arrowsmith, W. "The Criticism of Greek Tragedy." In *Tragedy: Vision and Form*. Ed. W. Corrigan. San Francisco: Chandler Publishing, 1965.

Austin, J. L. "A Plea for Excuses." In *Philosophical Papers*. Ed. J. O. Urmson and G. Warnock. London: Oxford University Press, 1961.

Bancroft, F. *Slave Trading in the Old South*. New York: Ungar, 1959.

Bator, F. "The Anatomy of Market Failure." *Quarterly Journal of Economics* 72 (1958).

———. "The Simple Analytics of Welfare Maximization." *American Economic Review* 47 (1957).

Beecher, H. K. "Scarce Resources and Medical Advancement." *Daedalus*, Spring 1969.

Berelson, B., ed. *Population Policy in Developed Countries*. New York: McGraw-Hill, 1974.

Bernard, W. *American Immigration Policy: A Reappraisal*. New York: Harper, 1950.

Bickel, A. *The Least Dangerous Branch: The Supreme Court at the Bar of Politics*. Indianapolis: Bobbs-Merrill, 1962.

———. *The Supreme Court and the Idea of Progress*. New York: Harper & Row, 1970.

Black, C. *Capital Punishment*. New York: Norton, 1974.

———. "Due Process for Death: Jurek v. Texas and Companion Cases." *Catholic University Law Review* 26 (1976).

Blum, A. *Drafted or Deferred: Practices Past and Present*. Ann Arbor, Mich.: University of Michigan School of Business Administration, 1967.

Bobbitt, Philip. "Strategies of Abolition." *Yale Law Journal* 84 (1975).

Boulding, Kenneth. *The Meaning of the Twentieth Century*. New York: Harper & Row, 1964.

Bradford, D. *Deferment Policy in Selective Service*. Princeton, N.J.: Department of Economics, Princeton University, 1969.

Brooke, R. "The Soldier." *The Collected Poems of Rupert Brooke*. New York: Dodd, Mead, 1915.

Brooks, C. "Introduction." In *Tragic Themes in Western Literature*. Ed. C. Brooks. New Haven, Conn.: Yale University Press, 1955.

Brown, P., and Corfman, E. "Moral-Political Values: An Historical Analysis." In *Population Policy and Ethics: The American Experience*. Ed. R. M. Veatch. New York: Irvington, 1977.

Buck v. Bell. 274 U.S. 200 (1927).

Burke, Edmund. *Reflections of the Revolution in France*. Oxford, 1907.

Burt, Robert. "Why We Should Keep Prisoners from the Doctors." *Hastings Center Report* 5 (1975).

Cahn, E. *The Moral Decision*. Bloomington, Ind.: Indiana University Press, 1955.

Calabresi, G. "Access to Justice and Substantive Law Reform: Legal Aid for the Lower Middle Class." In *Emerging Perspectives and Issues in the "Access-to-Justice" Movement*. Ed. M. Cappelletti. Vol. 3, Florence Access-to-Justice Project Series. Dobbs Ferry, N.Y.: Oceana, 1978.

———. *The Costs of Accidents*. New Haven, Conn.: Yale University Press, 1970.

———. "The Decision for Accidents: An Approach to Nonfault Allocation of Costs." *Harvard Law Review* 78 (1965).

———. "Reflections on Medical Experimentation in Humans." *Daedalus*, Spring 1969.

———. "Transaction Costs, Resource Allocation, and Liability Rules: A Comment." *Journal of Law and Economics* 11 (1968).

Calabresi, G., and Melamed, D. "Property Rules, Liability Rules, and Inalienability: One View of the Cathedral." *Harvard Law Review* 85 (1972).

Callahan, D., ed. *The American Population Debate*. Garden City, N.Y.: Doubleday, 1971.

Cappelletti, M., ed. *Emerging Perspectives and Issues in the "Access-to-Justice" Movement*. Vol. 3, Florence Access-to-Justice Project Series. Dobbs Ferry, New York: Oceana, 1978.

Cappelletti, M.; Merryman, J. H.; and Perillo, J. *The Italian Legal System*. Stanford: Stanford University Press, 1967.

Cavanaugh, F. *Immigration Restriction*, Washington, D.C.: Catholic University, 1928.

Cavitt v. Nebraska. 396 U.S. 996 (1970).

Central Advisory Council for Education (England). *Children and Their Primary Schools*. Vol. 1. London: Her Majesty's Stationery Office, 1967.

Chutkow, Paul. Associated Press article. In *New Haven Register,* February 28, 1977, p. 17.

Coase, R. "The Problem of Social Cost." *Journal of Law and Economics* 3 (1960).

Costantini, A. Interview with G. Calabresi, July 4, 1973.

Costituzione Italiana. Florence: Vito Majorica Press, 1971.

Davis, W. H. "Overpopulated America." In *The American Population Debate.* Ed. D. Callahan. Garden City, N.Y.: Doubleday, 1971.

Deutsch, J. "Neutrality, Legitimacy, and the Supreme Court: Some Intersections between Law and Political Science." *Stanford Law Review 20 (1968).*

Donovan, Patricia. "Sterilizing the Poor and Incompetent." *Hastings Center Report* 6 (1976).

Duerenmatt, F. *The Visit.* N.Y.: Grove Press, 1962.

Duncan v. Louisiana. 391 U.S. 145 (1968).

Durgnan, P., and Clendenen, C. *The United States and the African Slave Trade, 1619–1862.* Stanford, Calif.: Hoover Institution, 1963.

Dyck, A. J. "Population Policies and Ethical Acceptances." In *The American Population Debate.* Ed. D. Callahan. Garden City, N.Y.: Doubleday, 1971.

Ehrlich, P., and Holdren, J. P. "Population and Environment." In *The American Population Debate.* Ed., D. Callahan. Garden City, N.Y.: Doubleday, 1971.

Elliott, R., et al. "U.S. Population Growth and Family Planning: A Review of the Literature." In *The American Population Debate.* Ed. D. Callahan. Garden City, N.Y.: Doubleday, 1971.

Euripides. *Bacchae. The Complete Greek Tragedies, Euripides V.* Ed. D. Grene and R. Lattimore. Chicago and London: University of Chicago Press, 1955.

Euripides. *Hippolytus. The Complete Greek Tragedies, Euripides I.* Ed. D. Grene and R. Lattimore. Chicago and London: University of Chicago Press, 1955.

FBI. *Crime in the United States.* Washington, D.C.: U.S. Government Printing Office, 1975.

Ferster, E. Z. "Eliminating the Unfit: Is Sterilization the Answer?" *Ohio State University Law Journal* 27 (1966).

Freund, P. "Introduction, Ethical Aspects of Experimentation with Human Subjects." *Daedalus,* Spring 1969.

Fried, C. *An Anatomy of Values.* Cambridge, Mass.: Harvard University Press, 1970.

———. "The Value of Life." *Harvard Law Review* 82 (1969).

Friedlander, P. "Israel." In *Population Policy in Developed Countries.* Ed. B. Berelson. New York: McGraw-Hill, 1974.

Friedman, Milton, and Savage, L. J. "The Utility Analysis of Choices Involving Risk." *Journal of Political Economy* 56 (1948).

Friedman, R. P. "United States Compulsory Service Systems." In

Compulsory Service Systems. Ed. R. P. Friedman and C. Leistner. Columbia, Mo.: Artcraft Press, 1968.

Furman v. Georgia. 408 U.S. 238 (1972).

Gates, P. *History of Public Land Law Development.* Washington, D.C.: U.S. Government Printing Office, 1968.

Gideon v. Wainwright. 372 U.S. 335 (1963).

Giovanetti, S. Interview with G. Calabresi, June 20, 1973.

Gregg v. Georgia. 428 U.S. 153 (1976).

Gunther, G. "The Subtle Vices of the 'Passive Virtues': A Comment on Principle and Expediency in Judicial Review." *Columbia Law Review* 64 (1964).

Gutman, H. *The Black Family in Slavery and Freedom.* New York: Pantheon, 1976.

Handlin, O., ed. *Immigration as a Factor in American History.* Englewood Cliffs, N.J.: Prentice-Hall, 1959.

Haviland, J. W. "Experiences in Establishing a Community Artificial Kidney Center." *Transactions of the American Climatological and Clinical Association* 77 (1965).

Herr, S. "Civil Rights, Uncivil Asylums, and the Retarded." *University of Cincinnati Law Review* 43 (1974).

Hershey, L. *Outline of Historical Background of Selective Service.* Washington, D.C.: U.S. Government Printing Office, 1952.

Huizinga, J. *The Waning of the Middle Ages.* London: E. Arnold, 1924.

In re Cavitt. 183 Neb. 243 (1968).

Institute of Medicine. *Disease by Disease toward National Health Insurance? Report of a Panel: Implications of a Categorical Catastrophic Disease Approach to National Health Insurance.* Washington, D.C.: National Academy of Sciences, 1973.

Jurek v. Texas. 428 U.S. 262 (1976).

Kalven, H. "Comment on Maki v. Frelk." *Vanderbilt Law Review* 21 (1968).

————. "A Special Corner of Civil Liberties: A Legal View I." *New York University Law Review* 31 (1956).

Katz, A. "Process Design for Selection of Hemodialysis and Organ Transplant Recipients." *Buffalo Law Review* 22 (1973).

Katz, J., and Capron, A. M. *Catastrophic Diseases: Who Decides What.* New York: Russell Sage Foundation, 1975.

Kaufmann, W. *Tragedy and Philosophy.* Garden City, N.Y.: Doubleday, 1968.

Kerr, D. N. S. "Regular Hemodialysis." *Royal Society of Medicine Proceedings* 60 (1967).

Koeninger, R. "Capital Punishment in Texas." *Crime and Delinquency* 15 (1969).

Laird, M. *Report to the President: Progress in Ending the Draft and Achieving the All-Volunteer Force.* Washington, D.C.: U.S. Government Printing Office, 1972.

Lattanzi, G., ed. *I Codici Penali.* Milan: Giuffrè, 1963.

Leach, G. *The Biocrats*. New York: McGraw-Hill, 1970.

Lewis, A. *Gideon's Trumpet*. New York: Random House, 1964.

Life. November 9, 1962, p. 102.

Lindsay, C. "Our National Tradition of Conscription: Experience with the Draft." In *Why the Draft? The Case for the Volunteer Army*. Ed. James C. Miller. Baltimore: Penguin Books, 1968.

Lockmiller, D. *Enoch H. Crowder, Soldier, Lawyer, Statesman*. Vol. 27, University of Missouri Studies. Columbia, Mo., 1955.

Lorenzo v. Wirth. 170 Mass. 596, 49 N.E. 1,010 (1897).

Mantovani, F. *I Trapianti e la Sperimentazione Umana*. Padova: Cedam, 1974.

Mayer, L. A. "U.S. Population Growth: Would Fewer Be Better?" In *The American Population Debate*. Ed. D. Callahan. Garden City, N.Y.: Doubleday, 1971.

Mead, Margaret. "Research with Human Beings: A Model Derived from Anthropological Field Practice." *Daedalus*, Spring 1969.

Merryman, J. H. *The Civil Law Tradition*. Stanford, Calif.: Stanford University Press, 1969.

Meyers, D. *The Human Body and the Law*. Chicago: Aldine, 1970.

Michael, J., and Wechsler, H. *Criminal Law and Its Administration*. Chicago: Foundation Press, 1940.

Michaelman, F. "The Supreme Court and Litigation Access Fees: The Right to Protect One's Rights—Part I." *Duke Law Journal*, Vol. 1973.

Mill, J. S. "Bentham." In *The Philosophy of John Stuart Mill*. Ed. M. Cohen. New York: Modern Library, 1961.

Miller, James C., III, ed. *Why the Draft? The Case for the Volunteer Army*. Baltimore: Penguin Books, 1968.

Millis, W. *Arms and Men: A Study in American Military History*. New York: Putnam, 1956.

Mooney, Gavin. Letter to Guido Calabresi, from the Economic Adviser's Office of the Department of Health and Social Security, dated 5 June 1973, on file at Yale University Law Library.

Moore v. City of East Cleveland, 431 U.S 494 (1977).

"Moral Problems in the Use of Borrowed Organs, Artificial and Transplant." *Annals of Internal Medicine* 60 (1964).

Moynihan, D. *The Negro Family: The Case for National Action*. Washington, D.C.: U.S. Government Printing Office, 1965.

Muramatsu, M., and Kuroda, T. "Japan." In *Population Policy in Developed Countries*. Ed. B. Berelson. New York: McGraw-Hill, 1974.

Murdock, E. *One Million Men: The Civil War Draft in the North*. Madison, Wisc.: State Historical Society of Wisconsin, 1971.

———. *Patriotism Limited: 1862–65*. Kent, Ohio: Kent State University Press, 1967.

Musgrave, R. *The Theory of Public Finance*. New York: McGraw-Hill, 1959.

New York Times Co. v. United States. 403 U.S. 713 (1971).

New York Times. June 30, 1977, Section A, p. 14.

———. "Muskie Calls for Changes in Unfair Draft System." February 18, 1969, p. 4.

———. M. R. Killingsworth. "Topics: Civilian Service Instead of Draft." February 15, 1969, p. 28.

———. "James Donovan Urges That Women Be Drafted." February 23, 1969, p. 41.

———. "Yale Head Scores Inequities of Draft." February 29, 1969, p. 27.

———. R. Semple. "Nixon Asks Draft Lottery with 19-Year-Olds First." May 14, 1969, p. 1.

———. W. Turner. "Criticism and Evasion of Draft Grow with Unpopularity of Vietnam War." May 14, 1969, p. 20.

———. "India State Is Leader in Forced Sterilization." August 13, 1976, Section A, p. 8.

———. "Alleged Sterilization of Indians Denied." November 24, 1976, p. 12.

Newsweek. June 11, 1962, p. 92.

Nichols, D.; Smolensky, E.; and Tideman, T. N. "Discrimination by Waiting Time in Merit Goods." *American Economic Review* 61 (1971).

Nixon, R. "Changing Rules of Liability in Automobile Accident Litigation." *Law and Contemporary Problems* 3 (1936).

Noonan, J. "Unintended Consequences: Laws Indirectly Affecting Population in the United States." In *Aspects of Population Growth Policy.* Vol. 6. Ed. R. Parke, for the United States Commission on Population Growth and the American Future. Washington, D.C.: U.S. Government Printing Office, 1972.

Note. "The Case for Black Juries." *Yale Law Journal* 79 (1970).

———. "Patient Selection for Artificial and Transplanted Organs." *Harvard Law Review* 82 (1969).

———. "Scarce Medical Resources." *Columbia Law Review* 69 (1969).

Nozick, R. *Anarchy, State, and Utopia.* New York: Basic Books, 1974.

Nutter, W. "The Coase Theorem on Social Costs: A Footnote." *Journal of Law and Economics* 11 (1968).

Pannain, R. *Diritto Penale.* Torino: Unione Tipografico, 1962.

Parke, R., ed., for the United States Commission on Population Growth and the American Future. *Aspects of Population Growth Policy.* Vol. 6. Washington, D.C.: U.S. Government Printing Office, 1972.

Pollara, F. "Trends in U.S. Population." In *The American Population Debate.* Ed. D. Callahan. Garden City, N.Y.: Doubleday, 1971.

Population Council. "India" in *Country Profiles,* May 1976.

Posner, R. "Review of *The Costs of Accidents.*" *University of Chicago Law Review* 37 (1970).

Powell, Lewis. "Contributory Negligence: Necessary Check on the

American Jury." *American Bar Association Journal* 43 (1957).

Ramsey, P. *The Patient as Person: Explorations in Medical Ethics.* New Haven: Yale University Press, 1970.

Rawls, J. *A Theory of Justice.* Cambridge, Mass., Harvard University Press, 1971.

Redbook. November 1967, pp. 80, 133.

Relf v. Weinberger. 372 F.Supp. 1,196 (D.D.C.1973).

Robbins, R. *Our Landed Heritage.* Princeton, N.J.: Princeton University Press, 1942.

Rodell, F. "Goodbye to Law Reviews." *Virginia Law Review* 23 (1937).

————. *Woe Unto You, Lawyers.* New York: Reynal & Hitchcock, 1939.

Sanders, D., and Dukeminier, J. "Medical Advance and Legal Lag: Hemodialysis and Kidney Transplantation." *U.C.L.A. Law Review* 15 (1968).

Scribner, Belding. *Newsweek,* June 11, 1962.

Sewall, R. B., "The Tragic Form." In *Tragedy: Modern Essays in Criticism.* Ed. L. Michel and R. B. Sewall. Englewood Cliffs, N.J.: Prentice-Hall, 1965.

Skinner v. Oklahoma. 316 U.S. 535 (1942).

Spengler, Joseph J. "Population Problem: In Search of a Solution." *Science* 166 (1969).

Stevens, R. *American Medicine and the Public Interest.* New Haven: Yale University Press, 1971.

————. *Medical Practice in Modern England.* New Haven: Yale University Press, 1966.

Stigler, G. *The Theory of Price.* 3d ed. New York: Macmillan, 1966.

Taylor v. Louisiana. 419 U.S. 527 (1975).

Tobin, J. "On Limiting the Domain of Inequality." *Journal of Law and Economics* 13 (1970).

Tribe, L. "Trial by Mathematics: Precision and Ritual in the Legal Process." *Harvard Law Review* 84 (1971).

Tyler, P., ed. *Immigration in the United States.* New York: H. W. Wilson, 1956.

United States Bureau of the Census. *Historical Statistics of the United States.* Washington, D.C.: U.S. Government Printing Office, 1960.

United States General Accounting Office. *Treatment of Chronic Kidney Failure: Dialysis, Transplant, Costs, and the Need for More Vigorous Effort. Report to the Congress by the Comptroller General of the United States.* 1975.

United States National Advisory Commission on Selective Service. *In Pursuit of Equity: Who Serves When Not All Serve.* Washington, D.C.: U.S. Government Printing Office, 1967.

United States Selective Service System. *Annual Report of the Director to the Congress.* Washington, D.C.: U.S. Government Printing Office, 1967.

————. *Legal Aspects of Selective Service.* Washington, D.C.: U.S. Government Printing Office, 1969.

United States v. Holmes. 26 Fed. Cas. 360 (C.C.E.D.Pa. 1842).

van Pragg, P., and Lohlé-Tart, L. "The Netherlands." In *Population Policy in Developed Countries.* Ed. B. Berelson. New York: McGraw-Hill, 1974.

Walton, G. *Let's End the Draft Mess.* New York: McKay, 1967.

Westoff, C. "United States." In *Population Policy in Developed Countries.* Ed. B. Berelson. New York: McGraw-Hill, 1974.

Wicksell, K. "A New Theory of Taxation." Trans. and repr. in *Classics in the Theory of Public Finance.* R. Musgrave and A. Peacock. London and New York: Macmillan, 1958.

Wilson, M. A. "Doctor's Duty to his Patient." *British Medical Journal.* March 11, 1967.

Wittgenstein, L. *Tractatus Logico-Philosophicus.* Trans. D. F. Pears and B. F. McGuinness. London: Routledge & Kegan Paul; New York: Humanities Press, 1961.

Wittke, C. "Immigration Policy Prior to World War I." In *Immigration and the United States.* Ed. P. Tyler. New York: H. W. Wilson, 1956.

Woodson v. North Carolina. 428 U.S. 280 (1976).

Wyatt v. Aderholt. 368 F.Supp. 1,382 (M.D.Ala. 1973).

INDEX